# GARDEN *to* ORDER

*Books by Ken Kraft*

*Land of Milk and Omelets*
*The Birds and the Beasts Were There*
*Give Father a Hard Knock*

# GARDEN
# to ORDER

## Ken Kraft

### INTRODUCTION BY
## Pearl S. Buck

DOUBLEDAY & COMPANY, INC.
GARDEN CITY, NEW YORK, 1963

Library of Congress Catalog Card Number 63–7692
Copyright © 1962, 1963 by Ken Kraft
All Rights Reserved
Printed in the United States of America
First Edition

# Contents

# AN APPRECIATION

To use a plant breeder's word, this book is a modern hybrid. It is a home gardener's handbook in part, packed and crammed with practical know-how from many experts. In part it is also a swift history of some big genetic break-throughs that touch on the daily lives of all of us. Again, scattered here and there you will come across a number of excellent recipes you may do well to try, even if you have no garden. And if you have, you may be amazed at some of the strange and wonderful things our grandparents grew in their gardens—and which in many cases you can grow today.

Here is a sampling of what you will find in these pages:

. . . A practical, easy way to grow luscious salads in the dead of winter.

. . . The most popular flower and vegetable in American gardens today. Also the most unpopular vegetable—and why it doesn't deserve to be.

. . . How to create your own hybrid flowers and vegetables at home, without special equipment.

. . . Forty free gardening aids for the asking.

. . . The discovery that the most enthusiastic gardeners are doctors.

. . . How to grow durable and beautiful baskets, ladles, and sponges in your garden.

. . . The lima bean that cost $1000.

. . . How to garden "defensively" in case of war.

. . . The average life expectancy of garden seeds, and a simple way to store them for years if necessary.

. . . The seven best places to get reliable gardening guidance.

. . . Plants that *prefer* poor soil.

. . . How to live more deliciously out of your own home garden.

. . . Thirty-eight ways to get better garden photographs.

. . . Thirty-four beautiful flower bed plantings that are literally good enough to eat.

. . . What you'll be growing in your Space Age garden of the future. And tips, gardeners' secrets, anecdotes, and ideas by the hundreds.

The authority for most of the informative and the technical areas of the book is the long-time world leader in the business of selling garden seed by mail, the W. Atlee Burpee Company of Philadelphia. In part, the book is also a history of this seed house, for it spans the vital years in this country's life between an almost utter reliance on European seed, and a complete independence married to the rather new science of genetics.

Through its first forty years an intensely interesting man owned and ran the company, having started it when he was eighteen. He was W. Atlee Burpee, and he died away back in 1915, so that I never knew him. Yet, in the course of writing this book I have become so well acquainted at secondhand with Mr. Burpee (as I have termed him here, while usually referring to his chief successor and son, David Burpee, by last name only, in newspaper style) that it has become an increasing pleasure to feel I am doing some kindness to his memory merely by showing a part of this country's seed business history through his work. "My old seedsman," many of his customers affectionately called him, though he was only in his fifty-eighth year when he died, and dozens of them named a son after him. Mr. Burpee would send the child a little silver mug, and he occasionally visited some of these namesakes during his peculiar grasshopper train journeys across country. He knew bitter personal tragedy but he seemed able always to laugh at such simple jokes on himself as when he once ordered a meal item by item in a small-town restaurant and overheard the astounded waiter telling the cook there was a dude out there who wanted to eat in courses. Though flattered when Elbert Hubbard, the glorifier of business progress, lauded him in *The Fra,* Mr. Burpee continued to write his catalog in longhand, and by coal oil lamp in his home long after electric lights were in general use. Apparently he thought more clearly that way.

Since 1915 his shoes have been filled by his son David, who was devoted to his father and who runs the big seed house in precisely the same one-man way. He appears often in these pages and was of vast help in putting his records, staff experts, and his own time at my disposal for the year the writing required. However, it is likely that he will not care much for some of the things said here, and also would have put more emphasis on some other things had he been doing it. My object has been simply to turn out as useful and readable a book for gardeners as I would have liked to have when my wife and I were buying Burpee seeds to plant a big farm garden in Missouri just after World War II. I told of that experience in a book, *Land of Milk and Omelets,* and because David Burpee read it, we later became acquainted, and this led to the present book, planned to be a garden book all gardeners could enjoy and use, whether they cultivated an acre or a window box.

My thanks are due the Burpee people as a group for really splendid help in putting together a book that could mean something to the gardener looking for useful answers to many gardening problems, but who gardens mainly because he likes to, and wants to learn to enjoy it more. If he also has a curiosity about modern plant breeding and the growing of his garden seeds, he'll find something about them here, not in technical language but mostly in terms of people.

Everyone, from the Mexican workers laughing and waving at us across Red Man zinnia fields at Santa Paula, California, to the officers of the firm, was unfailingly willing and able to shove the job along. I am very grateful and have tried to repay them through accuracy and clarity in telling the story of *Garden to Order,* and making it offer what the house of Burpee has built its reputation on offering—help, comfort, and good things for the home gardener.

*Ken Kraft*
Big Sur, California

# FOREWORD

There are certain occupations in the world designed not only for practical use and necessity but also for the delectation of mankind. Such is the practical art of gardening. To plant seeds in spring is an urge universal unless repressed by long habit and an unfavorable environment, but the urge alone supplies only the energy. The materials are a proper soil and excellent seed. My friend, David Burpee, has for many decades advised on the soil and provided the seed, and for this God bless him.

There is even more to gardening, however, and again this master gardener provides the ingredients for our profit and pleasure. His work has led him into important discoveries in genetics. The laws of life apply to the vegetable world as significantly as they do to the animal world and they are the same laws. When a scentless marigold can be bred, when genetics carefully pursued lead to the production of a white flower where one never was, this means basic discovery. Those of us who know David Burpee know him as a scientist whose work is as valid and important as any other, but we know him also as a man of many ideas and wide interests. Anecdote and incident enrich his conversation, and he produces ideas as lively as his seeds. He denies that this book, *Garden to Order*, is a biography, with which statement I agree, in the hope that some day he will write that volume. Until that time, however, this book will serve as biographical. It reveals an important and interesting personage in a field increasingly important, as we move slowly but steadily toward the discovery of the unity of life in that unified field of which Einstein dreamed.

*Pearl S. Buck*

# *1* THE WONDERFUL SEEDS

A fifth-grade schoolboy came into the little public library in fertile Carmel Valley, California, one day last fall munching a very juicy apple. The library is anything but formal, but books are books, so the librarian steered her young client to a chair to finish his apple before pawing any of the stock. He chomped with such enjoyment that at apple's end he had nothing left but two seeds. He then presented himself before the librarian's desk. "That," he declared, "was the best apple I *ever* ate," and taking one of the two seeds from his hand, he placed it on the desk. "Now—you plant that one and I'll plant this one," he said with utter confidence, "and you and me will have the best apples *anybody* ever ate."

The biggest mail-order seed house in this world, W. Atlee Burpee Company of Philadelphia, Pa., does not sell apple seeds (they do not come true to variety, as those in the seed business put it, though the company did in 1880 offer a quart of apple seeds for 40 cents), but while the business of selling seeds tends to make seedsmen matter-of-fact about them, even they now and then grow bemused at the mystery and wonder of their merchandise. Victor R. Boswell, horticulturist with the United States Department of Agriculture, put it this way in the department's 1961 *Yearbook of Agriculture:*

"Researchers are conducting more inquiries into seeds today than ever before, and still our wonder grows.

"Why does a very dry seed become so well protected and so insensitive that it can tolerate sharp, deep-freeze temperatures for years . . . ?

"A light-sensitive seed, while dry, may be so well protected and so insensitive that it is quite unaffected by daylong exposure to sunlight, yet, after it becomes moist, it may respond to a light exposure from a flash lamp as short as one one-thousandth of a second. Exactly what chain of events is set in motion by that flash, and how?

"Why do some seeds require alternating temperatures in order to grow, while others do not?

"Why do some seeds live for decades and scores of years, while others, apparently as well protected, die in 2 or 3 years?

"Why do some small plants produce seeds that are much larger than the seeds of some much larger plants?

"Why does one kind of seed develop completely in a few days while another takes years?

"How is it that seeds are so wondrously different among species, and yet all are quite evidently evolved to accomplish exactly the same thing?"

The fact is you buy seeds utterly on faith. A shoddy seed, hastily matured, of trashy parentage and grown solely for cut-rate sale, can look exactly like a good seed. Cutting a seed open tells you nothing of its quality and ruins the seed to boot. You must plant it to find out. And if it is no good, you have lost a season, and your work, and some faith.

No seedsman was more tenderly aware of the faith factor than the original W. Atlee Burpee, and while he was building his business into the giant of its kind, he kept pounding away in his annual catalog at the indispensable need for seedsman honesty. So conscious was he of the seed-buying public's willingness to be fooled that at times he went charging in against his better judgment to save them from themselves. One such time was around the turn of the century when a craze for growing ginseng root to sell the Chinese trade was sweeping through the country.

Mr. Burpee took a wry view of the fad and of its promoters, and was standing aloof from the profitable trade in ginseng seed. But finally goaded into action by requests for seed from customers, he burst forth in his 1904 catalog. "We," he wrote sternly, "are opposed to '*get-rich-quick*' booms . . . and would advise our friends to consider the special requirements of this plant before investing largely in its cultivation. . . .

"The plants require an equable temperature, comparatively cool, *constantly moist and shaded.* They grow very slowly; seedlings take from five to seven years to reach marketable size. The crop requires considerable labor in keeping the beds stirred and free from weeds,—*during all these years. . . .*

"*Were the claims made for* GINSENG *cultivation true, we could easily make millions a year at* FORDHOOK FARMS, *with less than half the thought or constant work now given to the seed business!*"

To back up this opinion, Mr. Burpee then quoted a U.S.D.A. bulletin warning the public of fraud in some ginseng seed and root sales, one shyster having been caught selling turnip seed as ginseng seed, at a 1400 per cent markup. Furthermore, the bulletin pointed out, the annual U.S. export trade in ginseng was less than a million dollars, about 170,000 pounds, and since it could all be grown on seventy-five acres or less, even a little success in ginseng cultivation would glut the market and topple prices.

Having done all he could to save his customers from their own scheming, Mr. Burpee added a final touch typical of him. "After these 'Warnings,'" he thundered in blackface type, "if you still desire to try the culture of GINSENG, we shall be willing to advise you of price at which you can procure the true seed and roots,—knowing that then you will not expect to 'get rich quick,'—at least from any representations of ours!"

But man seems always to have been intrigued, bedazzled, and sometimes betrayed by seeds. For more than a thousand years gardeners believed they could change the taste of vegetables by merely doing something to the seeds that grew them. A popular way was to soak the seeds in milk. This doesn't change a thing—and yet a modern technique of treating seeds or plants with a chemical that does change the end result seems just as weird. Luther Burbank said of the seed that it was "the most awe-inspiring wonder of the universe." In her book *Westward the Women,* Nancy Wilson Ross remarked on how pioneer wives contrived to smuggle into the scarce space of Conestoga wagons a few bags of flower seeds while their men's backs were turned.

Such devotion to floral beauty under hardships could not surprise David Burpee, the present head of W. Atlee Burpee Company. Frequently so carried away by enthusiasm for his new things that he called a variety of zinnia on its introduction in 1951, for instance, "the loveliest new flowers ever created," Burpee also has occasional twinges of uneasiness at taking too much credit from nature. If such twinges strike him just before he rises to give one of his frequent talks before garden clubs, he quiets his conscience by apologizing in advance for what he is about to claim. "We don't really create, in plant breeding," he has said in this vein. "We combine. The process is something like thinking. That is, you must start from something known, and so a thought is never completely original. It is a combining of things known, to produce something new."

In the work of producing something new, Burpee's can take a good deal of credit over the eighty-six years the house has been in business. Its most lasting success to date has been a cabbage, Burpee's Surehead, which was discovered growing in Europe and was introduced into the United States by W. Atlee Burpee in

1877, his second year in the seed business. The cabbage is still carried in the annual catalog, as are such other early introductions as Golden Self-Blanching celery (1884); Iceberg lettuce (1894), which proved so popular that the name is loosely appropriated by produce dealers for New York and Imperial varieties as well; Netted Gem cantaloupe (1881), even better known, to seedsman Burpee's displeasure, as Rocky Ford because growers at Rocky Ford, Colorado, so labeled crates of it and the name caught on. Among later vegetable introductions still going strong are Golden Bantam sweet corn, two varieties of fine bush lima beans, and a splendid white radish found in China. All in all, 274 new vegetables had been introduced by Burpee's as of 1962, 75 of which are still carried in the annual retail catalog. Since about 1940 most of the house's new vegetables have come about through controlled crosses, and these hybrids include, among Burpee's exclusives, several tomatoes, a wilt-resistant cucumber, a Zucchini squash, an eggplant, a watermelon, and a cantaloupe.

Hybridizing has also accounted for a spangle of Burpee flower triumphs with petunias, marigolds, zinnias, snapdragons, sweet peas, and nasturtiums.

Another tool in getting new things has been the chemical treatment with colchicine. This hasn't got anywhere with vegetables, but it has produced superb new snapdragons and, along with crossing, it brought forth so spectacular a string of descendants of the black-eyed Susan that Burpee named the newcomers "Gloriosa daisies," and is selling them like hot cakes.

Burpee's has never, since soon after its start, belittled its seeds by selling them cheap. True, in the beginning the inducement that was used to sell flower seeds to penny-wise farmers' wives was the statement, "The cheapest flower seeds ever offered," and the price per ten-packet lot was 25 cents. For that sum a flower-starved prairie homemaker in 1879 could get seeds of, for example, aster, sweet alyssum, balloon vine, canna, an ornamental grass, lupine, sweet pea, petunia, sweet william, and verbena. Two years later Mr. Burpee, cheered by the response, offered a much bigger list of flowers, all at one price—now 5 cents a packet. After another two years the flat price was scrapped and the 1883 flower gardener paid from 5 cents per packet on up to the dizzy height of 50 cents, though seed of only one flower brought that figure, a geranium said to be colored golden and bronze.

This price pattern persisted (on introducing the sensational Burpee bush lima bean in 1890, for example, Mr. Burpee charged 75 cents for a packet of exactly four of the scarce beans), and the son and successor of the founder has stayed generally with the policy. Toward the end of his life, W. Atlee Burpee said in a newspaper interview: "What nonsense that competitors must be enemies. . . . Make it a point to compete in quality rather than in price." In practice, Mr. Burpee, an excellent competitor himself, managed to get some mileage out of both points. "Burpee's seeds cost more but are worth far more," he repeated doggedly over the years until loyal Burpee customers would probably have felt betrayed if their hero had suddenly announced he would no longer be undersold.

His son, while proud that his seeds bring a higher price than those of some rivals, is operating in a rougher economy than his father was. Thus, when his pride in his costlier seeds happens to collide with his competitive urge to slash some prices, the resulting mental struggle is a fascinating sight. Clamping one of his long cigars, Burpee veers far to the pro or con side of the question, then scuttles back to safe middle ground again. If he is operating in conference, his geeing and hawing is accompanied by an anxious firing of questions at everyone in sight. After going through a prolonged struggle of this kind in 1961, he finally decided in favor of lower prices and the 1962 catalog warbled the news that readers would find no prices advanced, and 419 prices reduced.

One thing that makes such price-shaving possible is the company's broad production facilities, a nice example of vertical diversification. More than one seed company is merely a seller of seeds. Burpee's sells seeds till the world looks green, but it also raises them—on its own land, on leased land, and through contract arrangements, to a total of about four thousand acres. It harvests, cleans, measures out and packages them, advertises them and mails them. In addition, and in some ways more importantly for human needs, it researches seeds, and in the ways previously mentioned and with other techniques it helps keep nudging forward the frontiers of usefulness.

Without a sizable return it could not spend much money experimenting. In 1961 sales came to $6,500,000, continuing to keep the company the Sears, Roebuck of the world's seed trade, a position it has held for about seventy years. For the past twenty years the net profit on sales has averaged 2.39 per cent. The company is a closed corporation, stock being owned by David Burpee, his brother W. Atlee Burpee, Jr., and the brother's son W. Atlee Burpee III. David Burpee, the undisputed head and mainspring of the business, holds a little more than 67 per cent of the stock, dividends on which have ranged from nothing to $6.00 since incorporation in 1917. Dividends were skipped during ten separate years, in each case so that the money could be used for expansion, as when branches were opened in Clinton, Iowa, to serve Midwest customers, and in Riverside, California, for western business. Depressions have not caused any dividend skips, and indeed, seeds are called a good depression business; in tight times more people plant vegetable gardens, and flowers from seed cost far less than those raised from nursery stock. This gardening pattern was true during the depression of the 1930s though less markedly than in prior slumps, when public relief measures were on a much smaller scale.

The value of home gardens in such periods was a point well used by W. Atlee Burpee, and in the late summer of 1893, as he wrote in his bold and angular longhand the copy for the next year's catalog, he was mindful of the current hard times. "Economy is the order of the day," he declared in the foreword. ". . . It is our purpose simply to emphasize a self-evident fact, that proper economy suggests more attention to the garden. The butcher's and grocer's bills can be reduced to the health of both person and purse by greater care and forethought in cultivation of the Vegetable Garden. Some of the sweetest pleasures and the most refining influences can be gathered around the home by more attention to the Flower Garden, so often sadly neglected in the hurry of modern life.

"True economy for 1894, if generally practiced along the lines of careful culture of the garden, will certainly tend largely toward a quick return of the time, sure to come, when plenty shall again crown this broad land."

The seedsman was speaking from a pinnacle of experience unusual for a man of thirty-five. He had already achieved two ambitions worth any mortal's efforts. In less than seventeen years he had built from scratch the world's biggest business of its kind, and just a few months before he sat down to write its next year's catalog, he had become the father of a son who would carry on the business with such enthusiasm and skill as to make it five, then ten, then fifteen times as vast as when he took over.

# 2 THE FOOT OF THE OWNER

"I'm the oldest Burpee employee—since January 1, 1914," David Burpee occasionally says. He also did part-time work for the company for about ten years before that, usually during summer vacations. Some of these periods were spent working as a roguer—one who walks the rows of plants and destroys poor or nonconforming ones—and some were spent traveling in Europe with his father on an annual search for better vegetables and flowers.

Burpee's own enthusiasm for the seed business undoubtedly helps boost *esprit de corps* in the organization, which is not unionized though operating in an age of unionization, and has no formal pension plan or many other fringe benefits in the form of written commitments. Still, morale appears generally good, and one employee, famous in company annals for his devoted management of their Floradale Farms, Lompoc, California, was so thoroughly a part of the company that he once exclaimed at Burpee himself on the conclusion of a good Floradale year: "Boss, I'm proud of you." He was William Hoag, and by the time of his remark he had grown from a youthful unskilled hand in the Philadelphia headquarters building into a nattily leather-booted expert at seed growing. A few weeks before his death, which unexpectedly followed hospitalization for an organic trouble, Hoag earnestly told Burpee, "After this operation I'm going to be a better man for you than ever," a sentiment not usually upper-most in an ailing worker facing a physical crisis. It was also Hoag who was so customarily keyed up by the triumphs of his com-pany that he generously credited everybody else with the same perception. Thus, when curious motorists on country roads near Lompoc in 1945 were observed frequently slowing down for a better look at flamboyant fields of the not yet introduced tetra-ploid snapdragons, Hoag exulted: "People came time and time again just to awe at them."

As his father did, David Burpee runs the business largely by feel. Rather than management by committee, his remains a personal-command technique. Aware that this does have its dan-gers, he set up in 1960 what he called a planning committee. This was done at the suggestion, on request, of a cousin, George W. Burpee, a nationally known executive engineer and a man whose judgment the seedsman, nine and a half years his junior, respects. The planning committee was intended as a device by which David Burpee might start shucking off some executive cares. Since important decisions in every branch of the firm's operations still rest with him, however, the planning committee's plans can and do go oft awry. While its six members, mostly department heads, chew over problems in the ground-floor conference room of the Philadelphia headquarters building at Hunting Park Ave-nue and Eighteenth Street, Burpee himself, if not buzzing about the country on business, can frequently be found snug in his farmhouse study at Fordhook Farms, Doylestown, Pa., with his hand firmly on the company wheel. His attitude toward the planning committee seems hopeful, tolerant, and good-humored. "I'm not a terribly aggressive person," he has been heard to say, then adding, "except in business."

His aggressiveness in business was of early growth, fortunately for him, since at age twenty-two he had to take over the company and contend with a sticky management problem involving the

only two executives left after the death of W. Atlee Burpee in
1915. These two, both mature men, had been at such constant
odds that by that time they were no longer speaking to each
other. During conferences at young Burpee's insistence as the active executor of his father's estate and consequently head of the
business, each of the embattled pair behaved as if the other were
invisible, and addressed only Burpee. Unable finally to abide
even the other's presence, one man then resigned, and Burpee
brought in some fresh young blood, set the company up as a corporation with himself as president, and was on his way without
interference.

As a result of his personal drive, Burpee's relations with his
staff people today are somewhat akin to those a relaxed four-star
general might have with a string of youngish captains, majors,
and—here and there—colonels. For one thing, no one ever has the
slightest doubt who's in charge. Burpee obviously believes in the
adage, "The foot of the owner manureth the land," and so is on
the move a good deal of the time. A good example of him in action takes place when he jets from the East during one of his
thrice-yearly trips to California where, besides Floradale Farms,
he has another growing farm at Santa Paula and a branch office
at Riverside. His travel comes to thirty thousand miles most years,
and has hit fifty thousand. In August of 1961 he swooped down
on Floradale for a critical appraisal. The weather was summery—
warmer than it ordinarily is in the cool Lompoc Valley, which is
tempered by fog drifting inland from the ocean about six miles
away—but Burpee stuck to a Philadelphia uniform of collar and
dark red tie and a conservatively cut gray suit, instead of the
sports shirt and work pants his California staffers use. He was
shod, however, in country shoes—heavy, high-top tan ones. He
wore no hat, but he usually doesn't wear one anywhere; gray at
the temples, the rest of his hair is black, with only a small bald
spot at the back.

Since Floradale is a spready enterprise of some 650 scattered acres, the total varying by the amount of ground being leased or on which crops are being grown under contract, an inspection tour begins by driving (or "motoring," as Burpee habitually calls it) to the fields to be walked through. Along with his research assistant Jerome H. Kantor, the Floradale manager, Walter Manfrina, plant breeder Ellwood Pickering, and two guests, Burpee planted his tall, spare frame in a company station wagon, and chatted of this and that en route. This casualness fell away as soon as the party arrived at the first check point, a field of cosmos. Springing out of the wagon, Burpee strode off between rows, his carriage semimilitary, hands clasped behind him as he bent slightly forward from the waist, peering at the blooms growing seed for future gardens. He was trailed by the rest of the party, most closely by Kantor, whose title fails to convey many of his duties.

Presently Burpee stopped. So did everybody else. "People think cosmos are too sprawly," he announced. "Jerry—have we tried to make tetraploids out of cosmos?" Kantor told him they had tried but the results were no good. One frequent effect of tetraploiding (doubling of chromosomes) is a dwarfing of plants. "Let's try again," Burpee said in a no-nonsense tone, and Kantor made a note on a thick pad of paper he carried.

At a stop to check test rows of snapdragons, one of the guests, a woman, exclaimed over the fine blooms, but Burpee belittled them as past their prime. Like home gardeners the world around, he told his guest she should have seen them a week before. A few minutes later, he called on her to settle a difference of opinion. Among the open-pollinated marigolds there had appeared one variety with a raffish appearance, like a tousled head just risen from the pillow. Though somewhat taken with it, Burpee was giving ear to objections from Kantor, a man of nice sensibilities who found the disorderly-looking marigold depressing. "Do you think it's worth keeping?" Burpee asked his guest, and to Kantor's pain, she voted for it, remarking that a professional flower arranger she knew often tousled some blooms for certain effects. Burpee looked happy and thought up a name on the spot. "We'll call it Ruffian," he said. A persistent brain picker, he keeps his staff men busy taking notes, and his own pockets gradually fill with items he jots down when there is no one he can dictate to. At such times they usually share the pocket space with seeds, for Burpee is a believer in the sample as the ideal form of advertising. Since his products are low-priced compared with, say, cameras or watches, he can give away samples the way John D. Rockefeller used to give away dimes. No figures are available for comparison, but it seems likely that Burpee's giveaway rate would have given Mr. Rockefeller shudders. He is seldom found in public without packets of seeds bulging his pockets, and during field trips he may reload several times in a day.

While having luncheon one noon in the dining room of a guest ranch he favors in southern California, he was informed by the waitress that she had been unable to find any Burpee seeds on sale in the nearby town. (By far the most of Burpee's seeds are sold by mail, but a few are offered in some retail stores.) A chatty and generous man, Burpee frequently inspires a kind of vicarious company loyalty in people he meets, and the waitress added that she had chided the erring storekeepers, one and all. Touched, Burpee reached into his pocket and presented the woman with a dollar's worth of his prized Gloriosa daisy seeds. The next day at lunch he impulsively gave her another batch. A personal friend who was so dazzled by the sight of forty acres of the daisies that she declared she was forthwith going to tell all her friends to plant them, found herself abruptly presented with the whole fat wad of packets Burpee was just then carrying —around twenty dollars' worth.

Although Burpee has mentioned, without rancor, that his wife says he asks everybody for advice and then takes his own

2

(his father was charged with the same trait), there are exceptions. One occurred at the next point in the tour of Floradale as the party inspected test rows of petunias. "Oh, I love this one," the woman guest cried, stopping beside a plant with light pink flowers. Burpee gave it a cold look, and a curious silence fell upon his staff men. The guest, a gardener and flower fancier of considerable experience, declared she thought the pink petunia was outstanding. "All right, all right—mark it," Burpee said glumly, and Kantor, who was nearest, grinned and slipped a paper-band noose around the stem. Burpee, he told the guest as the boss marched away, cared little for pastel tones in petunias, and it was always a struggle to get him to approve one.

The tour had begun late in the morning and was interrupted at this juncture for the drive back for luncheon, served on a plank table in a sheltered corner of the manager's house grounds. His wife, Myra, had prepared fried chicken, scalloped potatoes, an aspic, tossed salad, cake, and ice cream. She served it, all hands helping, then took her place at the table as hostess. Like army wives, the wives of Burpee staff men are expected to rally around and help keep the wheels turning. The head man's wife is no exception, as Fordhook swarms with special-events visitors several times each year. Burpee women employees also turn their hands to extracurricular tasks that need the gentle touch; a young woman hired for her scientific brains hops into fresh jeans and shirt when there are luncheon guests at the farm where she is plant breeding, slaps skin freshener on her tanned cheeks, and becomes mistress of the ceremonies. At the Santa Paula unit, when someone thought of making catch-all bags from purse-sized seed sacks for gifts at flower shows and such, it was not necessary to scour the town for a seamstress. A pretty girl in the office left her typewriter for ten minutes to hem the sack top and insert a drawstring that worked like a charm.

During the inspection-tour luncheon the woman guest who had offered her advice on the marigold and the petunia, volunteered some more, crying that she was terribly disillusioned to find, on a table in the heart of a great growing farm of the greatest mail-order seed house in the world, not one single measly home-grown vegetable. Even the salad makings had come from a market in Lompoc. Burpee was not noticeably disturbed by this cobbler's-children comparison, and ate heartily of the store victuals. Had the visitors been there during World War II they would have had no cause for complaint: manager Hoag had grown a flourishing victory garden in the front yard where everybody passing by could get a mouth-watering look and see that Burpee seeds did indeed grow.

As the inspection tour resumed after the meal was over, Burpee paused on his way to the station wagon to eye a bed of verbena in front of the Floradale office building. It looked pretty good to the visitors, but Burpee and his staff men shrugged in unison and admitted it was a failure. They had been working with it, a tetraploid plant, for about five years, hoping to get a good bedding plant, but the verbena stayed stubbornly tall.

Proceeding to the fields again, Burpee had Manfrina stop the car for a closer look at some more evidence of trouble he had just glimpsed. This, occurring in a stock-seed block (producing seed that would be planted the next season to supply seed for sale), showed up in stunted and wilted leaves. None of the party could say what was causing it, and Burpee asked Kantor if they could get someone at the University of California to help. Seedsmen, like other farmers, frequently turn to faculty brains to help out in such diagnosing, as well as in prescribing.

Some vegetable seed is produced on the Burpee Floradale acreage but its specialty is flowers. The firm grows about eight hundred varieties there, scattered over plots miles apart, so it takes quite a bit of Burpee's motoring along dusty roads to oversee even a few of the blocks. One of the pet projects—the Gloriosa daisies—came next on the tour. As the party clambered through part of the forty acres growing Gloriosa daisies, a good deal of variation showed up in their coloring—a natural result of the shaking up that the hereditary factors got during development—and Burpee called for paper markers on some plants ("We need more of these yellows"). The seed from marked plants would be saved for stock seed so that there would be more yellow flowers in the next plantings and, later, in home gardens. "Jerry, make a note," Burpee said a few minutes later. "'Select some plants for more definite or darker markings, some for striped or variegated.'" He paused to ask his woman guest's opinion on the decidedly dark-flowered daisies (she was enthusiastic), and then concluded the snatch of dictation: "'In all cases, select for bold, straight, broad petals. Avoid droopiness. Look for small plants with large flowers.'" He stood for a while with his hands behind his back, looking over the rippling, tawny flowers that had brought home an All-America award and were now some of the biggest sellers in the catalog. The guest asked what effect frost would have on them, and Burpee told her that even a heavy frost would not harm the roots. "We had thought they were annuals," he explained cheerfully, "but they turned out to be perennials."

Deer tracks were seen in the next field, near a tree-bordered creek, and the deer had been impartial, nipping off Mr. Burpee's valuable flowers as willingly as they strip any California suburbanite's posies. None of the men seemed upset by the raid, and Burpee, who is so cool toward hunting that his staff men don't talk about it in his hearing, took the deer in his stride. "We're working here on male-sterile marigolds," he told his guests. Such a flower, in which there is no possibility of self-pollinating, is highly useful to the hybridizer, offering an excellent chance of getting bees to do the work.

Of another field of marigolds the car passed, Burpee remarked that they were behind time, and also that some roguing was needed. He credits his early experience at roguing with sharpening his eyesight; he has been known to spot, while on horse-back, a four-leaf clover in the sward below.

Presently the party came across one of the few workers they had met, Burpee's twenty-year-old son, Jonathan. Wearing a straw hat and dark glasss, he was using a tool resembling a chisel on a hoe handle. To his father's question of what he was doing, Jonathan said he was roguing out dark singles (from among a test planting of cosmos). Burpee the father looked spellbound for a few moments and then strode on without comment, as if it was Jonathan's headache, not his. The younger Burpee's work at that moment was part of a project he had been doing that summer—trying for a cosmos that would bear nothing but fully double flowers that would produce seeds true to type. Originally a producer of single flowers, the cosmos through a mutation showed up one year with a double-flowered plant. Its descendents had both single and double flowers on the same plants, and it was these that Jonathan was working with, under the guidance of a plant breeder. The chore was a little reminiscent of one his father had undertaken when he was around Jonathan's age—a search for a yellow sweet pea. The search was unsuccessful, so David Burpee never collected the $1000 promised him if he found the yellow sweet pea. It never has been found, by the way.

Though Jonathan had no such glittering inducement, he appeared immersed in his work. His relations with his father on the latter's summer visits to Floradale are a nice problem in balance. During the working hours of the day they are as chief and under-ling. But since both live in a little frame cottage that David Burpee's father built for him in 1911, things change when they enter the doorway.

When David Burpee occupied the cottage as a youth he had a Japanese cook, who made more money than he did. Today, Jonathan cooks the food and the millionaire seedsman washes the dishes. Neither is enchanted with the other's performance, the son taking the view that a good dish washer uses something more than plain water, and the father questioning whether the human stomach was intended to get its morning bacon from a skillet brimming with the grease of many fryings. "What," the elder Burpee suddenly asked his woman visitor during the tour, "do *you* do with the stuff?"

"Pour it in a coffee can," she said at once.

Burpee seemed puzzled at the simple solution. "Uh—then what?" he asked.

"Well, when it's full you can throw the can in the fire," his guest suggested.

"Throw it in the *fire!*" he cried. "Then what would we make our coffee in?"

It took a few moments for his guest to clear up the seedsman's confusion between a coffee can and a coffeepot. Since coffee beans are not listed in the catalog, they had never, naturally, been favored with Burpee's most earnest scrutiny.

# *3* HOW IT STARTED

In 1872 an English pedigreed-poultry fancier visiting in New York City took the train to Philadelphia expressly to meet a fellow fancier for whom he had conceived an enormous respect. He and the Philadelphian knew each other only through correspondence as fellow-subscribers to some British poultry magazines. At the moment, though, this purely paper acquaintance seemed to the visitor only a minor drawback; surely two gentlemen breeders of pedigreed birds could quickly get to know each other over some good cigars and brandy. The Englishman was in for a shock. When he arrived at Philadelphia his American poultry wizard seemed to be nowhere in sight and there was only a fourteen-year-old boy to greet him. "Ah, my lad," said the Englishman, "would you be the son of W. Atlee Burpee, the famous poultry authority?"

The boy held out his hand. "I am the son of Dr. David Burpee, sir," he said. "*I* am W. Atlee Burpee, the poultryman."

Four years later, at age eighteen, the child poultry prodigy had learned so much about the merits of purebred livestock as well, and also about farm seed, that when a wealthy young Philadelphian proposed they go into business together to sell these commodities, he was eager to try it. The partners set up shop in 1876 but it was an unhappy partnership and no better when a third

man was admitted, so young Burpee pulled out in 1878 to go into
business for himself. He dated the start of his business as 1876,
however, the date the Burpee company uses today. Still, if he
had wished to, he could have justified an even earlier date: In
1875, the birthdate, incidentally, of the telephone, young Burpee
had offered a line of fowls and livestock by mail order, his own,
spare-time business while he was a student. His attractive 16-
page catalog was titled, "W. Atlee Burpee's Catalogue of High-
Class Land and Water Fowls." It would seem that he dated his
seed business strictly from the first year he handled seeds, perhaps a reflection of his character, which was singular for its
probity.

So far as his father and grandfather were concerned, he had
no business going into business anyway. They were medical men
and expected him to follow suit. The grandfather, Dr. Washington Lemuel Atlee, was a widely known surgeon who, though by
no means the first to perform an ovariotomy, had by the time he
died in 1878 performed a prodigious, for then, 378 of them, in
spite of such an uproar from some of his colleagues when he began that he was called a murderer. A nimble-minded man with a
quick tongue, Dr. Atlee gave as good as he was sent, and gradually argued his critics into submission. Later on, when a Canadian
medical student of the 1850s studying in a class the doctor was
conducting at Jefferson Medical College, Philadelphia, asked
to marry one of his daughters, Ann Catharine, her father again
had no trouble finding words. "If you want the girl," he said
in effect, "you'll have to take Philadelphia too." To the student,
David Burpee, this seemed reasonable; his home was in Sheffield,
New Brunswick, but the Burpees had originally settled in Rowley,
Massachusetts, after emigrating from France in 1639. In French
the family name came from the phrase *beau pré*, "beautiful
fields." Young Dr. Burpee took his bride home to meet the folks,
and when they returned to Philadelphia to live, four years later,

as the Civil War began, they had a three-year-old son they had named after his grandfather, Washington Atlee Burpee.

The Atlees were of old English stock; the name is said to go back to a certain Sir Richard at-the-lea. (For coincidence collectors—"lea" refers to a meadow, as did the last syllable of "Burpee" in the French version, a rare combination for a man who became a seedsman.) Sir Richard probably spelled his lea "ley," the more usual form during the twelfth century, and his estate was called Fordhook, presumably from a ford across a river bend. Some seven hundred years later, W. Atlee Burpee took the ancestral estate name for his own estate near Doylestown, a few miles north of Philadelphia. According to Atlee family tradition, Sir Richard befriended Robin Hood, whose Sherwood Forest was hard by, and not only befriended him but gave him his daughter, Maid Marian, to wed. This version is considerably more confident than those of most scholarly investigators of English legend, hardly any of whom care to say for sure just who Maid Marian was or even whether the girl ever existed.

It is unlikely that Washington Atlee Burpee spent any time pondering the problem. Even as a boy he was as practical as pants, as well as bright, and busied himself (after whacking the "Washington" in his name down to a more manageable single initial) at down-to-earth interests, particularly the poultry on which he became such a specialist. By the time he took up the study of medicine at the University of Pennsylvania when he was seventeen, he was actively in business selling and exhibiting his fancy breeds of chickens, geese, turkeys, and pigeons, and reporting for various trade journals as an authority. The medical education lasted only a year and then broke up under the impact of a two-way strain. One factor was the young man's dislike; as he wrote a sick friend years later, excusing himself for not visiting at the hospital, "Nothing is more depressing to me . . . I had to give up the study of medicine, which I studied for a year, because I could not endure seeing the suffering when I attended the operations with my grandfather." The other thing involved in his withdrawal was the partnership proposal previously referred to.

It was made by August S. Benson, Jr., who put up $5000 as his contribution, against W. Atlee Burpee's five years of experience and study in the field. This was in June of 1876. According to the young Mr. Burpee's account about two years later, Benson grew discouraged over the cost and time of getting the business established, and after fourteen months they took in the third partner, William Henry Maule, to share the expense. Though he was a boyhood—and lifelong—friend of W. Atlee Burpee's and the same age, then nineteen, the new partner lined up with Benson in opposing "every plan I had to increase trade," Burpee said later, and the next year, on April 29 of 1878, Burpee withdrew. The firm had spent $3500 more than it took in its first year but paid expenses the second one.

Two days later, Dr. David Burpee loaned his son money to set up his own business, W. Atlee Burpee & Company, despite his regret that the lad was deserting medicine. The new company made $2500 its first year, repaid Dr. Burpee his loan the next year, and grew thereafter like a weed. Or like Burpee seeds, its founder would probably have preferred to say. The business started at 223 Church Street, expanded into adjoining buildings, and then moved to 475–77 North Fifth in 1883. A larger structure was built on the site in 1898, and warehouse space on York Avenue was used. The move to the present sizable headquarters building at Hunting Park Avenue and Eighteenth Street was made in 1936.

For the record it should be said here that despite a fairly long tenure in the field, Burpee's are by no means the U.S. pioneer in the seed trade. The oldest house in the business is ninety-two years Burpee's senior. It is the D. Landreth Seed Company, organized in 1784 in Philadelphia, a comparatively small firm. But there were seedsmen in business in this country a good sixty-five years earlier than the early Mr. Landreth, though these entrepreneurs gradually vanished from the scene and left no mark of their passing. They were the dim beginnings of the U.S. seed industry. Seed growing was itself just then starting to grow. In north Europe acreage was being set aside here and there for the still novel purpose of letting crops go to seed. Slowly, over a span of eighty-odd years, this new branch of agriculture spread across an ocean and took root in North America. At about the time the Landreth company began, garden seeds were also being sold by the Shakers. Members of this religious sect, superb husbandmen, may have been the first to offer seeds in small paper envelopes—the cornerstone of today's big mail-order seed business, which could not, of course, get under way before there was an adequate mail service, a nineteenth-century development. A kind of self-imposed watch dog of the seed industry as a whole was also a nineteenth-century development—the American Seed Trade Association, started in 1883. It has, among other things, helped effect plant disease control through treatment of seeds, and also certification for trueness of variety.

It is the opinion of the present head of the Burpee seed company that seeds originally got into the business through the barn door, so to speak. He thinks they were probably offered as a means of raising feed to feed the high-class birds and animals the partners had for sale. On withdrawing from the partnership and setting up shop for himself, W. Atlee Burpee lost no time in expanding and promoting the seed end of his business. He began issuing a separate seed catalog almost at once, and in two years it was plain that here was the real future of the firm.

The 1880 catalog, or *Burpee's Farm Annual,* as it was called for years, devoted twenty-nine pages to seeds (against eight the year before), and offered a dollar's worth of vegetable seeds in a collection for 25 cents. Bargain hunters who responded got a packet each of Paragon tomato, New Excelsior watermelon, Ovoid mangel, Green Prolific cucumber, Nimble Six Weeks' turnip, Large Round Viroflay spinach, Golden Yellow Summer Turnip radish, Sutton's Student parsnip, Varigeted lima beans, and Mammoth Tours pumpkin (a specimen of which was reported weighing in at 220 pounds). To push this introductory package deal, the enterprising Mr. Burpee offered a sewing machine to anyone who would take orders for three hundred of the 25-cent boxes. The sewing machine, said to be patterned after the Singer, was a $22 value. Also, of the $75 the volunteer salesman was to collect for the three hundred orders, he could keep $15. The response to this tempting offer may have been partly responsible for what the editor of a Philadelphia farm magazine saw when he dropped in on Mr. Burpee that spring and "found him in his private office reading the morning mail while a confidential clerk counted and opened the letters. This one mail alone numbered upward of *four hundred letters,* and yet there were several more mails still to arrive the same day. . . ." Mr. Burpee was then not quite twenty-two years old and had about thirty-five more years of life ahead of him. By the time it ended he was known all over the world, and by any standard except its length he had enjoyed the good life, in the grand Late Victorian manner.

Also in the Victorian tradition, he was conservative. He refused to have electric lights installed in his Fordhook Farms home or, for a long while, a telephone, and held out against an automobile until his last year, when he gave in and bought a big Packard. In religion he was a kind of conservative rebel, disapproving of some tenets of his church (Presbyterian) and of the Biblical "Eat, drink, and be merry." Once when his realistic son David, then a boy, said he had decided it would be good if young people could be shown it paid to do right, the father vigorously disagreed, on the ground everyone should do right for right's sake. "Even," he added heroically, "if heaven and hell were reversed."

Though the son took a spotty view of going to hell for being good, he nevertheless so generally admired his father that even where he could not follow in his footsteps, he remembers them with affection. "Father," he once said, "believed that the way to travel was slowly." On summer seed-buying trips to Europe he often took a leisurely cattle boat, and for train trips across the United States it was his custom to buy a thousand-mile ticket and get off every place he took a notion to. He would then hire a horse and buggy and visit any of his customers who lived around there, causing them to run and tell all their friends that Mr. Burpee had come all the way from Philadelphia to see their gardens.

The son David travels more swiftly on his appointed rounds than his father did (though about the same annual distance), and except in broad principles and certain details, his life has little in common with that his father led. One of the mutual details is tobacco. Like the original seedsman, his son smokes cigars at the rate many persons smoke cigarettes. W. Atlee Burpee's brand was called Flora de Cable, a name that seemed depressingly apt to friends who made the mistake of accepting one of these ropes, as they regarded them. Mr. Burpee thought them splendid, and bought them in lots of a thousand. Just the same, he offered son David a handsome reward—$1000—if he would not smoke before he was twenty-one, and since David didn't plan to smoke anyway, being a serious-minded distance runner in his youth, he won the reward with the greatest of ease. A few years later a fellow clubman in Philadelphia told him he was missing a lot of pleasure by not smoking, so he forthwith went to the club cigar shop and said "Corona Corona," the only thing he could think of at the moment when asked what he wished. A 65-cent smoke at that time, it was the biggest cigar in the case and a somewhat advanced subject for a beginner. The natural assumption is that young Burpee smoked about a finger of it and staggered outside for fresh air. Not at all, according to the experimenter himself. "I smoked it all the way down and felt fine—because," he now says, "I smoked it s-l-o-w-l-y, see?"

He has been smoking cigars at various speeds ever since, and feels slightly undressed without several in his pocket, usually Webster queens when in the East, or a long blunt shape in the Santa Fe brand when he is on the West Coast. It may be significant to note here that the $1000 he got for abstaining from tobacco until he had passed twenty-one is essentially still in his and his company's hands today. At the time his father presented it, young Burpee was also receiving a second $1000 in the form of a matured building and loan fund investment. This had been built up over ten years from interest his father had been paying him on a still earlier $1000 which he got when he was ten years old and which the astute lad had immediately invested in the family business, to his father's joy. But by the time he was twenty-one and was getting his hands on the couple of thousand in cash, young Burpee had another notion. "I'm going to buy the Barney Reel place," he told his father, referring to a twenty-two-acre farm that adjoined Fordhook, and he added that he had an option to buy for $3200. And where, the elder Burpee inquired without enthusiasm, was he going to get this $3200? "I've got this $2000 to start with," the son said promptly, and then appalled the old man by announcing, "and I'm going to draw my $1000 out of your business. For the $200 balance on the farm, I'll put on a mortgage." It ended up with the father forking over the $200 as a loan, and the son instantly arranging to rent the farm to him. It is still being operated as part of Fordhook's five-hundred-acre expanse.

By the time he engineered this land deal with the Burpee company, David Burpee was an active participant in its affairs, having dropped out of Cornell a few months before, when he grew worried about his father's declining health. So courtly looking and handsome a man that for years a seed house in India had printed his picture on its stationery purely for the tone it lent, W. Atlee Burpee began in 1914 a series of fruitless vacation trips in quest of relief from a liver ailment from which he was growing haggard. His son David was with him almost constantly during this period, at the father's request. It made a close relationship closer, but it kept the son from getting some of the experience he very soon needed in running the business, when, in the late fall of the following year, 1915, W. Atlee Burpee at fifty-seven was finally brought home to Fordhook to die.

David Burpee was then twenty-two. His scholastic background was casual—some early private tutoring, public schools, three and a half years at Culver Military Academy (his own choice, when a magazine ad showing a student on horseback caught his eye), a semester at Cornell University (where he sampled around by attending genetics classes for information, not college credits, and pledged Delta Upsilon fraternity). In any case, he was clearly the heir apparent to management of the big company; W. Atlee Burpee, Jr., a year and a half younger, did not have David Burpee's concentrated devotion to the seed business, and a still younger brother, Stewart Alexander Burpee, was sickly from birth and died young.

If a thumbnail analysis of David Burpee's character, made in his mature years by a business acquaintance, is correct, it may shed some light on his behavior when younger. "Frank and outspoken, but basically reserved," this size-up ran. "He has an orderly, practical mind. Good sense of humor and imagination, and wants what he wants when he wants it. Well adjusted, and not bound by tradition." As a boy, he was certainly not bound by at least one Fordhook tradition; his father bred and sold aristocratic collies, but David's favorite dog, and the one he still remembers with longing, was a mongrel on the loose who won his way into the lad's heart by stealing half a ham from the kitchen the minute he arrived at the farm, and eating it on the front lawn. He named the dog Don, and it slept on his bed, helped him wake up at 4

A.M. to run a muskrat trap line, and was so great a ratter, weasel killer, and brain that it passed into legend, becoming the hero of a serial saga for the eventual delight of David Burpee's children, Jonathan and Blanche.

As might be supposed, vegetables were—and are—a big thing on the family dining table at Fordhook. (In 1915 a New York *Sun* garden writer had dinner there and remarked that "Judging from the variety of vegetables and fruits served, everything in the trial beds was sampled.") At age six the future head of the seed house displayed evidence of his practical head about food. Noticing that his parents seemed to enjoy many vegetables he did not, he made up his mind to taste everything. Beets were the first things he grew to like during this noble experiment and are still his favorite vegetable. The last to give up the struggle were cucumbers, and he still doesn't care greatly for them. Carrots came somewhere in between, and today he occasionally gives voice to a plaintive complaint because when dining out, he is often served carrots but seldom served beets.

He was learning the seed business when he was still just a child, through such chores as gathering seed, and later learning to rogue the rows. Some summers he traveled with his father, usually on the annual European tours of discovery. When he was sixteen his father offered him the $1000 he never collected, to find the yellow sweet pea he never found. (His conscience hurt him for years, he says, because he slyly pinched a few pods of a likely-looking specimen at Kew Gardens, an unsettling act for a boy who occasionally wondered if he would discover he had a call to become a missionary.)

When he entered Culver he was seventeen, a lanky, handsome youth who liked to run, and ride horseback, and who had no interest whatever in studying his head off. There he became so good a half-miler that the coach wanted him to train for the Olympics. He also did trick riding, slept outdoors in a tent in the

Indiana winter to harden himself, and so enjoyed his breakfasts at the training table that he could recite the menu half a century later: five eggs, five slices of toast, beefsteak, hot cereal, milk. His school nickname was "Big Burp." W. Atlee, Jr., who also chose Culver, was "Little Burp."

The brief spell at Cornell followed three and a half years at Culver, and it was when he came home in 1913 for the Christmas holidays that David found his father looking so ill he dropped out of school to be with him. The elder seedsman was in a slow decline, still running the business as usual to the eyes of most observers, but distracted about his condition. He made his regular trip to Europe in the summer of 1914, and the whole family went along. Toward the latter part of the trip a kink was thrown into the plans by W. Atlee Junior's becoming ill of appendicitis in London. The father went on home, leaving David to look after the others and to finish up the summer's business with a trip to Germany.

Two or three days later, the Kaiser's troops marched into Belgium, Europe broke into flames, and from mid-ocean David received a wireless couched in his father's typically restrained language: BETTER NOT GO ON TO GERMANY AT THIS TIME. A business friend in Ireland advised the young man in more emphatic fashion. DO NOT NOW UNDER ANY CIR-CUMSTANCES GO ANYWHERE, he roared by wire.

It was a historical moment of dramatic importance to the United States seed industry—and consequently to every American family. As Europe moved into war, Europe abruptly stopped growing seeds. American seedsmen were flung entirely on their own devices. Out of that necessity an infant American seed-growing industry sprang into a quick, gangling adolescence and then a hurried maturity. W. Atlee Burpee lived on only long enough to see this revolution beginning. He was entering his fortieth year in the seed business, and to mark it he was getting together an anniversary supplement to the 1916 catalog. Some work on this—an eighty-page booklet of pictures, descriptions of the business operations, and reprints of articles—and some work on the catalog was all he had time left for. In August he gave David power of attorney to act as he saw fit, and never went back to the office. Without any specific instructions, the young man took over his father's old desk and, with a total practical experience of a few weeks in one minor department months before, took charge of the biggest mail-order seed business on earth. Death came to its founder three months later, on the day after Thanksgiving, November 27, 1915. As the chief executor of his father's estate, David Burpee continued to run the business, and in 1917 it was made a corporation with him as president and his brother W. Atlee Burpee, Jr., as vice president and treasurer.

# 4 GOT A PROBLEM? HAVE A BOOKLET

On looking over a sample of handwriting by the original Burpee seedsman, an amateur graphologist remarked that it showed a man whose character blended gusto and drive with generosity, tolerance, and a desire to help others. If true, these traits may have been somewhat responsible for a strong desire by W. Atlee Burpee to teach. This took the form of instructive booklets, and they are a sideline business that the Burpee seed company has been in ever since.

At present, the list of how-to information for the home gardener runs to thirty-eight titles, and anyone ambitious enough to study them all could end up with a groundwork in horticulture approaching a professional level in its practical aspects.

Since the tendency today is to break down the information quite specifically by titles, the booklets are much more compactly written than they used to be, and are also more properly called leaflets. Burpee's calls them bulletins, in the Department of Agriculture manner. It sends them free on request, or for fuller answers to questions gardeners are always writing in about. It sometimes mentions certain titles here and there in the catalog pages, and in some years it has run the whole list—a reckless move, sure to result in a rash of requests, "Please send me *all* the bulletins," from certain catalog readers, many of whom turn out to be about ten years old.

Today the information is written by anonymous experts on Burpee's staff. In the very early days it was W. Atlee Burpee's custom to do the job himself, and later he hired it done. He wrote his first instructive booklet at so tender an age that it was out enjoying a nice sale even before he was in business as a seedsman. The title was "The Pigeon Loft, How to Furnish and Manage It," and the chances are that many of the eager middle-aged pigeon fanciers who paid their 50 cents for a copy of the expert's advice would have been flabbergasted to find he was younger than their own sons—just seventeen. He followed up the success promptly with a companion booklet, "The Poultry Yard, How to Furnish and Manage It." He was an expert on that too, and even though he seemed in a rut on titles, both booklets flourished and sold for years.

By the late 1880s the seed part of Mr. Burpee's business was so much bigger than the livestock part that it behooved him to start teaching his customers how to help his seeds grow. This time, instead of writing the instructions himself, he had other people do it, the other people being at first some of the customers themselves. He managed this by offering cash prizes for essays on certain "how-to-grow" subjects. Then he assembled the prize essays into booklets which he sold for 30 to 50 cents each in most cases, or gave away on request by crediting the requesters with 10 cents per $1.00 order for seeds, to apply against booklet purchases.

One of the more expensive early booklets was a 50-cent one titled "How and What to Grow in a Kitchen Garden of One Acre," and it can serve here as a handy contrast with what today's gardeners can get from Burpee's along the same lines.

The kitchen garden booklet came out in 1888, the first year such helps were offered, and was co-authored by the first and

second prize winners of essays on the subject, a Mr. E. D. Darlington (who later became superintendent of the Burpee growing
farm at Doylestown, Pa.) and a Miss L. M. Moll, with a preface
by Mr. Burpee mentioning with his usual blunt vigor that "some
of the methods described are unnecessarily laborious," and that
some varieties recommended had been surpassed by better ones,
but presenting the booklet as nonetheless the most complete and
practical treatise on general gardening yet published. This did
not prevent him from peppering the pages with occasional wry
footnotes: "We must differ with Mr. Darlington as to the usefulness of the winter radishes. Their fresh, pungent taste is very
refreshing." "The reason here presented [by Miss Moll] for not
growing late cabbage, because the worms might damage some
of them, is quite original, and about equal to not planting any
potatoes, because the bugs might eat the tops. . . ."

Running to 198 pages, the booklet discussed at leisure the
proper situation for the garden, soil treatment, the layout, seed
purchasing and seed saving, hotbeds and coldframes, tools, planting, manure and compost, and—at greater length—the sorts of
things to grow.

Strictly speaking, Burpee's has no modern equivalent of this
booklet. To cover the same ground, you would have to ask for
sixteen of the current leaflets. Armed with these, you would have
a less chatty wad of reading matter but a good deal more information, more casually set forth but done with a scholarly flair. Soil
treatment, for example, is covered by a leaflet titled "Soil Care
and Fertilization." A request, whether or not with a seed order,
will bring it to you free, and the same goes for the others. Each
year, Burpee's mails out several thousand of their little leaflets.
Planting of the garden is handled by "Suggestions on Seed Sowing," and another leaflet wrestles with an allied problem, "Damping Off—How to Prevent It."

Of these sixteen leaflets the most general is "Growing Garden
Fresh Vegetables," and it makes short work of such things as the

old debate over the just-right situation for the garden. "As long as you have a sunny spot," it says, "where the soil is fairly rich and well drained, you can raise your favorite vegetables." This is possibly an acceptance of the inevitable, since few home gardeners who send for the leaflet have a choice of many spots, or are staking off anything like the 208-foot by 208-foot square the 1888 booklet recommended as a family garden plot that would accommodate everything but the pumpkins.

The size plot recommended by the current leaflet is scarcely more than one-fortieth the extent of the old one—20 by 55 feet. In fairness it should be added that the old one was about half in small fruits. None are included in today's suggested plot, which calls for twenty-two kinds of vegetables as compared with double that number and more varieties in the 1888 garden.

It does not follow that today's vegetable space of one-twentieth the old one will yield only a twentieth as much food, however. For one thing, it is more closely planted, since the horse-drawn cultivators formerly used took two or three times the clearance that hand cultivation needs between rows. Also, more concentrated growth stimulants and more effective pest fighters have increased production for the home gardener just as they have for the market gardener. Even more important is the boost given by new varieties of vegetables, most notably by hybrids. "We used to plant fifty feet of squash," one backyard gardener said recently. "Then a 25-foot row grew the same amount. Then we cut it to ten feet when newer varieties yielded more, and now we put in only two or three plants and are still getting all we can eat."

Today's family that plants the 20- by 55-foot garden will eat very well indeed, with decent care of the plot and any kind of luck. It will have coming to the table spaced over eight months, say, such salad plants as lettuce, endive, radishes, and cucumbers; greens will come from chard and spinach; sixteen staked tomato plants will furnish vine-ripened fruits enough to keep a family of four or five eating platters of freshly sliced ones every day through the heavy-bearing season, with some over for canning, and tomatoes are nearly foolproof canners. The garden will supply sweet corn to the table for two months or more from three varieties that span the season; and nourishment at a peak of flavor forever unknown to those without a garden will come pouring in from lima beans, snap beans, Brussels sprouts, broccoli, squash, cabbage, peppers, eggplant, kale, cauliflower, beets, carrots, onions—and a little parsley for garnish, flavor, and health.

The vegetable garden leaflet includes a planting-date table and diagram for spacing, in a form far easier to use than in the original booklet, where it took good eyes and close study to make it out. Both of them, though, make mouth-watering reading, likely to drive hungry gardeners a little frantic in the dead of winter. If you had been living in 1888 and paying heed to Burpee's booklet, you would have been planting a few oddities such as hops (the blossoms were used to make yeast), hundred-pound watermelons, and both globe and Jerusalem artichokes; you would have been informed by the booklet that carrots were little used as table vegetables but would be found very palatable in soups and stews, that lettuce was mistakenly known as a salad, "as *salad* means anything that is served in a green state . . . onions, tomatoes, cabbage . . ." And speaking of cabbage, you would have planted over one thousand feet of row, taking up nearly as much space as five entire gardens of today; by burying the late cabbages upside down in the garden under earth and straw, you would have had fresh cabbage all winter. You can still store cabbage this way in a cold winter climate. Here are the instructions from the 1888 booklet, written for the Philadelphia vicinity:

> The cabbage is quite hardy and will stand considerable frost in the fall without damage, being rather improved in quality by it. By the third week in November they should be pulled

up, root and all, the outside leaves wrapped closely around the head and stood side by side, on their heads, on a well drained piece of ground. Dry soil is then thrown on these heads to the thickness of five or six inches and the roots left sticking out of the top; this covering should be firmly packed, to prevent the entrance of water, and a small gutter should be dug round the heap to carry it off. If, after the cold weather has set in and the ground is slightly frozen, the heap is covered with three to four inches of corn fodder or litter, it will prevent the covering from freezing so hard, and will greatly lessen the work of getting out the head when wanted for use.

In general, the modern leaflets make the whole job of gardening seem much easier. An 1896 successor to the vegetable garden booklet took seven mortal pages just to talk about planting times: "No precise rules can be laid down." . . . "North America is divided into a number of clearly defined life areas." . . . "The Transition Zone is the belt in which Boreal and Austral elements overlap. . . ." By contrast, the current leaflet on vegetable growing wraps up the whole subject in a short paragraph: "In the Southern and Pacific Coastal areas, hardy varieties such as peas, lettuce, spinach, chard, beets, carrots, onions, radishes, cabbage, cauliflower, and broccoli can be planted in the fall. In the rest of the United States . . ." and so on.

Other early booklets offered by Burpee's included several addressed to the market gardener; one on insects, some on flowers, one on the annual work at Fordhook Farm (later "Farms"), a collection of technical papers presented in 1893 at the World's Auxiliary Horticultural Congress in Chicago, a booklet for child gardeners, and a vegetable cookbook. Current helps for gardeners from the house of Burpee do not range over so wide a field, which seems a pity if only from the standpoint of liveliness.

Burpee's today do not cater specifically to tots with the urge

to garden, for instance, but in 1912 W. Atlee Burpee rocketed off
on an experiment of this kind by commissioning a garden book
writer, Edith Loring Fullerton, to do a how-to gardening booklet
for children. Mrs. Fullerton turned out a whimsical but practical
thirty-two-page book titled "Small Gardens for Small Folks," and
illustrated with photographs of her own three gardening youngsters nicknamed by her Mousie, Pigeon Pie, and Sunny Jim. Mr.
Burpee confidently had a quarter-million copies of the booklet
printed, and backed them up with a new departure in seedsmen's
practices by setting up a children's department and offering
miniature packets of seeds for children's gardens at 2 cents each,
or twelve for a quarter with the booklet thrown in. Admitting
that a certain number of canny adult gardeners would probably
sneak in at the children's rate, Mr. Burpee came right out with
it in the 1913 catalog and showed himself fairly canny too: "It is
necessary to risk possible loss of trade if we would really help the
children,—many of whom are likely to remain customers of our
children, when all are no longer children." The little booklet was
popular enough to need reprinting, and presumably some of
Burpee's customers today were in rompers when they first
planted Burpee seeds from 2-cent packets.

The cookbook came out in 1890 and enjoyed a brisk distribution for a few years. Offered only as a premium on seed purchases
and not for sale, it was written at W. Atlee Burpee's invitation by
Mrs. S. T. Rorer, principal of the Philadelphia Cooking School
and in her day a nationally known authority on cooking. "As an
illustration of how thoroughly the subject is treated," said an ad-
vertisement about the book, "we would mention that it gives
forty ways of cooking potatoes." Mrs. Rorer even had a recipe
for potato pie: "To one cup of mashed potatoes add one pint of
milk and the yolks of three eggs, well beaten. Mix and add one
cup of sugar and the juice and rind of one lemon. Turn this into
a deep dish lined with paste, bake in a quick oven thirty minutes.
Beat the whites of the eggs until light, add three tablespoons of

powdered sugar and beat white and stiff. Heap this over the pie, put back in the oven a few moments to brown."

The author laid down some interesting ground rules on vegetable cooking generally. "After water has boiled for a time," she informed readers, "it parts with its gases and becomes hard, and most vegetables are better cooked in soft water." A few lines farther on, she made a distinction: " . . . All green vegetables must be cooked in hard water, and all dry vegetables in soft. A teaspoon of common salt added to a gallon of water hardens it at once. A half teaspoon of bicarbonate of soda to a gallon of water renders it soft."

Mrs. Rorer confined her recipes to vegetable dishes, though she gave advice on whatever came to mind: "Broiled or baked blackbirds may be served with the salad course . . ." "Corn must never accompany poultry or game . . ." "Boiled mutton (of course) must have caper sauce, boiled rice, cauliflower, or stewed cabbage." Even etiquette came in for attention. "While perhaps it is rather unusual to give recipes 'how to eat,'" the cooking school principal noted, "it is certainly an art to know just how to eat corn. Score every row of grains with a sharp knife, spread lightly with butter, dust with salt, and with the teeth press out the center of the grains, leaving every hull fast to the cob. Corn thus eaten will not cause trouble or produce indigestion, as the hull is the only indigestible part."

By contrast, the lady had a way of cooking asparagus that did at least make that vegetable easy to mange. She called the dish "asparagus peas," and after cutting off the tender tip ends of the stalks, boiled them hard for a quarter-hour and served them up in a white sauce. The recipe inspired no confidence seventy years later in a homemaker living in the Big Sur, a California region noted for superb cooks. "Anybody who'd do that to honest asparagus," said the Californian crisply, "ought to be sentenced to *eat* it."

You cannot get a vegetable cookbook or any other kind of cookbook from Burpee's today, but leaflets on many other subjects are yours for the asking, and the annual seed and bulb catalogs also have a good deal of gardening information spotted on pages of the plants referred to. The quickest way to get leaflets is to write the company office nearest you:

W. Atlee Burpee Company
Philadelphia 32, Pa.

W. Atlee Burpee Company
Clinton, Iowa

W. Atlee Burpee Company
Riverside, California

Here is the complete list of the current thirty-eight leaflets, by code number and title:

GN–38  Soil Care and Fertilization
GN–34  Suggestions on Seed Sowing
GN–35  Damping Off—How to Prevent It
GN–41  Greenhouse Gardening
GN–43  The Lawn—Construction and Maintenance
GN–40  Growing Garden Fresh Vegetables
GN–9   Beans
GN–7   Cabbage and Related Crops
GN–8   Sweet Corn
GN–12  Celery
GN–15  Cucumbers, Squash, Pumpkins and Melons
GN–48  Mushroom Spawn
GN–16  Peas
GN–10  Pepper and Eggplant
GN–13  Vegetable Root Crops—Carrots, Beets, Radishes, Turnips, etc.
GN–14  Rhubarb Roots, Onion Sets, Asparagus, Horse-Radish

GN–11   Salad Crops—Lettuce, Endive, etc.

GN–17   Tomatoes

GN–22   Annuals

GN–19   Aster Culture

GN–21   Snapdragon Culture

GN–26   Pansies—Directions for Growing over the Winter

GN–27   Geranium Culture

GN–28   Fall Sowing of Larkspur

GN–20   Petunias

GN–23   Fall Sowing of Sweet Peas

GN–36   Sweet Pea Culture—Spring Sowing

GN–37   Annuals and Perennials for Fall Sowing

GN–18   Biennials and Perennials from Seed

GN–42   Plants for Shade and Partial Shade

GN–24   Spring Flowering Bulbs—Daffodils, Tulips, Hyacinths, etc.

GN–29   Forcing Spring Flowering Bulbs for Indoor Bloom

GN–30   Hardy Garden Lilies

GN–32   Summer Blooming Bulbs and Roots, Gladiolus, Dahlias, Cannas, etc.

GN–31   Tender Bulbs—Tuberous Begonias, Gloxinias, Caladiums, Callas, etc.

GN–45   Rock Gardens

GN–46   Growing Herbs

GN–54   House Plants and Their Care

In addition to the leaflets, there are two other gardener aids, handy little folders such as Mr. Burpee used to call vest pocket guides. They are:

> Planning Your Vegetable Garden
>
> Planning Your Flower Garden

Each is a quick reference to the growth pattern and uses of the most popular vegetables and flowers.

# 5 COUSIN LUTHER

When David Burpee mentions Luther Burbank today he is apt to call him "my famous cousin." The relationship has occasionally been taken with a grain of salt by some seedsmen rivals and some newsmen, possibly because Burbank seemed to them to have become a Burpee cousin by a sort of spontaneous combustion. In a letter dated October 20, 1900, for instance, Burbank wrote to W. Atlee Burpee to thank him for hospitality during a Burbank business tour to the East Coast, and nothing was said about kinship, though Burbank was highly complimentary, remarking, "A careful seedsman's experiment grounds, like yours, it seems to me, are far more useful than any of the colleges or public experiment stations, as it is all practical work. Your Fordhook trial grounds were the best of all my Eastern object-lessons. . . ."

Nine years later, W. Atlee Burpee sprang to Luther Burbank's defense when the *Rural New Yorker* suggested that the plant wizard was something of a fraud. It was an opinion voiced from time to time by certain Burbank critics. Others objected mainly that he was not scientific in keeping careful track of his plant breeding steps, while still others gave him credit for bringing mass production into the selection and discovery end of American horticulture, but said he permitted exploiters to claim far more for his creations than their performance under differing climatic conditions justified. David Fairchild, head for many years of the Department of Agriculture's Office of Seed and Plant Introduction, and a personal acquaintance of Burbank's, pointed out in his book, *The World Was My Garden* (Charles Scribner's Sons, New York, 1938), that Burbank "grew up as a commercial nurseryman and spent his life in an atmosphere where plants meant money, and where exaggerated claims such as those in many nursery catalogues were the rule, not the exception. This early training unfitted him in many ways to handle scientifically the large amount of plant material which he grew and imported. Consequently, I am inclined to believe that he had little control over the circumstances resulting in the exploitation which brought him a certain degree of disrepute in scientific circles."

W. Atlee Burpee seemed to have no reservations about Burbank's achievements; his letter of protest to the *Rural New Yorker* was a sizzler, and he stated that he knew Burbank was utterly honest. He did not, however, mention anything about being a cousin of any degree to him, nor did he ever make capital of this unique distinction.

David Burpee, nonetheless, has no blocks about explaining the cousin setup if asked. Luther Burbank, he says simply, was a great admirer of W. Atlee Burpee's integrity, calling the company the most reliable seed house in the world, and in one of his letters to the elder Burpee, Burbank said, as accurately as David Burpee can recall, "I now want to claim cousinship with you. My grandmother in Rowley [Massachusetts] was a Burpee." Presumably Mr. Burbank became Cousin Luther forthwith. Since Rowley, a little community in the northeast corner of the state, was where the first Burpees settled after coming to the New World from France, and since "cousin" is a term of great stretching power, there seems no reason to belabor the point. Today one of David Burpees' regrets is that as the young head of his business he did not realize his opportunities and take time to run up to

Santa Rosa more often when in California and visit Cousin
Luther. Certainly the two had things in common. Both were after
results of benefit to humanity and were also interested in showing
a profit; both were good showmen and salesmen. The house of
Burpee handled certain Burbank developments from time to
time, with mutual benefit.

In 1926 the plant wizard died and Stark Bro's Nurseries of
Louisiana, Missouri, largest business of their kind in the world,
then and now, were privileged to buy up the rights to his creations and to the various developments in progress, as specified
by Burbank before he died. Stark's are still growing some of Burbank's things, including his July Elberta peach, Grand Prize
prune, Mammoth Cardinal and Great Yellow plums, and their
letterhead carries the notation: "Burbank Central Experiment
Grounds." In addition to the nursery stock, however, Stark's also
found themselves with a trunkful of Burbank's flower and vegetable seeds, included in the estate. Having only a minor interest
in the seed business at the time, and finding even that interest
dwindling, Stark's in 1931 washed their hands of seeds and made
a deal with Burpee's to take over the Burbank trunk, or "Treasure
Chest" as it was referred to in the resulting publicity. Burpee's
were proud and happy to get hold of Cousin Luther's old trunk,
and their 1932 catalog announced the purchase:

## LUTHER BURBANK'S PLANT EXPERIMENTS
## TO BE CONTINUED BY US

Luther Burbank, known as the plant wizard of the world,
was a cousin of W. Atlee Burpee, and the two men had much
in common. Both were masters in the creation of new varieties of plants that were better than those in use. Mr. Burpee
built up the largest mail order seed business in the world,
while Mr. Burbank confined his efforts almost exclusively

to his garden work, selling his seeds only in a modest way. How natural it was that this past year (summer of 1931) arrangements were made whereby we took over all Mr. Burbank's Flower and Vegetable experimental work, so it can be continued and developed. We also will have the exclusive distribution of the seeds from Luther Burbank Flower and Vegetable productions. This year a limited number of varieties are offered on page 160, in the back of this book. Everyone knows of the marvelous work of this world-famous hybridist, and we feel sure our customers will quickly and generously avail themselves of these Burbank seeds. From Mr. Burbank's numerous letters to us we quote: "I remember well my former visit to your wonderful Floradale Farms . . . where I saw so much of interest to me."

Prefixed "Burbank" in each case, there were on the initial list sixteen flowers and six vegetables. Over a six-year span the list gradually withered until in 1938 it disappeared entirely. Some of the Burbank flowers and vegetables continued to be offered for a while, but they were carried in the body of the catalog. Today the only plants carrying the old plant wizard's name in the Burpee catalog are Burbank's hybrid tritoma and the Luther Burbank zinnias, and the zinnias aren't the zinnias Burbank produced. However, they were developed as a continuation of Burbank's hybridizing, and were named for him in memory of his pioneer work on these flowers. They are part of Burpee's Super Giant line. The ones called Burpee's Giant Hybrid zinnias also owed their pioneer breeding to Burbank's work, as do the zinnias named for David Burpee.

For the record, it should be added that Luther Burbank's name also appears in the current catalog heading one of a group of collections under the general designation: "Burpee's Special Flower Seed Blends." Here are listed: "Luther Burbank's Favorite Flowers. Celosia, centaurea, cynoglossum, gypsophila, helichrysum, larkspur, miniature zinnias and others. Delightful blend of flowers on which Luther Burbank worked years ago." Thirty-five cents buys you the whole packet.

Recently when he was asked exactly what he had gained from the Burbank trunk, David Burpee seemed to find the question a hard one. Nor could he recall what the treasure chest had cost him. There is magic still in the Burbank name, however, and the Burpee company continues to operate a subsidiary called the Luther Burbank Seed Company, using it for some offerings of seeds as premiums in other people's merchandise, such as packages of breakfast food.

Not long after the Burbank list vanished from the Burpee catalog, the Post Office issued a Luther Burbank memorial stamp, one of thirty-five in the Famous Americans series. This was in 1940, and David Burpee lost no time in buying some. He wasn't sure what use he would make of them, but he thought he'd better buy while he could, so he picked up a hundred thousand. This safe but no-interest investment cost him $3000, the stamp being a 3-cent one. To date, only about one-third of Burpee's Burbank memorial stamps have been used, most notably on invitations to the New York premiere of the Luther Burbank zinnias in 1948. The remainder are stored in the office safe till Burpee thinks up some more good ideas for using them, especially now that they need the help of another stamp to carry a letter by first-class mail.

Lest anyone is tempted to feel sorry for a man saddled with all those old stamps, it should here be noted that in addition to still being perfectly acceptable at any post office, the 3-cent Luther Burbank stamp has become sufficiently prized by philatelists so that it is now worth around 8 cents over the counter. This is not a phenomenal jump, in the stamp world, but as an investment it is equal to a tidy 8 per cent annual return to Burpee for each and every year since he bought the stamps.

# 6 HOW TO LIVE OUT OF A GARDEN

For the collector of Americana the early Burpee catalogs teem with goodies all once close to the hearts of the people. The seed business has always been extravagantly personal in its relations with customers, and even today the giant Burpee organization often gets chatty little notes such as one that came from a woman in New England. She regretfully asked David Burpee to take her name off his catalog mailing list after a forty-year tenure because she had decided to let her spry seventy-five-year-old niece do the family gardening now that she herself had turned ninety-nine. (Burpee's sent catalogs to both, with letters of appreciation.)

Despite such expressions of loyalty, the colorful modern Burpee seed catalog seems as impersonal as a brick when compared with the juicy ones W. Atlee Burpee used to write, much of them in his own flourishing longhand. Mr. Burpee's main aim was to educate the customers and get them all as whooped up about his seeds as he was, and once he got started writing, he could hardly stop. In his time, seeds were far more intimately a part of daily family life than now; its garden was the means of supplying many families with—besides food and flowers—medicines, kitchen equipment, entertainment, comforts, cosmetics, and even fuel. Surprisingly enough, the seeds that grew many of these wonders are still listed in the catalog. They are usually there for some reason besides utility but they can still do the old job.

The older catalogs were talking to a family audience so accustomed to doing for itself that it was nicely tuned to receive such catalog fare as Mr. Burpee's annual little lecture on popcorn: "Pop Corn," he wrote with his frequent emphatic capitals, "should be found in every garden, especially if there are children to enjoy it during the long winter evenings. It is a fact not generally known that pop corn pops best when more than one year old, and that, when well popped, it becomes twenty times its natural size; thus, a quart and a half will make nearly a bushel of popped corn." Our family's long winter evenings were enlivened not only by, one trusts, earnest study of the new year's Burpee catalog but also by the deafening fusillade of Burpee's popcorn, if the folks had paid attention to previous years' catalogs. Their seedsman even included a little picture of a popper, with the word that if it could not be found in the hardware store it could easily be made from a few cents' worth of wire netting. The old catalogs listed half-a-dozen or more popcorn varieties. Four are listed in the catalog now, three of them being hybrids, with an expansion up to thirty volumes. That is, a single quart will now get you a bushel.

While the children were growing popcorn for those winter nights at the fireside, father was sometimes bringing along a patch of tobacco for his own future comfort. Burpee's could offer him as many as fifteen kinds to choose from, including Persian Rose Muscatelle, "Introduced by us several years since from Hungary, whence it was brought from the gardens of the Shah of Persia," which produced a leaf so huge a man could hide behind it. Other varieties included General Grant, Havana, Gold Leaf, Gooch, and White Burley—which the catalog recommended as so ornamental it could be planted on the lawn and in shrub borders.

From fifteen, the varieties of tobacco seed offered by Burpee's have shrunk to none at all today. The nearest you can now come to raising your own cheroots is to plant a little nicotiana, and the catalog has even stopped calling it flowering tobacco.

Another little home-grown comfort now missing from the Burpee offerings is something that was called the soja bean. A legume primarily intended for livestock to graze, the soja bean was also sold by the 5-cent packet since it offered this kitchen-garden aid to the household: "This variety," Mr. Burpee advised his customers, "has been extensively advertised as the '*German Coffee Berry*,' the seed sometimes being parched and ground for use as coffee. Plants grow eighteen inches in height and are immensely productive, having small, round seed."

A plant also used for livestock grazing but having a bonus for the household was madder. Burpee's used to list it under the "Miscellaneous Seeds" heading, advising customers that the roots furnished a red dye. A pound of seed cost a dollar.

Occasionally the seedsman called attention to an extra utility possessed by a flower. For this reason nasturtiums used to appear twice in the catalog, once in the flower section and next among the vegetables, complete with recipe: "Nasturtiums of all varieties are useful for furnishing tender seed-pods which make delicious pickles. The seeds for pickling should be gathered while green and with a portion of the stem attached. Pick them over and place in a jar until filled; then cover them with cider vinegar that has been brought to the boil and is still warm, to keep for winter use."

Nasturtiums, of course, are offered in the current Burpee catalog, but also, surprisingly, you will find there the gourds which once were an important source of utensils for the home. The reason you can still find gourds in the Burpee catalog is not that they make lightweight and durable containers—which they do—but that they are pretty. They always have been pretty, and even in

1887 when advising his customers of the usefulness of gourds, Mr. Burpee also listed twelve varieties among flower seeds, in his department of annual climbers. Of the sugar trough gourd, which looked like an immense pear and was one of the most versatile, he wrote: "These are useful for many household purposes, such as buckets, baskets, nest-boxes, soap and salt-dishes, and for storing the winter's lard. They grow to hold from four to ten gallons each, have thick, hard shells, very light but durable, having been kept in use as long as ten years."

The nest-egg gourd produced smooth, white, egg-shaped fruits, and the old catalogs cautioned against growing it in very rich earth lest it produce nest eggs so lavish that nothing but an ostrich could use them. Both nest-egg and sugar trough gourds are still listed in the catalog. The dishcloth gourd, or luffa, can also be had from Burpee's today in its large-gourd collection, but the old catalogs were more explicit on its peculiar merits: "A natural dishcloth, and a most admirable one," they declared with enthusiasm and an illustration, "is furnished by the peculiar lining of this fruit, which is sponge-like, porous, very tough, elastic, and durable. Many ladies prefer this dishcloth to any prepared by art. The fruit grows about two feet in length, and the vine is very ornamental, producing clusters of large, yellow blossoms, in pleasing contrast with the silvery-shaded, dark green foliage . . . The dried interiors of these gourds have already become an article of commerce." The durable interiors were also popular as bath sponges, and are still seen in drugstores today, wrapped in cellophane and fetching about a dollar apiece.

By planting a few seeds of the dipper gourd families used to grow their own ladles, in sizes ranging from about one pint to three. The dippers came with curved handles unless the plant was grown on a trellis so that the fruits hung down. Either way, they had the advantage over metal dippers of handles that stayed cool while dipping hot liquids. As with the sugar trough gourd, the dipper gourd was prepared for use by merely cutting off the unwanted portion after the fruit had grown to the size needed. The dipper gourd is carried in the catalog today, in the "Big Gourds Mixed" collection, and there is also a little orange and green spoon gourd among the small-gourd listing. Of this one, the old catalogs had the following remarks: "Small fruits with slender neck four to five inches long. . . . By slicing off a portion on the side of the bowl and drying the shell, a spoon may be made. They will be found quite useful also in darning stockings and glove fingers, while the dry fruits with the seeds left in make fine rattles for the baby."

There were a couple of other highly useful household items Burpee's could supply you with once upon a time. Broomcorn was one. A type of sorghum, its panicles make the straw used to make brooms, "being firm and of good length," the catalog said, "and retaining the light green coloring when properly cured. Per pkt. 5 cts." Then, as now, broom straws were also useful for testing cakes to see if they were finished baking. The other item was an entertaining novelty as well as of, presumably, some practical use. It was offered under the name of the Resurrection Plant, and described in these terms under an illustration of a graceful whorl of fronds: "This is really one of the greatest curiosities of nature, and is, doubtless, well known to many of our readers. Imagine a bunch of withered looking, curled-up shoots, brown, stiff, and apparently dead, and resembling a bird's nest. Place it in a saucer of water; in half an hour what a transformation! The withered looking bunch has opened, and is now changed into a patch of lovely green moss, having the appearance of a genuine live plant. It can be taken out and dried, and the operation repeated to astonish your friends and visitors, and will keep for a number of years. It is so sensitive to moisture that, when placed outside, it will open on the approach of rain, and close during dry weather. In Palestine it is called Kaf Maryam, or 'Mary's Flower,' and has been known for many centuries." You could buy it from Burpee's for 15 cents then, but not for love or money today. Nor is broomcorn available from them, as it is considered a farm seed and the farm seed line was dropped a few years ago.

Headaches and fevers in the old days were taken into account when the garden was planted, and in his list of herbs Mr. Burpee was as particular to mention medicinal uses as culinary ones. Balm (*Melissa officinalis*) was recommended for fevers, in the form of balm wine or balm tea, and headaches were said to be relieved by a tea brewed from the leaves of thyme. Balm is not now carried in the catalog but thyme is, though no medical properties are attributed to it. The modern catalog does, however, go along with older ones in mentioning the use of horehound leaves for coughs, and it suggests catnip tea for the relief of nervous headaches. The older catalogs mention catnip as a mild nerve medicine for infants.

In ancient days some of the herbs and vegetables were given credit for a good deal more in curative powers than anyone has claimed for them lately. Pliny the Elder, Roman naturalist of the first century A.D., thought that anise (*Pimpinella anisum*) could restore youth to one's face and would ensure sweet dreams if fastened in a sachet to the pillow. Even in the oldest Burpee catalogs no such claims were ever made for anise, and certainly no such remarkable properties were attributed to beets as those that fifth-century Romans credited them with; they thought beets good for the cure of fevers, cancer, and bites from snakes and mad dogs. In the time of the first Queen Elizabeth of England it was said that bald men could very speedily grow a new crop by squeezing onions on their heads in the sunshine.

Compared with these, Mr. Burpee's herbs seem pretty mild. As a liniment for cuts and bruises, the fruits of balsam pear (*Momordica charantia*) preserved in alcohol were said to be valuable, and three other herbs were mentioned as useful medicinally—wormwood (*Artemisia absinthium*), a vermifuge and tonic, and an ingredient in absinthe; rue (*Ruta graveolens*); and tansy (*Tanacetum vulgare*). None are now carried in the Burpee catalog. In England it was once the custom to make cakes flavored with tansy, which is aromatic and bitter, at Easter; Samuel Pepys mentions a dish called a tansy, apparently flavored with this herb; it was a baked custard made of eggs, cream, sugar, and rose water.

Also among herbs in some of the old Burpee catalogs there occurred one said to be useful as a cosmetic. It was bene (*Sesamum orientale*), and oil extracted from the seeds was used to whiten and soften the skin. Only southern belles benefited, apparently, as the plant was too tender for the North. "The leaves immersed in a tumbler of water," the catalog added, "will make a mucilaginous drink very beneficial in cases of cholera infantum, diarrhoea, etc."

Herbs are still prominent in the Burpee catalog, fifteen (not including parsley and a new ornamental basil) being listed under the broad heading, "Aromatic, Medicinal, and Kitchen." Though their uses as seasonings are now most emphasized, one suggestion is made which the older catalogs omitted. It is in connection with true lavender. In addition to use of the dried flowers as a fragrance in the linen closet, they are also, says the description, used as a repellent to moths.

It may seem to be expecting too much of a vegetable garden to look to it for fuel. Perhaps the fuel was only a sort of kindling or fire starter, but still, it was one of the garden's crops at one time. The fuel was a by-product of sunflowers, the Mammoth Russian variety with seed heads from a foot to nearly two feet across. It was the strong thick stalks supporting these immense heads that supplied fuel. The seeds were fed to poultry, being a prime egg-producing ration, and the leaves were fed to cattle, so that nothing was wasted. The variety is still offered by

Burpee's, and the seeds still recommended as a chicken feed. The stalks can still be burned in stove and fireplace, too, but the modern recommendation is that they be valued as background or screen plantings.

In days of yore, gardeners had a more antic sense of humor than they seem to have nowadays. Or perhaps it was the seedsmen who had the sense of humor. At any rate there was a section in the old catalogs headed "Odd and Curious Vegetables," intended to furnish merriment to the customers. The *pièce de résistance* of the group was botanically *Scorpiurus vermiculatus*. Creeping plants with small yellow flowers, their fruit looked like curled-up caterpillars. "They are grown as curiosities," the catalog chortled, "and sometimes, as a harmless practical joke, are put into salads, for the purpose of startling those who are unacquainted with them." This from a man vigorously trying to popularize salads, to wit: "Nothing is more wholesome, and if you once acquire the habit, you will wonder how you ever enjoyed a dinner without a crisp refreshing salad!"

A couple of beans found a place in the odd and curious vegetables, too. One, the Ram's Horn bean (*Dolichos bi-confortus*), grew in a kind of coil, and the other, the Cuban Asparagus bean of the same genus, grew to be three or more feet long. A cucumber with the same tendency was listed by the jolly seedsman under the name of Snake cucumber. Growing to be as much as six feet long, they looked enough like snakes to keep the girls well out of the garden. "And," Mr. Burpee added frankly, "the quality is fair."

To include the smaller children in preparations for some of that winter-evening corn popping, there was a miniature variety called Burpee's Golden Tom Thumb. Its stalks grew only about as high as a man's knee, with ears no longer than his finger.

Cacti ranked as a kind of parlor entertainment in those times, and Burpee's could fix up the customers with no fewer than sixteen different kinds. This collection, all growing plants, cost two dollars and excited Mr. Burpee's enthusiasm. "Even when neglected for months," he wrote, "they will, after a good watering, not only begin to grow at once, but often commence to *bloom profusely.* The *perfume* of their flowers is, in many cases, *delicious,* and the seed pods of a *brilliant coral red,* ornamenting the plant for several months after blooming. They also increase in value as they get older, and, with proper treatment, a plant should last a lifetime. We know of several that are over 30 years old and reward their owner with several hundreds of flowers every season." If you are not impatient you can test these rewards today for yourself, as Burpee's still offers cactus. They now offer it in seed form only, and warn you that some kinds germinate slowly. A packet of mixed varieties (number not given) costs 50 cents.

For entertainment outdoors in former days you could get for a mere half-dollar a Japanese rose tree (*Pyrus malus Parkmanii*) about which Mr. Burpee grew lyrical: "It makes a small, finely-branching tree, with very glossy, wedge-shaped leaves, which become brilliant crimson in autumn, equaling in their tints the maple or woodbine. The blossoms are produced in clusters of five, on very slender stems, bending gracefully with the weight of the buds and blossoms. The buds are one inch long and are precisely the same as very slender *tea rose buds,* of a dark carmine color in bud, and lighter shades as they open. They are as double as an ordinary tea rose, and no one seeing them as cut flowers would ever suppose them to be anything else than tea roses. The tree has the habit of flowering on both the old and the new growth, and a shoot of the previous year's growth, loaded with its little roses is the most beautiful object conceivable. It has long been desired to have a tree rose, and this is realization at last. Of course it is perfectly hardy and easy to grow on all soils, being a crab apple. Its fruits are very small and bright colored, and hang on the tree till midwinter." Despite all this, the little rose tree soon disappeared from the catalog. His public, presumably, did not agree with Mr. Burpee, and he always knew when he was licked.

In years past, Burpee's customers were urged to grow their own insecticide. "Pyrethrum, the Insect Powder Plant," the catalog called it, and stated: "It has been fully demonstrated that the Persian or Dalmatian Insect Powder can be made from the ground leaves and flowers of the Pyrethrum, grown in this country, equal to the best quality imported. Large areas of the plants are grown in California, and the manufacture of the powder, which is certain death to insects, successfully conducted. We offer seed of both *Pyrethrum roseum* and *cineriafolium*." Seeds of this plant in the roseum species are listed in the modern Burpee catalog, and it is now regarded as a section of the genus Chrysanthemum. Though nothing is now said in the catalog of its bug-killing qualities, anyone is welcome to try. Commercially, it is the dried roots that are used to make insect powder.

Aside from the practical value of pyrethrum, the early catalog descriptions of how the seeds were originally obtained made such entertaining reading that they rivaled the dime thrillers of the period. "The powder has been in use for many years in Asiatic countries south of the Caucasus mountains," Mr. Burpee wrote in 1883. "It was sold at a high price by the inhabitants, who successfully kept its nature a secret until the beginning of this century, when an American merchant, Mr. Juntikoff, learned that the powder was obtained from the dried and pulverized flower-heads of certain species of Pyrethrum growing abundantly in the mountain region of what is known as the Russian province of Trans-Caucasia.

"As to the Dalmatian plants, the inhabitants are very unwilling to give any information regarding a plant the product of which they wish to monopolize. We have found great difficulty in obtaining even small quantities of the seed. Indeed, the people are so jealous of their plant that to send the seed out of the country becomes a serious matter, in which life is risked."

Despite the cloak-and-dagger atmosphere in which the seeds of the pyrethrum were originally obtained, Mr. Burpee took his usual detached and judicial air when judging the merits of claims made for the insecticide. His experience with it, he told customers, had been "so far quite satisfactory," but one of its advocates he thought went too far when he said, "To prevent the ravages of the weevil on wheat fields, the powder is mixed with the grains to be sown, in proportion of about ten ounces to about three bushels, which will save a year's crop." Mr. Burpee made short work of the claim.

"This," he snorted, "is simply ridiculous. We . . . fully appreciate its value as a general insecticide . . . but we are far from considering it as a universal remedy for all insects. No such universal remedy exists. . . ." Nor does it exist today, some eighty years later. But seedsmen can now supply you with many plants more resistant to insect damage. This resistance may be due to tougher stems that defy borers, odors that repel pests, and to other physical or chemical barriers. One of the best defenses against bugs is healthy growth. As for disease resistance, this is now a built-in with many new plants. There are snapdragons that rust seldom harms, asters that fight off wilt and yellows, tomatoes that are strong against fusarium wilt, mosaic-resistant beans and spinach. The list grows longer year by year—one of the seedsman's most valuable contributions to productive gardening.

# *7* THE SEARCH

In 1902 Burpee's introduced Golden Bantam corn, a vegetable so good and so quickly popular, it alone could have made a seedsman's reputation. Sixty years later it is still a delicacy, one so favored by some corn-on-the-cob gourmets that they consider all other varieties simply not worth the planting. Golden Bantam's beginnings are lost in mystery, and even the way Burpee's got it was rather casual.

"Eleven years ago," W. Atlee Burpee said, the year after he showered Golden Bantam on the world, "there lived near Greenfield, Massachusetts, an old gentleman who had a fancy for furnishing his friends with some choice early corn long before they had thought of having any ripe enough for the table—but he would never let any of them have any to plant. Since his death this variety has been kept pure and constantly selected by MR. J. G. PICKETT, also of Greenfield, Massachusetts. In the spring of 1900 our friend, E. L. COY, the veteran seed grower of New York, obtained for us all the seed Mr. Pickett could spare, which was less than two quarts, and wrote: 'You now own the very sweetest and richest corn ever known, and I am very glad to help you to its ownership. I came across this distinct new early sweet corn two years ago, when visiting at a cousin's in Greenfield,

Mass.—it impressed me as *the sweetest and most tender corn I ever tasted*. It is a deep yellow in color and very early.'"

Mr. Burpee paid Mr. Coy $25 for his scant two quarts of seed, one of the best bargains in gardening history. Little Golden Bantam with its precise eight rows of kernels was a success from the start. Rave notices began coming in from Burpee customers, and Golden Bantam quickly became a standard of excellence. In 1909 an upstart called Catawba was touted as "The First Real Rival Yet Discovered to Our Famous Golden Bantam." It soon settled down in an inferior position to the champion and today is no longer heard of.

A whole decade after Golden Bantam was introduced, the Chicago *Tribune* already announcing itself as the world's greatest newspaper, devoted its leading editorial to singing the praises of this ravishing corn, in phrases dripping with classical references and stuffed with adjectives: ". . . tenderest, sweetest, most luscious, honeyed, sugary, toothsome . . ."

Look in the Burpee catalog today, and though there are many rivals, including some brilliant hybrids, some of them crosses of Golden Bantam, you will find the original still headlined as "America's favorite sweet corn." The catalog, which has twenty-three other varieties to sell, says: "If you want a larger ear, an earlier corn, a more productive one, we have varieties for your needs, but if you want the best and sweetest for your table, it's true 8-rowed Golden Bantam."

Golden Cross Bantam, developed in 1927 by scientists of the United States Department of Agriculture and the Purdue University experiment station to get a sweet corn resistant to Stewart's Wilt, was the result of crossing two strains of Golden Bantam after each had been inbred and culled for several years. This kind of work on corn usually takes at least seven generations. By then the inbreeding had rendered each of the Golden Bantam strains so puny that a gardener wouldn't have given them row space. But when at last these two pitiful waifs were allowed to mate, the result was sensational—larger, plumper ears than the regular Golden Bantam, delicious and handsome. Released for trial in 1933, it quickly became the top sweet corn with planters. Burpee's sells it today for 25 cents a packet as "the standard hybrid for quality by which all others are judged." But the original Golden Bantam, at 20 cents the packet, is still Burpee's pet and gets top billing and a larger bull's-eye (the house's version of a gold star) than its cross.

This is as good a place as any to point out the immense importance of selection in plant breeding. In W. Atlee Burpee's day it was the seedsman's main reliance. Nature provided the breaks, and it was then up to man to keep sorting out the offspring of these new plants until he had a reliable best. Relatively recent, however, is the concept called individual plant selection. This means simply that instead of getting excited over one splendid ear of corn, say, the breeder judges the plant as a whole. As simple as this sounds, it came as a revolutionary change in the selection procedure, and is a much surer road to plant improvement than the individual-fruit method of selection, even though that one was quite probably responsible for the selection of such stars as Golden Bantam corn.

Like stars in some other fields, though, Golden Bantam had to be discovered by someone who could make it known to millions, or in time it would probably have been lost. Discovery, in fact, was once the classic and only method of finding new things for the garden. Historian Raphael Holinshed, chief author of the famed *Chronicles of England, Scotland and Ireland,* from which Shakespeare is thought to have got the background for his historical plays, told that in sixteenth-century England, "Delicate merchants, gentlemen, and the nobilitie . . . make their provision yearelie for new seeds out of strange countries." Somewhat more than three centuries later, when W. Atlee Burpee started selling seeds, this was still true, except that his customers were anyone with a nickel.

By then, at least on the seedsman's side, money sometimes seemed to be no object when there was a question of getting there first with a new wonder. In 1905 W. Atlee Burpee got a letter from a California lima bean grower saying he had discovered on his place two new bush lima beans so fine that he was going to auction them off to the nation's seedsmen. At this, there was no holding Mr. Burpee, who still had bells in his head over his triumphant introduction fifteen years before of the Burpee Bush lima—the first big-beaned *bush* lima ever known. He sped his general manager, Howard M. Earl, off to California with orders to bid $5000 for each bean if necessary, a loony figure to most seedsmen of that day, and no peanuts now, either. Mr. Earl played hard to get with the overshrewd seller, and eventually walked off with both bush limas for a thousand dollars each. Somehow, though, a rumor got around that Burpee's *had* paid five grand each. When the beans arrived in Philadelphia, Mr. Burpee clapped them into the office safe amid a deafening roar of publicity. By 1907 he had grown enough seeds of both varieties to introduce them, and he ran on about it for six catalog pages. He called one Fordhook Bush lima, and the other Burpee Improved Bush lima. Both are headliners in the catalog today, and Fordhook, which Burpee's now unequivocally calls the "most famous lima bean in the world," is served under its own name in good restaurants, and identified by it on frozen-food packages.

Seedsmen of W. Atlee Burpee's day never knew what better things might be growing around the corner or across the sea until they saw for themselves. What they were hoping to find was one of nature's happy accidents—the bush limas, perhaps a tomato that mysteriously ripened earlier than its surrounding acres of brothers and sisters, a sweet pea that sprang out beautifully ruffled in the midst of smooth-petaled ones. These geniuses among plants, variously called mutations or sports, freaks or crosses, were a boon to the discoverer in two ways. As the one to introduce a new thing, he enjoyed an exclusive franchise for a year or two—until rival seedsmen could raise, by planting his seed, enough of their own to sell. And in the second place, being known as the introducer of a good thing helped all his business. This made up for a lot of wild-goose chasing, too. Burpee's has willingly lost thousands of dollars on some expensive introductions and felt well repaid by knowing that gardeners around the globe that year were being told "Burpee's" when they asked where in the world their neighbors had got the seed for some new humdinger.

When the spring rush each year was over, it was W. Atlee Burpee's habit to take his slow boat to Europe and spend the summer sleuthing for novelties. When his sons were old enough to keep from under foot and learn something, he often took one or both along. David became the regular companion on these jaunts as he showed a zest for the seed business.

The usual procedure was to bring back for testing at Fordhook Farms the seed of any likely-looking new plant. However, the usual procedure was on rare occasions plowed under if something looked so good that Mr. Burpee couldn't wait. This took quite a bit of soul searching, and when in 1912 he burst forth with an untried (by him) but promising new cabbage, he took more catalog space to explain his impetuosity than he did to explain the cabbage. Even then, he was still biting his nails. "Are we right," he implored his customers, "in deciding to make this one exception . . . ?" Thereupon he hurried to tell all:

> Last summer the writer (W.A.B.) with his eldest son, David, and friend, MR. HUGH DICKSON, the well-known seedsman of Belfast, spent many a strenuous day under the broiling sun of the driest summer ever known, inspecting seed crops in Great Britain and upon the Continent of Eu-

rope. In conversation with one of the most experienced growers of Cabbage seed we all three became interested in his
account of a most unique, new, early Cabbage, which he had
discovered several years ago in an "out of the way" country
that is seldom (if ever before) visited by seedsmen. Tracing
this Cabbage, which first attracted his attention upon the
city market, to its source, he persuaded the grower to sell
him some seed. . . . He had expected to introduce the variety as a leading novelty for 1912, but upon hearing our offer
of "a big price," based upon confidence in his expert judge-
ment as to its unique merits, he decided to place the introduction exclusively in our hands, with the right to name the
variety. . . .

Forthwith Mr. Burpee honored the discovery with the name
Fordhook, calling it Fordhook Mainstay-Early Cabbage, and sold
a hundred seeds for a dime, no more than three hundred (for 25
cents) to one customer. He also offered 119 cash prizes ranging
from $50 to "a clean crisp dollar bill" for the best postal-card re-
ports on what luck customers had with the cabbage. He added
that what he wanted was honesty, not favoritism, and the critics
didn't even have to buy seed or grow the cabbage—they could
give their impressions of a neighbor's crop if they liked. In fact,
anyone taking the trouble to write was promised, should he fail to
win one of the prizes, "a due bill for ten cents as a slight acknowl-
edgement."

It is a pleasure to state that although Burpee's own 1912 crop
of the new cabbage was a miserable failure, the variety became
a favorite with home gardeners, who liked the solid little (3- to
6-pound) heads, and Fordhook Mainstay-Early was a leading
variety for years.

Speaking of honesty in connection with novelties, an interesting example of it cropped up in 1903. Mr. Burpee had a new
lettuce that year, a variety called Giant Crystal Head. He had

purchased stock seed from the originator, tested it at Fordhook, and had harvested quite a heap of new seed for sale. But by then he had changed his mind. "Were we to copy the enthusiastic description of the German seedsman who sent out this 'new lettuce,'" he rasped in a catalog footnote, "we should have *an enormous demand for the seed*—because our customers know that they can rely on what we say. The fact is, however, that while it may do differently in Europe, it would take an exceptional expert to distinguish it as grown from the 'originator's' costly packets from our own famous ICEBERG in a neighboring field. . . . Possibly some of our customers 'may have better eyes' than we, hence the seed of this so-called 'CRYSTAL HEAD' has been saved carefully, and we shall be pleased to send a packet FREE, *if requested*, to any purchaser of our original ICEBERG."

Whatever the German seedsman's lettuce was, the prized cabbage was very probably the result of a mutation. As such, it was literally a cabbage in a million, for it has been noticed that this is the over-all rate at which you can expect beneficial mutations within a generation. A mutation in the strictest genetic sense, as defined by geneticist Jerome H. Kantor of the Burpee organization, is "A suddenly-induced change brought about by a change in the structure of the molecules making up the genes in the chromosomes. Or a very small portion of the chromosome may be lost (or deleted), or inverted. The heredity will differ to the extent of the genes involved." The genes are, of course, the carriers of heredity in both plants and animals, and the cause of a change may be chemical, or it may be physical—such as a change in climate. Man has been able sometimes to speed up the mutation rate by using such dodges on plants as X-ray treatments, applying chemicals, and heating or chilling them. However, the results are still pretty unpredictable, and some natural-born mutations continue to be very useful. It was such a mutation that gave Burpee's one of its prides, Fluffy Ruffles sweet pea, a 1928 introduction. Before that, though they had bred sweet peas with lovely ruffled petals, they could not fix the character, as they say, and so after a couple of years the offspring would start bouncing back to the plain old petals. But Fluffy Ruffles bred true, and so this mutation became the grandame ancestor of all other colors of Burpee's ruffled sweet peas.

A mutation, by the way, is usually an extreme change in some respect. Sometimes it is so extreme that it kills the plant outright. If the victim lives through it, the mutation may show up as a complete change in the color of flowers borne, a new resistance to disease, difference in growth habit, or a change in an edible thing produced—as with the cabbage. Most mutations are harmful to the plant, but unless by rare chance a canceling mutation follows, the change induced is very apt to be there for good. Or, as Kantor has put it: "Another qualification of a mutation is that it is not usually reversible in action. The easiest way to explain this is to compare it with an egg. You can boil an egg but you cannot unboil it."

Seedsmen, of course, have no patent on finding new cabbages or whatever. Anybody can look for them—or look simply for something that to him is new and novel. While shopping one day in 1919 in a little Italian village market, Katherine Mansfield, an avid gardener as well as a noted writer, was elated merely to find out what Zucchini squash were. "Zucchinis are not cucumbers," she triumphantly wrote to her husband, John Middleton Murry. "They are a kind of elongated pale yellow marrows. . . . I don't at all see why we should not grow them in Sussex."

In a more scientific vein, another amateur was probably the first seed collector in the United States. He was Benjamin Franklin. If you like rhubarb pie you may thank Franklin. He brought rhubarb to this country, from Scotland, among his introductions. Thomas Jefferson was passionately interested in seeds and plants and was always trying out something new from far parts of the earth or sending off seeds gathered on his own estate. If he had to, he stole a little novel seed here and there, like almost any gardener, if there is no other way. Both these men were, of course, highly skilled observers and scientific experimenters, but such talent is not a must in the search for better plants. The Henderson bush lima bean, an excellent long-time standard and still carried by Burpee's, was found along a roadside in Virginia in the 1870s by an elderly Negro man taking a stroll.

Today most of the seeds that gardeners in the United States plant are produced in the United States, but when the house of Burpee started, and for about twenty-five to thirty years after, they came from Europe. And the map of Europe was speckled with seed-growing localities, all specialists in their lines. England was not among the leaders, for though it has been called the garden capital of the world, England's rainy, cool climate is bad for most commercial seed growing. Rain can sterilize flowers, and can swell seeds till they burst their coats and are ruined. On the Continent, conditions for producing seeds were more favorable, and Germany, for example, was noted for petunias and to a lesser degree for snapdragons. It was there that was developed the so-called balcony petunias, a name still seen in the Burpee catalog. Window boxes in many German homes overflowed with this beautiful flower, intended for just this use, and many varieties of the Giant petunias (*grandiflora superbissima*), and of the Big Fringed (*grandiflora fimbriata*) were hybridized in Germany. One reason for this early German progress in petunias was the abundance of expert hand labor at low cost, since in the case of the Giants particularly, plants were grown individually in pots, shaded in lath-houses, and each flower pollinated by hand.

Denmark has long been noted for cabbages and cauliflower, and another splendid locality for seed production was and is southern France. The Netherlands are famous not only for bulbs but for a general list of flower seed and for some vegetables—

spinach and cabbage especially. Bulbs are still such a specialty there that tulips, hyacinths, daffodils, crocuses, and others are often lumped under the heading "Dutch bulbs."

Typical of the important vegetables and flowers Burpee's found in Europe and introduced into the United States were Golden Self-Blanching celery, Copenhagen Market cabbage, and the Oxheart carrot, all still good enough to be listed in the current catalog along with fancy newcomers.

On observing how the catalogs come blooming forth each year with fresh new marvels for the gardener to try, some people have thought, as *Time* stated in 1960, that the seed business, like automobiles and some appliances, "is built on planned obsolescence." Such a remark cuts David Burpee to the quick. That there is obsolescence in plants, he agrees, but that it is planned, he denies.

It would be hard to prove differently. Certainly many and many brave new novelties of other years are no longer with us, but, going back an arbitrary seventy years and opening the Burpee 1892 catalog at random, here is the record on, as it happens, celery: ten varieties were listed as against three today. But of today's three, two have been carried along from 1892—Golden Self-Blanching, and Giant Pascal. In radishes there was a choice of thirty varieties in 1892. Today there are only fifteen, but five of these are among those carried seventy years ago. The same thing is true of many of the other vegetables, though novelties in flowers are not so lasting. The main reason for this is that merely a little newness will cause a flower novelty to catch on, but to win a place in gardeners' hearts a new vegetable must be importantly different and better than existing kinds. Consequently, new flowers fade faster under the shadow of still newer ones than do vegetables.

Sometimes, however, this is the flowers' own fault, a kind of *unplanned* obsolescence. In 1941 Burpee's made a great to-do over a new marigold they christened Wildfire, and the next year they beat the drums about something they called X-Ray Twins calendulas. Today you can't buy either one. Wildfire marigold, named too literally, got all out of hand by growing too tall in the face of a trend favoring more dwarfness in flowers, and the X-Ray Twins couldn't stand the hot summers usual in most of the United States.

In view of the severe regional testing Burpee's do on new plants before offering them for sale, the behavior of the calendulas was embarrassing. (The breeding technique used on them—a pelting with X rays to spur mutations—was a new one at the time.) In recent years Burpee's have made all their own test plantings of this kind, but years ago it was their habit to ask the customers for help. If you wanted to try out the latest novelty for them, Burpee's would supply you with a packet of free seed. The system worked fine, no doubt helped out by an engaging frankness on both sides, especially Mr. Burpee's side. In 1891 for example, he handed out 25,000 packets of a new squash, with this description printed on each packet: "Several years ago, in connection with a plantsman, we sent an Agent (a native Chinaman) to travel through the interior of China collecting seeds of Vegetables and Flowers which he might discover and which we could grow in America. The majority of these, on testing at Fordhook Farm, proved to be undesirable for American Gardens. One of the new Squashes, however, which we have named 'Der Wing' in honor of the discoverer, proved to be very distinct from any other we have ever seen. The Squash grows about 5 inches long by from 2½ to 3 inches thick at the stem end; running to a point at the blossom end. It has a rather hard and thick shell which is completely covered with warts; the color of the flesh is a very light yellow. The flesh is moderately thick and very sweet when cooked. It is a queer-looking, warty, hard-shelled little Squash, with which you could almost knock down a bull."

Sometimes, in searching for utterly truthful reports from outside seed testers, Burpee's have run into such unflinching veracity as that of one man who, on answering a routine questionnaire item—Was your season normal?—replied: "No. Weather here never normal."

Finding new plants by searching them out is now only one of the seedsman's methods, but it is still a useful one even if not of top importance. It was the basic tool with which the Burpee people worked in getting odorless marigolds, introduced by the house in 1937. There is no question that the introduction of the odorless marigold was a milestone in Burpee history, which is to say the seed business history. As most gardeners know, most marigolds have a decided odor, offensive to many persons. It is a characteristic not of the bloom but of the leaves, possibly a defense the plant built up against leaf-nibbling enemies. At any rate, it was one of the biggest problems David Burpee faced when he decided to see if he could remodel marigolds enough to make them America's sweetheart. The smell came from little oil sacs bordering the leaves, and Burpee's first move was to scour the globe for all kinds of marigolds and see if any were non-smelly. He got together 642 kinds. They all smelled.

Then, in the pattern of happy chance that seems to dog some people, Burpee got a letter from a man he had never heard tell of, an American missionary in darkest China, the Rev. Mr. Carter D. Holton. Out of a clear sky Mr. Holton wished to know if Mr. Burpee would risk $25 on one ounce of marigold seeds the Chinese called the Big Golden Aster. It may have come from Tibet, said Mr. Holton, and—oh, yes, its leaves didn't smell punk.

With jet-like speed, Burpee fired off the $25 and then waited for the slow mail from China. Months later it came: His houseboy, Mr. Holton reported, had housecleaned the $25 ounce of marigold seeds into oblivion, so sorry. But Mr. Holton would try to round up a few more seeds. He did, in time for next spring's planting, but what came up? A lot of scrawny, squint-flowered no-goods. These were Big Golden Asters to Chinese? Oh, the foliage was as pure as grass, all right, but crossbreeding this factor into decent-looking marigolds would take years. And then, spang among these few plants from the bit of salvaged seed the houseboy hadn't got at, there sprang up a gorgeous mutation, the one-in-a-million chance. It was a plant with fine big golden-orange flowers—"Crown of Gold," Burpee named it, no reference to William Jennings Bryan.

This would have been gravy enough to last most men for years, but at times Burpee is like the little boy who wants to win all the prizes at the party and have everyone love him too. "If I'm so lucky as to get an exquisite marigold sport in this little bit of a flower bed," said he to himself, "doesn't it stand to reason there might be an odorless-leafed sport somewhere in the 30 *acres* of other marigolds we have growing on the place?"

Well, there's only one way to find out if something smells, and that is to smell it. In the thirty acres there were over half a million plants. "Start smelling, boys," said Burpee, and off through the rows went every man on the staff, sniffing like beagles. For any-body else this wild gamble would have ended up with a crew of exhausted noses, convinced the boss was balmy. For Burpee it ended up with a second fine big odorless-leafed marigold, just as he expected. "Burpee Gold," he contentedly named it.

In the spirit of scientific inquiry and of prudent business he had it crossed with the Chinese wonder. The results were terri-ble, the children all turning out stinkers. But when crossed with regular marigolds, both the new odorless ones passed along their secret to some descendants in the second and following genera-tions. It is a good thing they did, for those who admire the odor-less kind. (Not everyone does, Burpee was flummoxed to find, when some gardening ladies said a marigold wasn't a marigold if it didn't reek.) In 1961 as Burpee was inspecting the Burpee Gold plantings at Floradale he got wind of some plants with smelly foliage, sure sign of a reversion starting (a "break-up" in seedman vernacular). But instead of having to sail into a big repurifying program, Burpee can afford to shrug it off and let Burpee Gold go. One of its descendants, the marigold called Hawaii, is better than either of the deodorized originals.

The Crown of Gold marigold wasn't the only thing David Burpee's missionary friend Carter Holton found for him in China. Helped along by the fact the grateful seedsman followed up his original $25 check with a couple of bigger bonuses, the gardening missionary kept on keeping an eye out for new things. You can find two of them in Burpee's catalog today in the vegetable section. One is the radish they call Burpee White, a mild and lovely thing that the Men's Garden Clubs of America named the best new vegetable in a decade. The second is a puzzler that seems to have started out to be lettuce and then changed its mind by growing a strong midrib. Burpee's called it celtuce, and when their head vegetable breeder at Fordhook tried to describe it to a bewildered garden club in 1941 he said it was good raw but when cooked twenty minutes and served with cream dressing or drawn butter, it tasted like lettuce, celery, asparagus, squash, chard, or spinach. Its discoverer, having had to quit China when the Communists moved in, is now a full-time member of the Burpee organization, their head salesman on the West Coast.

A third new Burpee vegetable might be mentioned here since it too was found through search and, as it happened, by another missionary in China. He was the Rev. Mr. E. L. Lutz, and on retiring he gave Burpee some seed he had brought from Chungking. Introducing it in 1944 Burpee said in the catalog: "In China the plant is known by several names, but these names are difficult to pronounce and not suitable for use in English or Spanish speaking countries. Therefore we have chosen the name 'Tampala,' by which it is known in India. Tampala is a horticultural variety of *Amaranthus gangeticus L.*" Since then, Burpee has changed the name to Fordhook spinach, and like regular spinach it has both devotees and detractors. Borrowing the well-known *New*

*Yorker* gag, one diner on first tasting tampala said that he said it was spinach and he said the hell with it. Actually, it is sweeter than spinach, has a slight globe artichoke flavor to some, and is highly nutritious. One of its converts, the mother of a large family, was heard to praise tampala to the skies. "And it goes so much farther than spinach, too," she said.

# *8* WHY HYBRIDS?

Except for continual selection, no matter what method of plant improvement is being used, the plant breeder's most single useful technique today is hybridizing. The word "hybrid" comes from the Latin *hibrida,* the offspring of a tame sow and a wild boar, which sounds dynamic. So are the new hybrid flowers and vegetables. They get up and grow, start producing sooner and then keep it up; flowers are prettier, vegetables usually taste better, and both are full of vitality.

Breeding to produce pedigreed, performance-guaranteed, first-generation hybrids is a technique of fairly recent broad usage. It dates only from the late 1930s even though hybrid corn, the first example of it, has been widely grown since around 1925 and was developed some fifteen years before that. However, corn is much easier to work with than other vegetables, or even flowers: plant side by side the two varieties you want to cross, and then just cut off the tassels of the seed parent—the mother plant which will grow the hybrid seed—so that all the pollen comes from the tassels of the other. This gives you a controlled cross, and the key word here is "controlled."

Though geneticists differ on the exact definition of a hybrid, it can be said that basically it means an offspring of mixed parentage—usually parents of the same species but of different varieties (or breeds if referring to the animal kingdom). However, the word "hybrid" used to be used in plant circles to refer to any mixture that wasn't pure—a natural and uncontrolled cross originally made by insects, wind, or any old thing. This sort of hybrid was a kind of mongrel dog of plants. Like a mongrel dog, it might be splendid, but its trouble was that you could seldom get good repeat performance in the next generation. An example was a tomato that Burpee's named, in 1910, the Dwarf Hybrid (rather, the customers did, four suggesting the name and dividing first-prize money of $25). Though many planters of free sample packets turned in glowing reports on Dwarf Hybrid, W. Atlee Burpee had begun to look sternly on the high percentage of unsmooth fruits it produced, and finally decided not to sell the seed until by roguing out the maverick plants he could get a pure strain of smooth-fruited tomatoes. The story ends unhappily; Dwarf Hybrid wound up on the dump because it never did consistently come true from seed.

The seeds from today's fine first-generation hybrids won't come true either, and they aren't supposed to; far from making the originating seedsman unhappy, this trait brings gladness to his heart. It is a kind of grow-your-own-patent-protection for him, the only way he has to keep rivals from helping themselves to his discoveries. The seed trade is a wide-open, gimlet-eyed, last-one-in-is-a-rotten-egg kind of industry, and a hard one in which to keep a secret a secret very long. The surprising consequence is that seed growers are more gentlemanly toward each other than you might expect. Each year in Lompoc Valley, California, for instance, where five firms plant hundreds of acres cheek-by-jowl, they get together beforehand to keep from planting varieties that will cross with what the other fellow will be planting in the next field.

To get back to hybrids, most hybrids in today's language are controlled crosses of specially selected, purified, and highly inbred parents. The seed resulting from such a cross will grow plants known as $F_1$ hybrids. The "F" stands for "filial," the subscript "1" meaning the first generation of offspring. If seeds from these hybrid plants were sown, the resulting plants would be $F_2$ hybrids, the next generation would be $F_3$'s, the next, $F_4$'s, and so on—and there would be a world of differences among them. Nevertheless, this kind of refining by replanting was formerly usual procedure among plant breeders in working with natural hybrids. They kept on selecting the best plants from successive generations until the assortment of characters (geneticists' term for "characteristics") they wanted were present and fixed—if they ever were. After that, the plants were expected to keep on coming true from seed.

In most cases today the hybridizer's efforts are directed mainly toward finding and purifying two strains of parent plants that, no matter how so-so they may themselves be, will produce absolutely marvelous children. This is the secret and the glory of the $F_1$ hybrid. Its production is a flexible and dependable technique, and the competition can't hop free rides on your work.

In the purifying that precedes the final cross, line breeding and inbreeding play large roles. In a thumbnail explanation, geneticist Kantor has described them this way: "Line breeding—one of the oldest tools of the plantsman—is merely reselecting so that characters already in mixed (or impure or heterozygous) condition may sort out and thus purify the strain. Inbreeding is only of value in heterozygous material. Since most organisms contain thousands of genes, it would take many, many generations to obtain a strain entirely pure for all characters. In practice, breeders purify material for only the important visible characters, and many minor traits are carried in impure form long after a new variety is introduced."

Incidentally, though man is now quite glib about juggling plant genes, it wasn't until the eighteenth century that he even knew plants had sex. Yet, the principle of bisexual reproduction in plants was being taken advantage of five thousand years ago by the Assyrians and the Babylonians. They got a heavier yield of dates by shaking pollen of the male flowers onto female ones. Since they didn't seem to do anything else with the technique, it is assumed they didn't really know what strong medicine they had hold of, and were approximately as vague as the people who used to cure warts by killing a toad.

The most important early work on which later hybridizing efforts depended was that of Gregor Mendel. This Austrian monk studied the inherited traits of crossbred peas in his cloister garden and in 1865 published the results of his observations. When they were rediscovered in 1900 they became the rock on which the science of genetics was built.

For a hybridizer life is seldom dull. Crossing a red flower with a white one of the same species may, he knows, give him both reds and whites in succeeding generations, but he may sometimes get pinks, or maybe stripes or polka dots. Each plant carries a kind of Saratoga trunkful of traits, stretching for infinite generations into the past. Old and almost forgotten characters may lie somewhere toward the bottom of the trunk, and when our hybridizer gets to fooling with it, he tumbles the trunk around and around until you never know what may turn up on top when the lid is opened.

The chances are the new plant will be a dud, or wildly impractical, or just no better than something already on hand. However, there is always a chance it may lead to something good, and a good hybrid really is good. Burpee's is, with reason, proud of its record on developing and introducing hybrids. Beginning with marigolds in 1939, it has since then pioneered in first-generation hybrids in other flowers, notably in petunias, zinnias, and snapdragons. Among vegetables, its first hybrid cucumber put cucumbers back into gardens where mosaic or mildew had long made it impossible to grow them. "The only thing customers ever complain about," David Burpee has said happily of his cucumber, "is that it bears more than they can eat." The firm was also first in America to introduce hybrids of eggplant, tomato (of which they have developed seven first-generation crosses now offered in the current catalog), Zucchini squash, and cantaloupe. Other hybrid vegetables the house has offered include two onions that can keep all winter, three sweet corns, and two watermelons, one of them so seedless you can eat it in the dark. Because hybrids combine quality with earliness, they have lavished delectable things on residents of short-summer regions by winning the annual race with the first frost, in the case of such tender vegetables as sweet corn and watermelons.

David Burpee's development of what he named, taking a deep breath, the Red and Gold Hybrid marigolds, would be outstanding for being the first first-generation hybrid flowers on the market even if they hadn't been anything else. He made up his mind to try for a tall red marigold by crossbreeding a French species with an African one, since the dainty French marigold had a monopoly on redness. So immediately he had made himself a big problem.

Even today most hybrid plants are not species crosses, but are crosses of varieties within the species. To take an animal example —if a Siamese tomcat mated with an Angora pussycat, the kittens would be variety hybrids. If, on the other hand, the Siamese fathered kittens of a panther, *they* would be species hybrids. This would be unusual, to say the least, but a more conceivable species cross, such as between a tiger and a panther, would be unusual too. Luther Burbank once said that while he had occasionally crossed species, among thousands of experiments, it could be regarded as nature's law that they were not expected to cross and many could not.

Burpee's problem number two was the way the marigold is built. Each bloom is really a bouquet in miniature, botanically a composite. What the rest of us call its petals, the botanist calls florets—separate little flowers—and in the marigold there can be as many as five hundred on the one stem. Trying to dust foreign pollen on such a thing with a tiny camel's-hair brush is plainly a hopeless job except on a small, experimental scale. But at this early stage Burpee was not even dreaming of first-generation hybrids in marketable quantities, which seemed as far away as the moon. He was merely hoping for a few little hybrid seeds which he might parlay into eventual truckloads by replanting their get, over and over. To help chart a course, he went to an expert—Dr. William Henry Eyster, geneticist at Bucknell University.

Working under controlled laboratory conditions, Dr. Eyster did manage to find a French marigold and an African one that would cross, and he grew a flower from the resulting romance. It was a nice tall red marigold, too, just what Burpee had been looking for, but it had one dismal drawback. It was as sterile as a paper daisy, an imperfect flower that could never set seed. To produce more, human hands would have to duplicate the laboratory cross by the thousands under field conditions each season. This would make the resulting seeds too expensive to sell, as Burpee had to prove for himself the next season by planting two acres of marigolds which were hand-pollinated, the seed parents caged in muslin to keep insects away. This resulted in 250,000 seeds, practically all no good. Only a very few grew nice big red marigolds, and they were as seedlessly sterile as Dr. Eyster's laboratory marigold.

Plant breeding, however, is something like chess; the more expert you get, the more possibilities you discover. David Burpee now began toying with the fact that about 50 per cent of some African marigolds are naturally male-sterile, as plant breeders say. They have only the female flower parts and do not produce pollen, the male factor in seed forming. The reason this now loomed importantly to Burpee was that if he could fix it so only the male-sterile African marigolds were grown for seed parents of the tall red hybrids, bees could do the pollinating because there would be no danger of any pollen reaching the Africans except from the rows of French marigolds that would be planted in between.

So . . . the next season five acres of African and French marigolds were planted in alternating rows, and of the Africans all but the male-steriles were ordered rogued out. A screen of sunflowers was planted around the field for privacy, and half a million bees were put to work crossing the marigolds when the flowers opened. The result was fifty pounds of seed and another headache: only about 28 per cent of the seed grew tall red marigolds. The aggravating other 72 per cent grew ordinary yellow Africans.

The Burpee men found the reason, finally, with a magnifying glass, right in the Sherlock Holmes tradition. The glass revealed that quite a few so-called male-sterile African marigolds, such as those that had been used here for seed parents, were not entirely male-sterile. They produced only a dab of pollen but it was so well located for easy pollinating of the neighboring female florets that it did the lion's share of that work. Result: Next season the roguers sallied forth carrying magnifying glasses in their overalls pockets. Through this closer inspection the percentage of true Red and Gold Hybrid marigold seed gradually rose until it leveled off at close to 90 per cent. Since the hybrids themselves become shades of yellow in hot weather (which was why they were named "Red and Gold") this 90 per cent purity was satisfactory.

Even at that, Burpee's wasn't making any money on Red and Gold Hybrids. Every dollar's worth of seed they sold was costing them two dollars to produce, so except for the satisfaction of doing it and the luster this gave to their reputation, they were losers. In trying to find a way out of this gilded trap they discovered that among the thousands of hybrid flowers there were a few that managed to make some seed. (Very few. Burpee's hardworking staff got one of their rare belly laughs out of this whole project when a couple of rival seedsmen made big plantings of Red and Gold Hybrids, confidently expecting to raise their own seed, and got nothing but exercise.) The persistent Burpee people planted the scarce seed they found among their own Red and Gold Hybrids, hoping that after a few generations they would have a good consistent seed-bearing strain. Alack, this hope also petered out. After a few generations these fertile hybrids had lost so much of their hybrid vigor they weren't worth fooling with. A word about this factor may be in order here.

One of the advantages of a hybrid plant is its vigor. Like electricity, this hybrid vigor is better recognized than understood. (Once a hopeful but very confused customer sent Burpee's a 25-cent order for "One pkt. Hybrid Vigor.") In pretty general terms hybrid vigor can be summed up by saying: A hybrid plant is apt to exhibit the strong points of each parent. The reasons for this are complicated and are still partly theory. However, scientists agree that hybrid vigor, or heterosis, certainly exists—a point confirmed by many a dirt gardener, including one California gentleman who seeded what he assumed would be a nice low border of some new Burpee hybrid flowers in front of his picture window, and in mid-season found himself peeping out through a muscular jungle. Well, there are low-growing hybrids too; you must pick the right variety for the job. But—and this is useful for gardeners to know—one of the reasons Burpee's keep ding-donging away about their $F_1$ flowers and vegetables is that hybrid vigor is always at its peak in the first hybrid generation, the $F_1$.

To go back for a last moment to Red and Gold Hybrid marigolds—the story finally came out right at the end. The big basic reason why it had been hard to cross African and French marigolds normally was that the two species had the fundamental difference of different numbers of chromosomes, the transmitters of heredity. But when science found a practical chemical means of doubling a plant's chromosome count, it then became possible to do this to some African marigolds and thus make them match the French species in this respect. These two crossed more easily, and though they still made almost no seeds, Burpee no longer grieved about it—the no-seed habit meant more flowers, and all season.

The experience gained in the Red and Gold project carried over into later work with other marigolds. Making use of some more exclusively female varieties, Burpee scientists developed their line of big Climax marigolds. And again, bees did the work, buzzing back and forth between alternate rows of a purified (by inbreeding) seed parent and a purified male-parent line. Since only the seeds from the female-parent plants are useful, the yield per acre is only about thirty-five pounds compared with a normal two hundred and up from most standard African varieties. This, plus a weekly or oftener hands-and-knees check of the fields all during the season to rogue from the female line all plants not completely male-sterile, keeps the seeds expensive. No $F_1$ hybrid seed, in fact, is apt to get cheaper to produce in time, even when the bees can be persuaded to help. Too much costly human labor is still needed, and the seed yield is too moderate to make for a lower-priced product.

Another story of Burpee's pure-line hybrids—here, hybrid zinnias—starts out sounding like a railroad yard. "Old 66 gave us the thing we needed," manager Al Condit of the firm's farms at Santa Paula, California, said. Old 66 is what they called a freak zinnia that was discovered about 1950 in Row 66 of one of the fields by plant breeder John Mondry. If it hadn't been quite so much of a freak it would have been rogued out as an off-type plant and forgotten, but it was such a crazy-looking thing that it got a more careful examination. It didn't look like a zinnia, not even like the little old eighteenth-century ones studied by, and named in honor of, a German botanist, Johann Gottfried Zinn. It didn't even look like much of a flower. It was more like a wad of yellowish cotton on a stick. But—just like the mother plants of the pioneering Red and Gold Hybrid marigolds—Old 66 was all-female, and that was terribly important.

As with marigolds, zinnia flowers are each a bristling cushion of florets, every one a separate little flower, and the physical job of cross-pollinating by hand and keeping track of results was slow and hard, impossible in commercial quantities. But having no pollen of its own, Old 66 could be the female parent of hybrids fathered, via bees again, by any normal zinnia. Or at least that was the hope. Such a cross did result in the introduction in 1960 of, to quote the Burpee catalog, "The first and only $F_1$ hybrid zinnia." If this seemed confusing to readers who saw on another page of the same catalog something called Burpee's Giant Hybrid zinnias (and introduced nine long years before) described as including "first and second generation hybrids," it was because you can get just so technical in a seed catalog and after that you lose the reader.

The older group of zinnias were hybrids, all right, but in their case the hybridizing could not be rigidly controlled. Furthermore, it was only one element in their background, something like merely one pinch of one of the seasonings in a curry. Their history stretched back for about fifty years, starting with Luther Burbank, then passing at his death to his head gardener, William Henderson, and finally to Burpee's, who bought Henderson's seed and carried on the zinnia work.

On the other hand, the new hybrid, Trail Blazer, was a hybrid in the modern manner—the first generation from the mating of purified, inbred parents. Obviously this technique, made possible in zinnias by the discovery of Old 66, brings volume and accuracy to their hybridizing, and Burpee's plant breeders have their fingers crossed, hoping they'll be getting some spectacular results. Trail Blazer itself, while an agreeable flower, is no ball of fire, its outstanding point being a resistance to mildew. This is a good, solid-citizen trait, however, and only the first, its creators feel sure, of many more that will dazzle zinnia lovers in this decade.

(For technical-minded readers who may wonder just how anybody can inbreed a one-sexed flower such as Old 66, these two

techniques are available: vegetative reproduction such as by rooting cuttings; and by pollinating them with normal plants in the
same line. This second method yields seeds that grow 50 per cent
66-type zinnias.)

While it is not hybridizing in the more extreme sense, the
method used to bring forth a sprightly 1961 introduction, Burpeeana Giant zinnias, is a more surefire if slow way to get a new
pretty. Here, shooting for dwarf plants with great big flowers, the
breeders began a decade ago to cross-pollinate pairs of plants of
the *same* variety to combine especially good characteristics. (Just
like people, no two plants of the same race are exactly alike
when you get down to details.) The succeeding generations of
the zinnias then went through severe selecting each year, during
which five per cent got a passing grade, until finally colors were
purified and the desired points fixed for good. Millions of plants
are grown during such a breeding marathon, and it is the technique that was also used to produce such other new flowers as
the Alaska, Hawaii, Mary Helen, and Mr. Sam marigolds, the
White Spire and Sunlight snapdragons, Barcelona larkspur, the
asters Scarlet Beauty, Blue Waves, and Charming, sweet peas
Gigi and Sachet, and a dwarf zinnia called Gold Tip.

It is a matter of some sorrow to imaginative seedsmen that the
public is sot in its ways about how a vegetable ought to look. In
flowers almost any novelty goes, but so far nobody has had much
luck peddling a curved cucumber, for instance, no matter how
good it may taste. People are so used to straight cucumbers that
curly ones repel them. To those who would defend this quirk on
the ground it is easier to slice a straight cucumber, the seedsman
has an unanswerable rebuttal: for easier slicing, plus easy peeling
and other merits, nothing could be finer than a square potato—but
try and sell one. Not that anyone has tried, or even developed
one, since so mild an innovation as a pear-shaped squash got
nowhere. "Doesn't look right," people said, and didn't stay to

taste. As has been mentioned, Burpee's have found that customers are true-blue faithful to their favorite vegetables, generally speaking, and no matter how good a new one is—hybrid or not—it usually catches on much more slowly than do good new flowers. Once it does, though, it usually lasts longer.

Creating a new vegetable by hybridizing is harder than getting a new flower. The new vegetable often requires basic structural changes in the plant, whereas with a new flower merely a new color may do the job—and the most easily varied part of the plant *is* its flower. Even so, to the eyes of the outsider, the physical job of hand-pollinating any flower whatever is one he can witness with his own eyes, and it certainly seems chore enough—and worse still when dealing with such insignificant little things as tomato blossoms, for instance, which nobody would bother with for a bouquet. You must snip off each and every little stamen on each flower of a female parent-to-be, catching them after they open and before the pollen is ripe, then gather blossoms from the male parent-to-be plant just as its pollen *is* ripe. And you have only just begun.

Now you must fix it so that human hands can act the bees' part, tipping the thousands of stigmas when they are ready—perhaps in three days—with grains of the chosen pollen. And to get those grains you must shake the pollen from the male parent—literally shake it, as if you were transported into a fairyland fantasy of childhood, shaking elfin saltcellars. It doesn't take much pollen to fertilize one blossom—so little that a hundred times as much would be a yellow speck on the end of your finger—but consider what it takes to fertilize the blossoms of even one acre of, say, Burpee's runaway success, Big Boy hybrid tomato. There are forty-five hundred of these plants to the acre, and each plant averages thirty fertilized blossoms. This means that the crews of high school girls who do the work during their summer vacations must fertilize on each acre 135,000 stigmas no bigger than a butterfly's antenna. As they do so they pull off with a pair of tweezers three sepals of each blossom to show it has been fertilized. Then on to the next, poking the stigma into a tiny hole in one end of a pollen-filled glass tube the size of a pencil stub.

If it were not being done, and matter-of-factly, by these tanned young girls in shorts against a backdrop of mountains in the Santa Paula Valley between Santa Barbara and Los Angeles, you would call it an undertaking far too finicky for practical use.

Even the pollen extracting has an unreal, Hans Christian Andersen air. Here, in the shade of a two-sided wooden shelter at the edge of the tomato field sit two Mexican women workers. They are talking across a narrow table, raising their voices because between them a little electric motor is buzzing. It is the motor from a used electric razor. On each side a thin, stiff, vibrating wire with a loop on the end sticks out, and as the women talk they keep dipping into bowls of tomato blossoms beside them, holding each blossom briefly inside the loop of wire nearest them. This is called "buzzing pollen." The vibrating wire loop shakes the ripe blossoms, and the pollen falls into a plastic vial suspended below the table. The vial is no bigger than one of your fingers, and to fill a vial is a good day's work for one woman.

All this precision work on a mass scale is of recent origin. Burpee's began their first experimenting with hybridizing tomatoes in 1937. The thing that triggered it was casual. David Burpee recalls that he was having a chat while riding home on the commuter train from Philadelphia one day with a staff man, Al Kempf, and Kempf happened to ask Burpee, out of the blue, why he didn't have a try at making some first-generation crosses of vegetables. Burpee, one of whose characteristics is the ability to smell a good idea the instant it shows up, grabbed this one and by the next morning W. C. Warfield, then in charge of vegetable breeding at Fordhook Farms, was starting work on what resulted in the Fordhook Hybrid tomato, introduced in 1945 and first of a prolific new line of garden goodies.

A different and simpler technique than in the tomato hybridizing is used on cucumbers, squash, and watermelons, because here the plants have the happy habit of growing two distinct kinds of flowers—one female, one male. Thus, twice a week in summer, a crew of workers go stooping through sixty acres or so of cucumbers, pinching the male flowers from each of three rows of plants that are to make the cucumbers for seed, so that they can be fertilized only by the pollen from the plants of the selected male-parent variety in the fourth row. This work is called deflorating, and the work of pollinating that follows is done by six hives of bees per acre, bribed to stay on the job and ignore the temptations of orange blossoms in nearby groves by plantings of borage among the cucumbers.

In the case of the hybrid watermelons Burpee's offer, there are so few female flowers that instead of deflorating the many male ones, it is less expensive to make the cross by hand and then protect the female flower from interference until it has set its fruit. To protect it, workers slip over it a gelatin capsule, exactly like the kind you take a powder in except this one is bigger and is called a horse capsule. As a bit of further experimenting, colored capsules are being tried, to see if by shading the blossoms from the southern California sun more than clear ones do, the fruit set can be improved. With clear capsules it averages about 50 per cent.

A still different method of hybridizing is the job of producing an $F_1$ petunia, say the variety Yellow Gleam. In the Burpee catalog, Yellow Gleam is listed among about fifteen so-called multiflora petunias, to distinguish them from ruffled-petal types, listed as grandifloras. For 50 cents you can buy a packet of 150 seeds of Yellow Gleam, described as "The deepest yellow of all petunias. Flowers grow 2½ in. across, clear lemon-yellow, darker toward the throat, the color becoming lighter in hot weather. Plants grow 30 in. tall."

Now, 150 petunia seeds are barely a pinch. It takes a quarter-million to make a single ounce. But to get those three-for-a-penny seeds to you, here is what was happening in the summer of 1961 in a greenhouse on the Burpee Santa Paula farms.

On four benches running the length of the greenhouse were rows of the petunia that becomes Yellow Gleam's seed parent, as plant breeders call a flower's mother. Altogether there were eight hundred to nine hundred of these plants there, each with a few flowers open when the day's work began. The work was being done by five high school girls, paid, as were the tomato girls, 75 cents an hour if this was their first year. They worked forty-four hours a week, and if they worked well and stayed for the summer they got a final bonus of 5 cents for each hour worked. Girls who had experience from the previous summer's work drew 80 cents an hour, with the same season-end bonus arrangement. At one end of the greenhouse a radio was yowling—a fringe benefit of inside work—tuned to a Los Angeles disk-jockey program. The girls, in the usual shorts and blouses, hair in curlers for the evening date and tucked under bandanas, chattered above the din as they dipped soft little brushes into vials of pollen they carried. Moving smoothly from one opened blossom to the next, they dusted pollen onto the stigma of each blossom after emasculating it. A petunia being bigger than a tomato blossom, the work trotted along. By lunch time the five girls had pollinated every receptive flower in the greenhouse, taking an occasional rest period, after which they washed their hands with alcohol if they smoked cigarettes; petunias are susceptible to tobacco mosaic, and alcohol kills the virus.

Girls, incidentally, have a monopoly on these jobs of helping to father hybrids, because boys foolishly regard it as sissy work. The illogic of this view has resulted in the lads' being employed by Burpee's in harder labor where, if they do try any monkeyshines, they at least won't bomb a few ounces of seed worth a few thousand dollars.

For the same reason, boys are not hired on the pollen-getting end of the job, which also seems to have the same effect on them as doing fancywork. Instead, a dainty little girl—Marilyn Condit, the manager's daughter—saunters with transistor radio in hand through rows of male-parent petunias in a field, and snips off the anthers at a table in a Quonset warehouse. These are dried in a drum with a light bulb hanging down inside, and the pollen is shaken out by another jackleg device—a sort of shimmying platform that holds a fine-mesh screen on which the anthers are jiggled loose of their pollen. If it isn't needed at once, the pollen is stored in a food freezer. It will keep for at least two weeks and probably much longer, but two weeks is the longest the Burpee people take a chance on.

An advantage of selling seeds instead of automobiles is that some of the old models stay in style for years and years. As an example, take the hybrid double nasturtiums Burpee's sprang on their customers back in 1934. It is a good example because, though there are plenty of older things in the catalog, the double nasturtiums in many colors were one of those star-spangled, work-and-win victories that linger sweetly ever after in its papa's memory. David Burpee was the papa, and when one of his competitors, seedsman John C. Bodger, introduced the original double nasturtium, Golden Gleam, Burpee examined it with the same interest and envy all of Bodger's other rivals were not bothering to conceal. It was not only "double"—having up to nine petals instead of the usual five—but smelled sweet and un-nasturtium-like. Any seedsman would have been entranced to have grabbed off this plum, as Bodger had done by following up promptly a lucky happenso when he spotted the lovely flowers in a bouquet a Mexican woman had picked in her garden and given to Bodger's niece. Probably the result of a mutation at one time, the double nasturtium walked away with an All-America award.

Once it was on the market it was fair game for all seedsmen. They all could buy and plant the seed and grow their own for sale eventually. Ah, but this would merely give them a place at the end of the parade. What they were all racing for, as they all knew, was to be among the first to offer the fragrant double nasturtiums in other colors besides the basic yellow of Golden Gleam.

Now, this, as any seedsman could have told you, was going to take at least three years. The first year they would grow the new double and cross it with standard single nasturtiums in various colors. Seeds from these crosses would then be planted the next spring and would produce hybrid nasturtiums that year in various colors, but virtually all of them with single flowers. The doubleness would be latent in them, as it is a recessive trait. But it would be there. Then, when seeds formed by these single-flowered hybrids were planted, they would, in the third year of work, grow both single-flowered and double-flowered nasturtiums. The double-flowered ones would be in the minority, but—and this is the really important point—they would breed true. The reason was that when a recessive trait, such as doubleness here, does appear, it can mean only one thing—that particular plant is pure in this respect (homozygous, geneticists say) and carries no factor for the other trait at all. Consequently it must breed true.

But if David Burpee had not come down with typhoid fever in the summer of 1933, it is most unlikely he would have scored his big scoop by being the first seedsman to offer the world double nasturtiums in a full range of nasturtium colors. As it was, the illness slowed him up, so that he arrived late for a summer inspection trip at his Floradale Farms, where a field of Bodger's babies were happily blooming. But Burpee was not so happy when he found that by some oversight the vital step of crossing the new doubles with standard single nasturtiums in many colors had not been done. By then it was July, and since the crossing was a fussy, painstaking affair that by then should have been almost finished, all Burpee could do was to hold his head. He was set back one full year. By the following season, 1934, every other seedsman could be in Stage 2, growing hybrid nasturtiums, while Burpee would still be back at the starting post, or at least still on the first lap. (And Bodger, with his head start as the introducer of Golden Gleam, could even be in Stage 3 by then, growing seed of the doubles in all colors for 1935 introduction.)

This setback for Burpee would have been more disastrous than it may sound. The biggest sales for a new flower usually take place the first year or two it is introduced, so that Burpee would miss out on the cream. Worse yet that the loss of face also should come, to a man many regarded as the world's champion friend to home gardeners. At this point, and with these thoughts flitting darkly through his head as he sat in a train taking him south from Floradale, Burpee, possibly wondering what Napoleon, a long-time hero of his, would have done, was suddenly inspired with the strategy of the impossible.

He would, he decided, positively not only refuse to lose the year he had already lost, but he would accomplish the whole entire three-year nasturtium project in less than one year. This was almost as ambitious as the little girl who said she intended to be married Monday and have twelve children Tuesday. The Floradale manager, Bill Hoag, had much the same feeling when he caught up with Burpee at Los Angeles by request and heard the plan. To get it going, Hoag would have to try to hire two hundred workers to toil among the Golden Gleam nasturtiums, cross-pollinating as fast as they could for a month, trying to make about fifty thousand crosses. Having been convinced long before that he was in a crazy business, Hoag went right ahead with this plan, got an acceptable forty thousand crosses, and as soon as the resulting hybrid seeds began forming, the next month, he zinged them off by air mail to Pennsylvania (in perforated boxes, as if they were kittens, so that the ventilation en route would ripen them). When they arrived they were planted at once in the Fordhook greenhouses, which had been stripped of their palms and other upper-class flora to make room. Ordinarily this planting would have waited till the spring of the next year, 1934. But by November of 1933 the seeds from the hybrid nasturtiums in the greenhouses were maturing, and *these* seeds— which normally would have been planted in the spring of 1935 to grow the second hybrid generation—were sent to Puerto Rico, Chile, Florida, and California, and were growing lustily even before 1933 was over, in the mild winter climates of those regions.

Burpee now knew that with luck he could by the next spring, 1934, deliver seeds his rivals wouldn't have till 1936. And luck, he felt, favored the brave, so he began accepting orders, at 10 cents per seed, when they began coming in as word of the man's recklessness got around.

The Puerto Rico and California plantings flopped because of bad weather at the wrong times, but the nasturtiums grew and seeded normally in Chile, in Florida, and in the Fordhook greenhouses. Burpee had also cannily asked an Australian seedsman friend, Eric Rumsey, to duplicate the season-telescoping on nasturtiums, and a good crop was formed down under. But all four crops amounted to just fifty thousand seeds, only half as many as Burpee had orders for, it turned out, so he had to pull one more rabbit out of his hat. He came up with the notion of rooting fifty thousand cuttings of the new nasturtiums and offering these at the same price as the seeds. With what some rivals have referred to as Burpee luck, this worked out gorgeously, almost exactly half the customers ordering seeds and half preferring rooted cuttings.

There was an interesting postscript to the story, relayed to Burpee by Rumsey following the Australian flower show at which Rumsey exhibited for the first time Australian samples of the brand-new double nasturtiums in many colors. One of the seedsmen attending the show was John C. Bodger, and when he came to the nasturtium display he stopped dead. As the man who started it all by discovering the original Golden Gleam, he no doubt felt it was carrying things a little too far to be not only beaten, but beaten two years too fast. As Rumsey told the story, he was hurrying forward to introduce himself to Bodger, whom he had long wanted to meet, when he realized that the well-known American seedsman was talking out loud to himself about the nasturtiums. "And," Rumsey reported to Burpee, "after listening for a few moments to what Mr. Bodger thought of the whole thing, I decided not to bother him by introducing myself for a while longer, say another year or two."

Another postscript to the nasturtium story was financial. Burpee lost about $12,000 on his expensive experiment. He lost it cheerfully, since he had gained a thundering lot of prestige for the house. He also picked up another bonus, in the form of a flower sport that showed up among the greenhouse-grown nasturtiums in the third generation. It was a nasturtium with fifty or more petals. But here the Burpee luck faltered—the glamour flower was sterile; no seed. The plant could be reproduced only by cuttings, or clones, as the horticulturists say. But as usual, Burpee came out on top again by turning a drawback into a sugarplum: since the glamorous nasturtium could not make seed, the United States Patent Office gave Burpee's the protection of a patent on it—something rare among seedsmen, who look enviously upon rose hybridizers in this respect. The patent got quite a bit of publicity, and as the result of a news story in the New York *Times*, humorous versifier Paul Showers was inspired to dash off the following for the old *Life*, issue of August 1936:

### Intimations of Immortality in 1936

A day was all that God required
To make the plants that He desired.
He brought forth trees, and herbs, and grass,
And so the springtime came to pass.
Today the laboratory sleuth,
Who probes His secrets, searching Truth,
Has found mutations in the genes—
If not the End—at least the means
To supplement Creative Will
With slow and scientific skill.
So forty thousand hot-house breeds
Are ravished of their crop of seeds,
And these are planted row on row
With careful trowel and loving hoe,
And horticulture's ablest brains
Keep watch for unexpected strains.
(For since man's methods aren't Sublime,
He has to wait on chance and time.)
At length the hoped-for Wonder comes:
Nasturtiums like chrysanthemums!
And man in puny imitation
Adds a bloom to God's creation.
However—
God made trees for man's delight
But Burpee wants a copyright.

Nothing daunted, Burpee went right ahead and named the
new variety *Tropaeolum majus Burpeeii.* Later on he found that
some of the super-blooms produced a little pollen, so even though
they still couldn't form seeds of their own, they could father those
of some other nasturtiums, producing seeds that grew 50 per cent
super-doubles. They were more of an interesting experiment than

a lasting thing, though, and are not now carried in the catalog, which continues to feature progeny of the big telescoping technique—a technique Burpee's have used from time to time ever since.

# 9  POLYPLOIDING AND SUCH

David Burpee is understandably pleased with what his plant breeders have done with snapdragons. These showy members of the figwort family began to be an important item with the company in the early 1920s. Up till then they hadn't amounted to a great deal, though W. Atlee Burpee listed species even in the early catalogs starting in 1880. But although it was a rather small staple, the snapdragon, botanically *Antirrhinum*, was an enduring one. It had a broad range of color, attractively shaped flowers, and it amused the children—the flowers looked like tiny dragons' heads, and pinching the throat made the "mouth" pop open. Snapping the dragon, they called it. In earlier days, simple folk took this to be a sign of influence with fate, and they planted snapdragons to help charm away any evil spells that might be heading their way.

If the popularity of the snapdragon were shown on a graph over the years the line would start shooting up more sharply in 1946. That was the year Burpee's celebrated the end of World War II by introducing the tetraploid snapdragon to a willing world. Though one will get you ten with any fair-minded betting commissioner if even today a single backyard gardener in a hundred has any clear idea of what a tetraploid plant is, Burpee's have patiently explained it in the catalog each year. In 1946 they did so in these words:

> Tetra Snaps are a new "scientific" creation—a new group of snapdragons originated through the treatment of the best diploid varieties with colchicine—a drug or chemical derived from the bulbs of fall crocus.
>
> Genetically, Tetra Snaps are known as tetraploid snapdragons for, when examined under the microscope, one finds that they have twice the number of chromosomes (the "container" of hereditary "genes") in their cells as regular or diploid varieties.

Probably feeling that this was a big enough dose of book learning for one spell, Burpee's did not go on to explain that, for instance, nature was producing polyploid plants (which includes tetraploids) long before man had crept out of his caves for good, or stirred earth with a stick to plant a seed. Freezing, for one, will sometimes turn a plant into a polyploid. So can very high heat. Mechanical injury may do the same thing, the scar tissue having the power to produce polyploid cells, under the right conditions. Man has aped nature and produced polyploid plants by belaboring normal ones with a blunt hoe. But compared to the use of colchicine, the hoe bit is vague.

Drop with an eye dropper, or apply with a spray, a dilute solution of colchicine on a flat of a hundred seedlings, and if it works at all it will work like the dickens. Some sorts of plants won't cooperate, and in the case of snapdragons, ninety-five or more of the hundred seedlings will fade and die. However, the few survivors will gradually pull themselves together, and most likely will grow up to produce some seed that will grow polyploid plants which will continue to breed true. It takes a few generations before they settle down and show what they can do, and even then they may not be worth keeping. But if they are good, they are very, very good.

A word about this colchicine: As the Burpee catalog says, it is derived from the bulbs of the fall crocus, *Colchicum autumnale.* It is a matter of record that other plants growing near a bed of fall crocuses have sometimes shown the polyploidy effect of the chemical on them. The thing that sparked the interest leading to experiments with colchicine came about through the disgust with bugs displayed one day by a Bulgarian scientist with the pun-provoking name of Doncho Kostoff. Kostoff was happily working in a greenhouse in 1931, experimenting with some egg-plants, when insects began buzzing him. Finally getting good and tired of being pestered, he fogged the place with nicotine sulphate, sending every bug to its doom. Later he was intrigued to find that many of his plants' seeds that were produced just after his nicotine counterattack grew offspring with extra chromosomes. Other scientists who heard about this were also intrigued, and though nicotine proved an inconsistent performer as a polyploidy agent, it led to the investigation of some related alkaloids. The pioneer work here was done by the husband-wife team of Dr. B. R. Nebel and Dr. Mabel R. Nebel of the Geneva Experiment Station, New York, and by Dr. Albert F. Blakeslee of the Carnegie Institution at Cold Spring Harbor, Long Island. They found that colchicine, once considered the sovereign remedy for relief of gout, was the alkaloid most effective in increasing chromosome numbers. So far, nobody is quite sure exactly how colchicine does it, but it does it better than anything else tested to date. Some of the other things that have been used to shock plants into becoming polyploids are sulfanilamide, the infection fighter in humans; chloral hydrate, a hypnotic; some of the hormone stimulants; and benzine.

The normal chromosome count varies from species to species of both plants and animals, and man has no special privileges here. He has twenty-four pairs of chromosomes, no more than a French marigold. Corn has ten pairs, petunia fourteen. Every chromosome in these paired sets is a kind of necklace of several genes (the controllers of inherited tendencies), and every cell in the plant or animal has the same number of chromosomes—except for the reproduction cells. These alone have one half the number, in order that after the reproductive cells from each parent have joined, the resulting tissue will have only the normal number of chromosomes for that species. Cells of body tissue are called diploid ( *di* for two, *ploid* for number), and reproductive cells, with half the number of chromosomes, are called haploid.

During cellular division as a plant grows, normal practice is for the chromosomes of each cell to double in number just before the cell splits in two, so that each of the two will come out with the normal number of chromosomes. Colchicine and other polyploidy agents trip up this process by preventing cells from going ahead and dividing after they have already increased their chromosomes. If they live through the treatment and resume growth, their new cells all have the same increase in chromosomes that the treatment caused to start. If this increase is a normal doubling, the resulting plant, instead of being a diploid like its parents, is called a tetraploid because it has four sets of chromosomes instead of two. Since affected plants may have various numbers of sets, the blanket term "polyploid" is used to mean "more than diploid."

Snapdragons in particular took to tetraploiding like ducks to water. When viewed alongside some regular ones, the tetraploid snapdragon looked like the campus queen next to her coltish kid sisters. Tetrasnap's flowers were larger and made more of a thing of themselves, being well ruffled and upstanding; plants were a trifle dwarfer and considerably huskier than the diploids, and the leaves were dark and glossy, almost leathery to the touch. Tetraploid snapdragons are, not surprisingly, now the most popular snapdragons on the market.

There are several other tetraploid flowers offered by Burpee's —marigold (first to be listed, and never outstanding), ageratum,

alyssum, gaillardia, phlox, zinnia, and their Gloriosa daisy. There
are also some natural tetraploids, as in petunias and marigolds.
Attempts to tetraploid zinnias consistently flopped for Burpee's
for a while, the plants all turning out sterile when they survived
at all, but in 1958 they introduced a tetraploid that was satisfactory, though not superb. They haven't had much luck with
scabiosa or cosmos. Also, you will search the vegetable section in
vain for any polyploid introductions. Of course polyploidy has
been tried on vegetables, but nothing very encouraging to
Burpee's has been produced by it so far. The reason may be that
our vegetables already have the ideal number of chromosomes.
That, in fact, is David Burpee's belief. He reasons that early civilized man didn't have time to feed his soul with flowers but was
fast to spot anything better in vegetables that cropped up. Thus,
if nature produced a good polyploid onion, man was there to
grab it and nurse the new variety along. This theory seems to be
borne out at times where there are one or more wild species of
cultivated plants available for comparison. It can sometimes be
shown that the cultivated one really is a polyploid. Wild wheat,
for instance, contains two sets of seven chromosomes each—
fourteen—while our bread wheat has six sets, or forty-two chromosomes (making it a hexaploid, as are cultivated oats also). Potatoes have been tetraploids as long as we have known them.
Cultivated strawberries are octoploids, having eight sets of chromosomes against two for wild strawberries, and many varieties
of pears and apples are tetraploids, or triploids (three sets of
chromosomes). Since there is a natural limit to the possible advantages of extra sets of chromosomes, and since it seems that
vegetables had pretty well reached that limit before plant breeders perfected their present polyploidy techniques, improvements
in vegetables must come about in other ways.

Though polyploid plants are apt to be better than their diploid
ancestors—that is, better for man's use because they are often

larger and stronger, prettier, and bear better-tasting fruits—peculiarly enough, these super-plants are also apt to be less fertile. And those polyploids with odd-numbered sets of chromosomes, such as triploids with three sets and pentaploids with five, are usually the least fertile of all. Offhand, this seems to be pure hard luck for the plant breeder: he develops a fine new plant and then it bites the hand that feeds it by refusing to set much seed, so he can grow a lot more in a hurry. Plant breeders, however, are used to disappointments and are a wily lot. Now and then they can yank a drawback inside out and turn it into an advantage. Seeds, they reasoned, are sometimes just a nuisance, such as when you're eating a watermelon. So how about a seedless polyploid watermelon? Burpee's now offer such a variety, and they have also crossed it so that it is both a polyploid and a hybrid. It needs a normal watermelon growing near, in order to set fruit, but the reward for going to this extra bother (Burpee's thoughtfully include a packet of seeds of a normal melon with each packet of the other) is, to quote the catalog: "A watermelon that is all edible but the rind . . . medium-large oval fruits, averaging 10–15 lbs. or larger, with solid bright red flesh of the sweetest flavor."

Also, every gardener who has wished his flowers would keep on blooming instead of insisting on going to seed can appreciate the merits of a polyploid variety that couldn't care less about the next generation, and goes grasshoppering gaily along with flower after flower the whole season through.

There is another side to the coin too. Sometimes a hybrid plant turns out splendidly but won't produce seed so that the breeder can experiment with its progenies. In some such cases, turning the hybrid into a polyploided hybrid sometimes startles it into becoming fertile.

In fact, if anybody ever organizes a society for the prevention of cruelty to plants, Burpee's are in for some rough times. Some plants need long days to bloom, and plant breeders think nothing of hurrying these long-day plants into bloom at the wrong season by turning on the greenhouse lights at some unearthly hour before sunrise, or of astounding short-day plants into flowering by clapping black bags over them while all their friends are enjoying the lovely weather. (Some examples of long-day flowers are sweet peas, carnations, snapdragons, and most perennials. Some short-day flowers: chrysanthemums, marigolds, asters, zinnias.)

Lengthening or shortening the exposure to daylight is so effective that one time a florist lost his Thanksgiving crop of football chrysanthemums because the city installed a new lamppost that shed a brilliant light on his greenhouse all night. It kept the chrysanthemums so busy making leaf growth they didn't get around to making flowers.

A few years ago it became all the rage to X-ray plants, not to explore their insides but to jolt them into extra mutations. It worked, but so far most of the extra mutations have been no good to man and less good to the plants.

Approximately the same results came from a much simpler dodge—that of using seed several years old. The mutations jumped way up, all of them bad. The lesson here for home gardeners seems to be: plant fresh seed. The longest-lived seed known, by the way, is that of the Indian lotus. Lotus seeds four hundred years old, found buried in peat at the bottom of a Manchurian lake, sprouted when their hard, waterproof coats were filed open. If Henry VIII had saved such a seed, Elizabeth II could plant it in the royal garden today and raise a lotus.

Many weed seeds, as any gardener can believe, snuggle in the earth for forty years and more, confidently waiting for somebody to spade up the spot for a few petunias. However, the live grain seeds said to have been found in the tombs of the Pharaohs make scientists laugh. During the 1930s somebody sent Burpee's a pea said to have been taken from King Tutankhamen's tomb, and it was planted at Fordhook. It sprouted and flourished, and turned out to be tough field type, of no commercial value. Barley which was said to have come from the wrappings of a mummy was actually from new barley straw used to pack the mummy for shipment to a museum. The flower seeds that keep best, in case you have some left over from last season and are wondering, are marigolds (2 to 3 years), poppies (3 to 5), zinnias and sweet peas (4 to 5), nasturtiums (6 to 7). Lettuce seed keeps quite well, and it is fairly safe to keep most vegetable seeds a couple of years if you don't keep them where it is warm and moist. Check the list in Chapter 12, "Seeds for War . . . and Peace," for the life expectancy of other seeds.

A seed can usually stand a lot more cold than the plant that produced it, though low humidity is the more important factor in storage. It is a matter of record that some cantaloupe seeds kept in a hot, dry office for thirty years grew good plants when finally sown.

Speaking of such resting, breeders have sometimes used ether on seeds and on plants, but ether doesn't put them to sleep. Just the other way around—it shortens their dormancy and speeds up seed sprouting. So, oddly, does an extract of the pituitary gland, the growth controller in animals. And thyroid gland extract has been used to hasten blooming time in some flowers.

In 1961 a small firm offered the public seeds treated with atomic energy, warning that though there was no radioactive hazard about the seeds, there was no telling what might come up, since the whole project was in the experimental stage. One effect of the treatment, when it worked, was sometimes to speed up growth; others were to increase yield, or plant size. Like X rays, the effect of atomic energy on plant life is to step up the rate of mutation. The attitude of the Burpee people toward this sort of treatment by radiation could be called one of hopeful pessimism. For one thing, they point out, most mutations are false alarms, no good for the plant or anything else. For another, irradiation is tricky, requiring a dosage low enough so it doesn't kill the organism or reduce viability below the legal limit if it is seeds that are being treated, yet high enough to increase the rate of mutations.

In the early 1950s Burpee's had the Brookhaven National Laboratories grow marigolds on Long Island in an isolated field that had been exposed to gamma radiation. Nothing of more than academic interest resulted. However, Burpee's were not completely discouraged, as evidenced by their 1962 catalog. In the listing of their Miracle marigolds, they stated that the seed had "been saved from plants that were the result of irradiated seed." The radiating was done for them by Nuclear Science and Engineering Corporation, Pittsburgh, a firm delving into peacetime uses of nuclear energy. The object of exposing the marigold seed was to see if it might boost customers' chances of finding a pure-white one.

Everything considered, seedsmen have come a long way since the justly famous horticulturist Liberty Hyde Bailey told seedsmen at the World's Horticultural Congress in 1893 that men could not do much to produce variations in plants, for it lay beyond their control and was up to nature. He recommended that, instead, they try to select for use those varieties that included in their good qualities a willingness to co-operate by mutating.

# 10 EVERYBODY LOVES A SEED CATALOG

Since they are largely a mail-order business, Burpee's have always taken enormous pains with their well-printed catalog. Their customers often show signs of feeling strongly about the book too, and on one occasion it acted as a kind of wonder drug. This was testified to by the user herself, and she was uniquely qualified to judge, being at the time the superintendent of a hospital in Highland Park, Illinois, and a registered nurse. She was Miss Marjorie Ibsen, a relative of famed Norwegian writer Henrik Ibsen. During a pneumonia wave in the 1930s every bed in the fifty-two-bed hospital had a sick person in it and Superintendent Ibsen herself was groggy with influenza.

Her personal low point, she recalled later, was the bleak January day when, too sick to rise, she had to run the hospital from her bed. And then on top of everything else, a traffic-snarling prairie blizzard came slashing in, and snowed out the ailing superintendent's one last bleak comfort—a view of the winter-quiet hospital grounds where for several seasons she had been nursing along flower beds and other plantings. But at dusk of that bad day, she recalled clearly almost thirty years later: "The night nurse brought me the late mail, and the one bright thing in it was the Burpee catalog. All through the blizzard that night while I stayed awake to handle emergencies, I lay in my bed and I read the catalog clear through, from asparagus to zinnias. I got out of bed the next day—and I knew that catalog was what cured me."

The story has a sequel. Shortly after her recovery, one of the hospital's regular clients, the wife of an Italian nurseryman, was brought to bed there for another childbirth and the husband told Miss Ibsen he was ordering a girl this time. Not one to pass up either a little jest or a bit of lagniappe, she promised Mr. Fiori a girl if he would promise to do a spot of gardening for her in the spring. He promised, the baby was a girl, and come spring, Miss Ibsen and her snug little hospital got themselves a whole blooming new flower bed, free for nothing and planted according to plans from Mr. Burpee's catalog drawn up the night of the blizzard.

Nowadays Burpee's send out somewhat fewer than two and a half million catalogs (plus about 400,000 fall bulb catalogs), a much heftier circulation figure than most national magazines have, but nearly a million fewer catalogs than were issued in 1950, their peak year in this respect. They could kick the figure any time to five million, the number of living customers, past and present, on their list, but the added circulation would probably not bring in enough orders even to pay the cost of the catalogs, which are running close to 25 cents per copy placed in a prospect's hands, and nearer 30 cents for foreign mailings. The average seed order today comes to just a little under $5.

Recent catalogs have been thinner than many of the old ones. The 1962 book totaled 98 pages plus 24 unnumbered ones in color, a far cry from the twenty-fifth anniversary catalog of 1901, which ran to 220 pages. It was exceptional, but not greatly so; many of the old catalogs were close to 200 pages long. The original catalog of 1876 had 48 pages.

By 1943 the catalog size, 6 by 9 inches, had become an awkward one for printers to deal with, so after fifty-seven years with it (size had varied a little during the company's first decade) they went, after much hand-wringing, to another size. The new one was three-quarters of an inch greater in length and in width. It was still small enough, Burpee's rejoiced to see, to be pretty sure to land on top when it and several competing catalogs, or some magazines, were stacked, as by a customer.

The modern Burpee catalog is highly informative, and a gardener can learn from it not only what varieties are best for his climate but how to make most of them grow. The old catalogs did not give a gardener as much cultural information, but when he finished reading one he must have felt he had had an intensive, thrilling, and exhausting visit with Mr. Burpee and Mr. Burpee's seed business. The elder seedsman seemed to permeate his catalog, much of which he wrote himself in pencil on Manilla sheets of catalog-dummy paper. Even when read today he steps out of the pages, fixes the reader with an earnest eye, and proceeds to give him the word.

When his sons became old enough to read, Mr. Burpee recommended the catalog to them as literature by means of a never-fail device. Each year at the family Christmas dinner table a copy of the brand-new catalog, hot off the press, was put at each place. The ones at the boys' places were unique, having book marks of one-dollar and five-dollar bills scattered through them. In searching for the treasure, their father reasoned, they would become interested in the business.

One of the first things you notice about the old catalogs is the far greater amount of background information they threw at the reader. W. Atlee Burpee not only liked being in the seed business —he was positive all his customers were fascinated by it and were hanging on his words to learn more. It is highly unlikely that Burpee's today would make a booklet of the technical papers read at a trade convention and confidently offer it to their customers for 10 cents. W. Atlee Burpee did just that. He titled it,

"Selection in Seed Growing," and advised his public it was "A book containing the papers contributed to the Horticultural Congress at the World's Fair, Chicago, 1893, by leading seedsmen of Europe and America, setting forth the advantages of high breeding in seeds intelligently conducted, with a resume of leading features in present methods of culture." It sold for years.

The nearest thing to this that Burpee's has done in modern times is a 160-page record of talks and panel discussions from a 1945 gathering at Fordhook Farms titled "Symposium on Horticulture of China," but the book was not for general distribution. Much of it was of interest only to the professional in horticulture, the program headlining such specialists as: Dr. Lela V. Barton, plant pathologist with the Boyce Thompson Institute for Plant Research; Dr. W. B. Mack, head of the Pennsylvania State College Department of Horticulture; B. Y. Morrison, in charge of the Department of Agriculture's Division of Plant Exploration and Introduction, and editor of the *National Horticultural Magazine;* Drs. T. P. Dykstra, S. W. Emsweller, and Roy Magruder of the Department of Agriculture; and Dr. Ardron Lewis, agricultural consultant of the International Training Administration.

Another thing the original Burpee seedsman doted on in his catalog was a tour of the store, as seedsmen call their headquarters. The old Burpee catalogs often ran page after page of wood engravings—frequently reprints from newspaper articles—showing what the headquarters looked like, inside and out. It looked like any other business establishment of that day—outside, solid and severe; inside, tall, dark, and cramped; the men in shirt garters, vests, and bartender haircuts, the girls ("All the good looking young women in Philadelphia," one of the visiting journalists rashly declared) sweeping the floor with their skirts, and everyone apparently dedicated to the proposition that Burpee's seeds had no peers. The 1905 catalog informed its readers that the house was so abreast of the times there were twelve telephones in its seven-story building.

As mentioned in Chapter 1, livestock was an important part of the business in the beginning, and continued to be a part of it throughout W. Atlee Burpee's administration. His successors dropped livestock for good in 1917, when the war made it hard to get feed. By then, Burpee's pedigreed lines of cattle, sheep, and pigs were a thing of the past, and the livestock consisted of only collie dogs and four breeds of chickens, none of them illustrated as of yore, when they had been shown in finely executed wood engravings.

Speaking of illustrations, it might be mentioned that the 1891 book was the first to use some wood engravings based on photographs. Until then, the flowers and vegetables, as well as the factory, were all shown by engravings made on the basis of artists' illustrations. The quality of the engravings was good, and the catalog used hundreds of them, the larger ones sometimes signed by the engraver. The doom of this ancient art could have been guessed by a study of the 1901 Burpee catalog, where appeared for the first time illustrations printed from engravings made by a mechanical process—photogravure. The colored pictures in the catalog today are from color photographs—1941 was the first year for this—but color is nothing new to Burpee's. Away back in 1884 they splashed out with three lithographed inserts—one of their new Cardinal tomato, and the others of dahlias and cannas, all in full color. Two years later the catalog covers bloomed for the first time, the 1886 book depicting on its front cover a Currier & Ives-type of harvest scene, and the back cover showing the head of a collie dog and that of a Cotswold ewe. The covers have been in color ever since. Front covers have run heavily to flowers, the earlier ones often including pretty girls or children; the high mark for charm in the latter class was reached in 1894 when Burpee's ran, under the title "Little Kitchen Friend," a painting of a sober little barefoot girl—or boy, some say, pointing out that on small urchins skirts knew no sex in that era—dragging in a wicker basketful of garden harvest.

The catalogs' back covers frequently showed views of the buildings where the business was conducted or of Fordhook Farms as if seen from a balloon. Vegetables also appeared on a good many back covers, and twice were given a more lifelike look by embossing; the famous Netted Gem cantaloupe was so honored in 1900, and a fingertip run over the 1903 back cover could detect each kernel of corn shown on an ear of White Evergreen and the leaves and blossoms of Matchless tomato.

One appeal of the older catalogs was a competitive one. W. Atlee Burpee believed in encouraging the customers to see what they could do with a packet of seeds, and to so encourage them he offered prizes. The prizes were nearly always cash, and he went in for quantity, preferring to reward hundreds of contestants moderately instead of enriching a paltry few greatly. Though he said he didn't want free advertising, he got a good deal of highly thrifty publicity by the simple device of offering cash prizes at every state and county fair in the entire nation to winners who grew their vegetables with Burpee's seeds. Prize placards mentioning that Burpee's seeds grew were furnished for the asking, and peeked out from among the mammoth squashes, watermelons, pumpkins, celery, tomatoes, cucumbers, and so on and on.

You didn't have to enter your candidate in a fair to try for some Burpee prizes, though. You could ship it direct to Philadelphia for Mr. Burpee's personal inspection. If it was too bulky (such as an acre of corn), the usual arrangement was to write the pertinent details and have them attested by a notary public or justice of the peace. In 1884 the system backfired, and the twenty-six-year-old Mr. Burpee was scandalized. "A Dishonest Winner," he bawled in the next catalog, and spilled the whole disgraceful story of an Illinois farmer who had forged the signature of a justice on a claim for such a harvest that it had sprung $90 from Mr. Burpee. The fraud was discovered when these winnings were reported in the next Burpee catalog, the country slicker's neighbors declaring he had grown all his prize crops in his head. Not mentioning the rascal's name, "out of consideration for the innocent members of his family," Mr. Burpee promptly had him charged with forgery. That ended for good any hankypanky on prize contests, and also spoke volumes for seedsman Burpee's fair dealing.

Though they get occasional kicks on such things as a standing 50-cent charge for packing bulb orders, Burpee's are, in the language of the retail customer, easy to do business with. That is, if something goes wrong with an order they make it right. This is implied in their guarantee, displayed in the catalog and similar to those of most seed companies, obligating themselves to the extent of the purchase price in case of complaint. Burpee's ask no questions, make no investigations, and promptly replace any seeds reported missing or substandard. Years ago they used to get a good many complaints from customers who had not received some packets they thought they had ordered but which they really had not. To cure this, Burpee's began returning the order blank with the shipment. To their pleased surprise it increased business, many customers sending in another order with the explanation: "I meant to ask for such-and-such also, but forgot." Just to prove you can't please everybody, though, last year a woman gardener, abashed at her extravagance, wrote in large letters across her $13.70 order: *"Tear this up.* Do not send it with order—my husband would faint."

At the time the $90 scandal blew up, the Burpee seed catalog was officially called *Burpee's Farm Annual,* the title it adopted in 1879 and kept for thirty years. In 1910 the title switched to

*Burpee's New Annual.* The "New" was dropped the following year, and the name *Burpee's Annual*—which lasted till 1929—became so familiar to the staff that they still refer to all catalogs, past and present, as "B.A.'s." After an interval of calling the catalog *Burpee's Garden Book*, the name changed once more, in 1935, to *Burpee Seeds*, its title today.

Aside from such things as title changes, the catalog has changed in character. There was a masculine vigor about the early catalogs that was in key with the prominence of vegetables in the front, followed by farm seeds, followed, finally, by flowers (which were usually interrupted by a listing of livestock). The 1900 catalog even had a little essay recommending that women take up gardening as a healthy novelty. Today, flowers lead off, and, logically, Burpee market research shows that it is now the woman who usually answers the special-offer ads in newspapers and magazines, automatically adding her name to the catalog mailing list. It is the catalog that then does the selling (hence the drab and matter-of-fact brown-paper seed packets).

Once the catalog is in the house, the man is exposed to it, and if he happens to pick it up he is frequently hooked. That is the Burpee reasoning, at any rate, possibly because in no other way can they account for cabbage, corn, and tomato seed appearing on orders from homemakers who started off toying with sweet peas and asters.

Home gardeners, Burpee's believe, number over thirty million in the United States. Hunters and fishermen together are said to total forty million. The probable incidence of duplication makes this a poor figure for comparisons, so, convinced they are catering to the nation's largest single group of enthusiasts, Burpee's occasionally try to find out something about seed buyers statistically. In one such try they were beguiled to find that their best customers were doctors. Burpee's were not sure what this meant but felt it couldn't help being good. (Their second-best customers, just to make it confusing, turned out to be the presidents of small-town banks.) Other probings of the catalog readers have led Burpee's to believe that often if you scratch a gardener you will find an intellectual. So far, they don't have much statistical proof of this, intellectuals being notoriously poll-shy, but they feel the trail is warm.

There is more concrete proof of such prosaic aspects of the business as how many members of the average seed-buying family order seed (one usually orders for everybody), how often they order (once a year), and when (late winter or early spring, creating an annual Burpee mad rush).

Considering that he had few statistics to guide him, W. Atlee Burpee showed a remarkable confidence in thinking he knew exactly what the customers wanted. Every year he came right out with it, splashing his guesses across the pink pages he ran in front of the regular listings. The catalog celebrating his twenty-fifth year in business carried thirty-three such pink-page novelties, though this was more than usual. Besides the brand-new things, Mr. Burpee plugged on the pink pages the recent introductions of which he was proudest, such as Burpee's Bush lima. It was still hitting the pink pages ten years after it was introduced. He was so sure of himself as a judge of plant merit that he blandly offered to supply his competitors' seeds to a customer if he "should order some variety that we do not catalog and insist that we get it for you (when we shall send it in its original package). . . ."

Today the Burpee policy on this point is not stated in words. In terms of deeds, the house tries to keep its customers happy. This boils down to: If you don't see what you want, ask for it—though the cost of handling such troublesome requests makes them shudder. Last year a woman gardener pining for an item she thought she remembered seeing advertised somewhere sometime, asked for a packet of yard-long beans. Burpee's have not carried the variety for years and do not recommend it for anything but as a garden eccentric. They filled the order just the same, having had a few beans on hand for test purposes. If they got many such requests they would very probably list the item again and be done with it.

In the effort to sidetrack such fancies, and particularly to increase the chances for gardening success, Burpee's put this mark, ☉, opposite the varieties of vegetables it particulary recommends. They call the mark a bull's-eye, and it comes in two sizes, big and little, when there is a choice of choices within a species. No bull's-eye is used for flowers since color is usually the important difference between varieties, and is plain enough, and also a matter of individual taste.

Such systems as the bull's-eye are sometimes criticized as subtle attempts to regiment the home gardener. Also, Burpee's list only about 60 per cent as many varieties of vegetables today as they did before World War II, and less than half as many flowers. But part of this decrease has come about in the effort to keep costs down by simplifying the operation—not merely through restricting the choice. Another argument for fewer varieties today is the increase in hybrid ones (forty-five vegetables and seventy-five flowers, compared with three of each before). By combining many good points a single hybrid can take the place of several old standard varieties. Both this factor and Burpee's bull's-eye system offer at least one quite useful feature—they make it much easier for the novice gardener, and for anyone in a hurry, to choose varieties most likely to succeed.

The quickest way to find anything in the catalog is to look in the index first. The listings in the body of the book are mostly alphabetical but many exceptions are made for promotional and printer's reasons. Flowers lead off, vegetables having been in back since 1935 except for four years, 1943–46, during victory garden importance. Though the vegetable pages are now only slightly more than one-third of the whole, Burpee's continue to sell more vegetable than flower seeds. Large orders from commercial growers account for this, however, while most flower seeds are bought by home gardeners. Seedsmen with sensitive palates deplore the attention such fripperies as skin diving, adult education classes, and television take from tending a little kitchen garden. They are acutely aware that fresh home-garden varieties of vegetables are as lusciously different from those most of us eat as a violin concerto is different from a washtub falling downstairs, and they are equally aware that the majority of U.S. citizens don't know this. Even special-offer ads on vegetable seeds in newspapers and magazines have usually pulled a poor response. They key ads to see how well they work, and to keep the customers from catching on the keys are linked to mailing room numbers in Burpee buildings. If you answer an ad, as mentioned before, your name goes on the catalog list. (If you simply want a catalog, you can get that, too. The house is so well known that a postcard addressed "Burpee, Philadelphia, Pa.," will reach them promptly.) In any case, they hope you will see some things you want, and send in an order. If you do, they then hope you won't make the most common mistake of all—that of using the catalog number of one thing with the name of another. (The number-plus-name system speeds up the handling of orders except when it lays an egg. When this happens, the order filler passes the buck upstairs, and the more experienced help hold what they call a buzz session, trying to read the customer's mind from his order blank. One that baffled the Riverside, California, branch was from an obviously venerable old western gentleman who ignored the catalog number entirely and then wrote his request in so shaky a hand it was all but illegible. A genius at decoding finally made it out: the old romantic desired some Love in a Mist.)

Here, clued by the other more frequent customer errors to avoid, are some things you *can* do to get the best and fastest service from Burpee's, or any other mail-order seed house:

Keep old catalogs if you are fond of them, but do order from the current one.

In any case, don't order from both of them on the same order blank. Things change from year to year.

Put any gardening questions, or any others you want to ask, on a separate sheet of paper. They can then detour to the Customer Service Department for answering while your order goes ahead and gets filled.

Send one order under one name for all the gardeners in the family. It reduces details for both you and Burpee's, and the fewer the details, the less chance of slip-ups.

Order flowers by the names shown in boldface type in the catalog. Common names often vary, or overlap between species.

Checks or money orders are best forms of payment, loose change the worst. Favorite currency: a dollar bill. Burpee's used to get so many stamps they had to hire a man just to sell them to banks and such to get their money in legal tender.

Some of the best buys in the catalog are among the collections ("$1.75 zinnia garden for $1. . . . Seven favorite flowers—$2 value for $1. . . ."). Burpee's offer these despite the fact you can never tell about a gardener. Sometimes when the best brains on the sales staff have noodled out a nifty package deal they are positive everyone will love, in come snarly letters from gardeners demanding to know who Burpee's think they are, trying to tell them what color flowers or kinds of vegetables they should like. Burpee's, who did not grow big by insisting on selling parsnips to carrot lovers, never argue. The customer may or may not be right, but right or wrong, they want him to keep on being the customer.

# 11 ACRES OF SEEDS

Flower seed growers have certain personnel problems not usually associated with farming. At Burpee's Floradale Farms in California the marigolds made one man sneeze so hard he finally had to be assigned to chores among the petunias and other innocuous blooms. Another worker developed severe headaches, also apparently only when among marigolds. Actually, such reactions to marigolds are rare, but one luckless fellow came up with an allergy that had no solution but utter departure; he, poor wretch, was sensitive to sunshine.

If flowers are apt to bother you, Burpee's is no place to work. The number of varieties the firm offered its customers in 1962 was 920, most of which by far it grew for itself. (It also offered 519 varieties of flower bulbs, but the majority are still grown in the Netherlands.) Vegetable varieties offered came to 377. Had you been determined to try out every last thing listed in the seed and bulb catalogs, you would have planted 1816 different items. Aside from owning a good set of calluses, you would by then have accumulated also the experience to understand a part of what David Burpee means when he says his business is the most complicated form of agriculture.

"A farmer is diversified if he has five or ten different crops," Burpee has said. "We have not five or ten, but over twelve hundred crops. And we are trying all the time to better them. And this whole job must then be carried through on up to the mail order catalog."

However, because of its splendid merchandising facilities, Burpee's can justify such expensive jobs as the intensive breeding done on double nasturtiums some years ago, to rush seeds to the customers ahead of competitors. "Furthermore," Burpee says when expanding his theme of the seed business complications, "we deal with living organisms. If a crop fails we lose a year—two years if the plant is a biennial in its second year, and this includes such commercially important vegetables as beets, cabbage, carrots, onions, turnips and cauliflower."

Partly as insurance against such disasters, the company, in common with other well-heeled seedsmen, keeps a spare stock of all seeds that, in the language of the trade, "will carry," meaning they have a life expectancy of more than a single year. "Most seeds," says Burpee with understandable relief, "carry very well." The seeds are kept in fireproof buildings—one on each of the three most important Burpee growing farms. The one at Floradale, for example, is of concrete blocks, so strictly functional that it looks like something the Army would have run up to store canned beans in. Burpee's call this building the stock-seed house. The cool California coastal climate is ideal for seed storage. The stock-seed house is about the size of two or three home garages, and to Burpee's the seeds stored in this one ugly little shelter are worth at least half a million dollars. Most of these seeds, in bags or brown paper envelopes and racked on shelves, are not the seeds you get when Burpee's mail your order. However, the main difference is merely a name difference. These stock seeds are what Burpee's plant to grow the flowers and vegetables that make the market seed they sell. And part of this market seed is saved out and becomes the stock seed for the next year.

Which brings up a question: Why can't you save your own seed from your own garden, and plant it next year? You can, you can. Your grandmother, or her mother, probably did. It won't work with first-generation hybrids (see Chapter 8, "Why Hybrids?"), but our grandparents didn't have them anyway. Well, then, if gardeners can save seed from the other, non-hybrid, flowers and vegetables, how does a seedsman such as David Burpee ever make a living?

The fact is he does pretty well, meets a payroll for more than a thousand employees in the busy season, and sells seeds hand over fist—something like thirty-two million packets a year. This isn't because home gardeners are too bone lazy to save their own seeds, and in fact some do and are very happy with them. Mainly, Burpee and other seedsmen do all right because they raise better seeds than most home gardeners can. Nature helps seedsmen by being as temperamental as a singed cat when it comes to keeping up the quality of flowers and vegetables that people fancy. Nature isn't a bit interested in seeing that the peas or corn you enjoy stay plump and tender year after year. If they want to get tough and skinny and drift back toward the original Adam of the species, that's O.K. with nature. Or they can cross, or grow sickly and die out entirely; nature in the raw is anything but a welfare state. Consequently, the seedsman justifies his existence by outfoxing nature and seeing that only the best-behaved plants provide seed and that the scallawags get pitched out. Besides selling dependability, the seedsman also drums up business through tempting the customers with new things by searching them out or by breeding.

Burpee's also do a good deal more for gardeners than to grow their seeds, as big as that job is. One of its boasts is that it was experimenting with and testing plants before the United States Government had any experiment stations. It may be truer to say that Burpee's were putting much time and money *consistently* in plant trials at an earlier date than the government was. The record shows that during the 1850s—possibly before W. Atlee Burpee was even born—the government set aside its original experimental plot, five acres in Washington, D.C., to test sorgo, and had granted land and appropriated funds for three crop-trial farms still earlier that century. Incidentally, the very first agricultural experiment station in this country was on ten acres which the city of Savannah, Georgia, provided in 1735 to see what subtropical plants might be introduced there. The venture never came to much. The first state to establish an experiment station was Connecticut, in 1876, the year W. Atlee Burpee went into the seed business.

In 1888, twelve years after he began, Mr. Burpee bought the original acreage of what he called Fordhook Farm, at Doylestown, Pa., about twenty-five miles north of Philadelphia, and was able to expand greatly the annual trials he had been running on other land in the vicinity and on Long Island. During Fordhook's first year he ran trials on over two thousand vegetables and on nearly fifteen hundred flower varieties. Some other big seed houses also ran such trials at the time, and on a comparable scale, but disinterested contemporary observers of standing in the trade regarded Burpee's as having no superior in their diligence to supply superb seeds.

Taking the customer to his heart with his usual manly enthusiasm, Mr. Burpee flashed frequent reports on Fordhook's trial grounds. In an 1894 flight of oratory he proclaimed: "Our system of trials furnishes the cable by which we anchor in the harbor of your good graces from year to year. Constantly repeated trials enable us to detect any fraying of its strands." While gardeners were still reeling from this fancy language, Mr. Burpee yanked them along on a fast verbal tour of the trials (which are done on substantially the same lines today):

". . . Seeds, after having been thoroughly tested for their germinating qualities and found satisfactory (all reputable seedsmen do this much), are sowed in rows ten feet in length in ground properly prepared for them. By the term 'properly prepared,' we mean treated precisely as any intelligent grower would work his soil having a good crop in view.

"We distinctly disclaim the employment of means or methods beyond the reach of any planter with a view to stimulating an unusual or excessive development; the plain truth is what we are seeking, consequently we do not 'tamper with the witnesses.'

"We must know precisely what our seeds will do for you, with your methods of cultivation, as on what they will do for you, *your way*, our reputation hinges.

"At the end of each row a stake painted white and bearing a number is planted—for instance, say No. 4618—and this number at once becomes a member of a vast and interesting family. No. 4618 is entered in a specially prepared register—where it came from, when it came, when it was sowed, when it came up, etc., etc.,—and from the time it has a visible existence above ground, its appearance, behavior, and general or specific characteristics are constantly and carefully noted in the aforesaid register. This register is an impartial history of its efforts at building a character, from germ to maturity, and on which record it must stand or fall."

The trial grounds on old Fordhook today see some tinkering that would astonish the original Burpee seedsman; but also almost all the things he was doing in the nineteenth century are still being done. An exception is the extensive testing of foreign-grown seeds; today we grow almost all our own seeds here in the United States. The trials system has these three broad purposes: to develop and to test new things; to plant everything in the catalog so as to make sure the customer is getting what Burpee's tell him he is getting; to try out competitors' seeds.

Among the things tested are many plants that come to seedsmen from the various state agricultural experiment stations, which work closely with the United States Department of Agriculture. Varieties high in disease resistance have frequently been among the outstanding developments from these sources.

In some years the Burpee research department has run as many as twenty thousand trials. This is a case where many are grown but few are chosen. Take marigolds, for instance; they are represented in the catalog with about seventy-five varieties, but if you visited the growing farms you would find no fewer than a thousand kinds blooming their hearts out to please Burpee. If he gets two or three topnotch novelties out of the whole shebang he will feel fate has smiled on him. As you can imagine, the work of keeping track of a year's trials, plus the seed handling and field operations, is tremendous. To supervise it, Burpee's maintain a staff of plant breeders, or geneticists, that is large even for as big a seed house as Burpee's. "We do a great deal more research for the home gardener," David Burpee has said, "than any seed house in the world." One thing that helps them is an organizational setup that has roots firmly planted from coast to coast.

The first non-eastern branch was a farm in southern (though not very southern) California, 160 miles north of Los Angeles, three miles west of Lompoc, and now a near neighbor of Vandenberg Air Force Base, due north. The farm lies in a windy valley and was so good a choice for seed farming that Burpee's were followed there by five other growers. W. Atlee Burpee bought the farm with the advice and help of his then sixteen-year-old son David, who soon found himself working there summers as a roguer. Mr. Burpee wanted the place in order to raise seed for sweet peas—a flower he called the poor man's orchid and did as much for in his day as his son David has done for the marigold —and to run it he hired a distinguished horticulturist, Edwin Lonsdale, and then asked Mr. Lonsdale to pick a good name for the farm. "Floradale," said Mr. Lonsdale at once, possibly from a fancy for his own last syllable as a caboose on the name of the Roman goddess of flowers. In 1944 the Burpee farm at Santa Paula, about ninety miles down the California coast from Floradale and twelve miles inland, was established to grow zinnias and other things that wanted warmer weather than the Lompoc Valley and its fogs from the ocean six miles away provided. These two farms and Fordhook are the Burpee big three today. For the sake of simplicity, Santa Paula is not much publicized, the term "Floradale" sometimes being used to embrace both California growing farms. Fordhook comes in a poor third on the volume of seed production but is important in trials and is still the showplace farm. Among them, they spread over about fifteen hundred acres of owned, leased, and contract land, though this figure shifts around from year to year. In addition, Burpee's operate a vegetable-seed farm at Los Mochis, Mexico, and grow more vegetable seeds, largely beans, at Twin Falls, Idaho. For several years they ran a farm, Sunnybrook, in southern New Jersey. Currently, Burpee's total acreage is a little less than four thousand. They used to operate farms in Lower California, Guatemala, and Costa Rica, too, but the weather in all three places was poor for seed growing. (In Costa Rica they were drenched with about twelve feet of rain a year, and had to build special houses to dry out their seeds.)

The other units of the company are the headquarters building in Philadelphia, and three sales branches—at Clinton, Iowa; Riverside, California; and a principally wholesale one at Sanford, Florida.

Burpee's scatter their farming operations widely because seeds are a finicky crop. Like hay, rain at the wrong time can ruin them, so the dry summers of California work out fine, and also help in producing seed free of diseases that humidity encourages. On the other hand, some California coastal valleys do have high humidity because of fogs, and this is good for such crops as cabbage and cauliflower, which shatter their seed all over the ground if the pods dry out before harvest.

Idaho is big on bean growing and has none of the bacterial blight that plagues beans in some parts of the east. This disease factor is especially serious in seed farming because crops going to seed must linger on in the fields until well past the market stage, giving more chance for disease and insects to attack them.

Here are the insecticides and fungicides Burpee's use for the more usual problems they meet every year:

| | |
|---|---|
| Soil insects (in greenhouse and flatting earth) | Methyl bromide |
| Soil diseases | (No chemicals. Crop rotation and use of resistant varieties.) |
| Damping off | Natriphene<br>Fermate |
| Aphids | Parathion<br>Malathion 5<br>Systox |
| Caterpillars | DDT 5-10 |
| Corn earworms | DDT |
| Cucumber beetles | DDT |
| Cutworms | DDT |
| Earwigs | Chlordane<br>Dieldrin<br>DDT |
| Flea beetles | DDT |
| Leaf hoppers | DDT |
| White flies | BHC-2 |
| Wireworms and nematodes | Ethylene dibromide (EDB), an 85% solution, 2½ to 5 gallons per acre. |
| Mildew    For Flowers:<br>           For Vegetables: | Kolodust<br>Karathane |
| Herbicide | 2-4-D<br>Neburon |

Although David Burpee does not need to make the annual seed hunt to Europe that his father made, the flung-out nature of the present Burpee organization keeps him traveling so much that at one time he owned his own plane. He bought this flying machine, a twin-engined Beechcraft with places for eight, after being stranded on the ground three times during World War II when someone with a higher priority nabbed his seat for a flight. To fly his plane Burpee hired a pilot and co-pilot who filled him with fierce satisfaction whenever they beat a commercial plane across the country. When they were on the ground between flights, however, they got on his nerves by phoning him every morning to ask: "What'll we do today?" Finding they didn't care much about hoeing weeds, Burpee set them to inventing, and they figured out a pollen buzzer. By then the war was over and priorities were no longer a problem on commercial flights, so Burpee gave up his airplane without regrets. This did not surprise his friends, who knew that he hates machinery and expects the worst from any mechanical device that gets a chance at him.

In this pattern, he once had to make an unscheduled stop in a little Virginia town when his car broke down on a trip to Florida. Checking in at a hotel, Burpee and his traveling companion, one of his vice presidents, proceeded on foot to their respective rooms, and the vice president's room being the first they came to, Burpee paused to see what the accomodations were like. They were unusual. Curled on the bed in scanty attire and sleeping like a baby was one of the hotel maids. As the vice president came churning back out, he found his way firmly blocked by Burpee, who dearly loves a little joke. "Now, Joe," he said, "you go right back in. Don't you know what this is? This is southern hospitality at its very finest." At times, in fact, it has almost seemed as if risqué situations lie in wait for Burpee in hotels. He once came marching back to the crowded lobby of one to report his room, No. 14, already occupied. He prefers ground-floor rooms, as did his father. "There is," he announced loudly, "a redheaded girl undressing in there." Impossible, the clerk whispered, but Burpee insisted. "She's flinging her clothes all over the place," he boomed. The mystery was cleared up by the horrified housekeeper, who discovered that Burpee had gone down the wrong corridor and started to enter a *second* Room 14, so numbered to duck unlucky 13 and reserved for the use of the maids. The redheaded girl was on her staff, the housekeeper informed Burpee, and was of high moral character even if she was an untidy undresser.

One time after a tour of the hundreds of plantings on one of the big Burpee farms, a woman visitor and a gardener herself could think of only one thing to say. "For pity's sake," she cried, "how do you know what to grow every year?"

As a matter of fact that was the one thing the farm manager didn't have to worry about. Every year the home office in Philadelphia looks at past sales and at novelties coming up, ponders on the mysteries of human nature and on some good and bad guesses it has made, and then shoots out what it calls a growing list to the farms. This list merely tells the managers how many pounds of seed of each variety will be wanted, and the managers figure out how many acres it will take. Since the original estimates are sometimes increased, managers play it safe by planting enough and then some.

They plant on paper first, making maps and filing them on poles hung from a rack, like newspapers at a library. Then before things get too final, the Burpee managers check with the managers for next-door seedsmen to make sure everybody's flowers and vegetables will be happy neighbors and won't trade unwanted pollen or hog all the bees, or misbehave in other ways. Since ideal seed-growing areas are rare and rival seedsmen tend to settle in the same places, there is as much need for neighborly good will as among six families in a two-family flat.

The land for seed crops is prepared in about the same way as for general farming. In some cases fields are pre-irrigated, and some are treated to kill damaging soil organisms or insects. Plowing and disking follow, and seed is planted at distances suitable for the particular crop. For the flowers grown at Floradale, for instance, where most of Burpee's flower seeds grow, two rows are planted 14 inches apart in raised beds, with 26-inch paths between beds. A side dressing of fertilizer is given at the rate of about five pounds per 100 feet of row after plants are thinned to the proper distances. This is the main and usually the only fertilizing that is done. Fertilizer formulas vary, those for marigolds being 16-20-0, 11-48-0, and 10-10-5.

The soil mixture used in the greenhouses and also for flats is made up of 50 per cent peat moss, 40 per cent sandy loam or silt, and 10 per cent coarse sand. To each cubic yard of this is added two pounds of pulverized "hoof and horn" (rich in nitrogen, which it releases slowly), two pounds of superphosphate, and one pound of sulphate of potash.

With the bulk of Burpee's seeds being grown in a mild California climate, the planting season does not wait for spring, but starts in the late fall and keeps right on until April or so. Since there is always something going on, frequently a surprise in the making, and since it is pretty hard to hide an acre of blooming flowers, you might think that there would be a good deal of spying among seedsmen, and possibly worse. There is amazingly little. Only once in its long history has Burpee's ever had anything swiped from it on a grand-larceny scale. This was a great heap of brand-new, first-of-their-kind nasturtium seeds—a dwarf variety of the doubles in all colors with which Burpee had stolen a march on all other seedsmen, including John C. Bodger, discoverer of the original double nasturtium from whence all others sprang. Burpee's new dwarf seeds were lying innocently in the field, spread on canvas sheets to cure, when one fine night they vanished, canvas and all, and were never heard from again.

Burpee, who has been heard to say he has his own ideas as to who the guilty parties were, priced the loss at $25,000 and put a detective on the trail, without results, and the next time he had something good just about ready for the taking, he asked for and got nightly protection from a couple of husky deputy sheriffs, as if he were growing dollar bills.

There is, to a point, some spying between seed houses, just as there is between automobile manufacturers and football teams. Some years ago, when a good many Chinese workers were employed by West Coast seedsmen, a visiting seedsman was usually greeted by the host seedsman with the remark: "Well, which Chinaman here is yours?"

If spying were much of a problem, though, the system of contract farming would probably not have come into use. It is an accepted way of growing seed—by arranging with private farmers to supply their land and labor, the seedsman providing the seed to sow, some supervision, and using his own roguing crews to weed out off-type plants. He then buys the seed crop at a price agreed on in advance. This guarantee of a ready market is popular with farmers, and sometimes it becomes hard to tell them from regular members of the seedsman's staff. The Burpee farm manager at Santa Paula, Al Condit, was puzzled once to notice extra beehives lined up at the roadside of one contract farmer's field as he drove by, and he stopped to ask about it. "Sh-h," said the farmer. "Those are nothing but empty hives, boy. But they sure do keep the tourists from stopping to pick the zinnias."

If you live in a seed-growing area, beekeeping can be a good business. In the Santa Paula vicinity in 1961, Burpee's hired 672 hives of bees to work on 191 acres, and paid $3.50 per hive for the bees' time. The beekeepers got to keep the honey, too. If bees are fond of a crop, as they are of regular, or open-pollinated zinnias, they work hard, and one hive (50,000 to 80,000 bees) will handle an entire acre. If they don't care much about something, though, such as the male-sterile Old 66 zinnia, which looks as attractive as a blob and hasn't any fragrance, even six hives per acre aren't always enough. Burpee staff men scratch their heads over this problem, and when someone wondered out loud if it might help to spray Old 66 with Chanel 5 or something, nobody laughed.

Fortunately for seed growers, bees seldom go gadding about, but keep on working the same field trip after trip. Just the same, Burpee's separate by at least a quarter-mile any flowers they don't want the bees to cross-pollinate. If the pollen is a kind that is carried by the wind, the separation has to be an entire mile or more. This situation is one of the big reasons why the seed farms are spread out. Just to touch base at each unit making up Burpee's Santa Paula Farms' four hundred acres takes hours of dusty backroad driving, and Floradale's various fields are so spread that the farthest fringes are twenty-two miles from each other.

Until he starts to harvest his crop a seedsman works the same way and uses the same machinery as other farmers. If for any reason they envied him up to then, they get over it as soon as they see the colossal headache seed harvesting is. Just as a for-instance, take tomatoes. A regular tomato farmer picks his tomatoes, and that does it; he has harvested the crop. The seed grower picks *his* tomatoes, too, and then . . .

runs them through a custom-built field thrasher which . . .
mashes the fruits . . .
dejuices them . . .
then seeds and juice ferment forty-eight hours . . .
are then washed clean . . .
and whirled in a sack in a centrifuge to remove water . . .
then dried on trays . . .
given a final machine cleaning, sacked up, and sent off to be measured out at last and finally packaged.

Pretty much the same rigamarole is gone through with pepper, eggplant, cucumber, cantaloupe, pumpkin, squash, and watermelon. One of the peskiest and most expensive seeds to harvest is that of a fairly unpopular vegetable—salsify, or oyster plant. It produces a large lavender flower, and when the seed ripens it will shatter and fall if, it seems to seedsmen, they so much as look at it. Every day, workers must go through the rows picking this temperamental seed by hand until it is all gathered. Years ago when a good many Japanese workers were employed on western seed farms, the salsify crop was often planted on the house grounds they occupied and was gathered as an in-between chore by the wives, who had the dexterity and oriental patience ideal for the job. Burpee's now grow their salsify in Mexico, where costs are low enough to justify it.

One of the hazards of seed farming is wet weather at harvest time. Since rain also hurts pollination, the dry California summers are just right for everything. Any paradise has its troublemakers, though, and at harvest time the birds of California—especially finches and sparrows—swoop down on such seed crops as lettuce and radish and eat themselves silly. So far, absolutely nothing has been found to shoo them, and nobody, including the U. S. Department of Agriculture, has any good suggestions except to harvest early and get what seed you can before the birds find out.

Like vegetable seed harvesting, flower seed harvesting is no bed of roses. Probably the champion pain is pansy seed, which shatters on the slightest provocation, but it has many competitors. Other seeds, such as dahlia, gaillardia, and geranium, actually must be flailed by hand, in the way harvesters were working in Chaucer's day. Yet one of the most feminine and delicate of flowers, the sweet pea, can be mowed, stacked, and threshed for its seeds like so much oats.

Had an efficiency expert invented seeds he would have made them all the same size. As it is, the variation is stunning, throwing another kink into harvesting. Nasturtium seeds, for instance, run from 160 to 200 to the ounce, which sounds pretty small until you find out that it takes 12,000 carnation seeds to make an ounce. And carnation seeds are big, compared to petunia seeds—they run 250,000 an ounce. And if you are feeling sorry for the petunia seed harvester, save your tears for the fellow who must account for a crop of lobelia seed; these bits of dark dust are so ridiculously tiny, it takes an astronomical 700,000 to tip the scale at a single little ounce.

Such diversity in seeds brings out the inventor in seedsmen. One day while idly watching his wife run the vacuum cleaner, Al Condit sprang into the air, more or less, uttering something like: "Eureka. Geraniums." Far from being off his rocker, Condit had suddenly seen the answer to harvesting the feather-light seed. Forthwith, he borrowed the family vacuum cleaner, and it worked, whooshing in the geranium seed the way a high school girl goes after a milk shake. After its rightful owner reclaimed her vacuum cleaner, Condit bought himself a secondhand commercial one for two dollars at the city dump, hooked it onto a little war-surplus gasoline engine, and was thriftily in business, independent of extension cords. The geranium seed haven't won a round since.

# *12* SEEDS FOR WAR ...AND PEACE

Although the garden seed business differs from most other businesses by doing well during depressions, it behaves like the majority in wartime. It goes a little mad trying to cope. A good deal of the reason for this is that during war, everybody —or so it seems—plants a food garden. Another reason is seed buying by the United States Government for export to allies and neutrals—done on a vast scale in World War II—and direct purchases by other nations. And then there is hoarding; the people who hoard anything they think may become scarce hoard seeds too, even though seeds are living things and eventually die in storage. As W. Atlee Burpee, Jr., has said, perhaps overcharitably: "Inexperienced gardeners would buy as much as a quarter-pound of tomato seed, whereas a packet would have been sufficient." The younger of the Burpee brothers, acting as the firm's liaison man on government seed buying during World War II, has vivid memories of the experience.

Speaking of Lend-Lease, he said later: "They bought at one time all the cucumber seed we had, besides a quantity we secured from a reliable competitor. I believe their total purchase of this seed was approximately a hundred thousand pounds, and I learned that it all went to Russia." Russia at the time was on our side, and cucumbers are greatly esteemed by Russians as a general-purpose vegetable.

Six other vegetables made up the bulk of Lend-Lease buying from Burpee's, most of it for England. These strategic wartime staples were onions, carrots, beets, peas, cabbage, and cauliflower. The last-named is a good example of what happens to normal seed demand during a war. In prewar days, Burpee's annual sales of a certain variety of cauliflower, Veitch's Autumn Giant, had been at most a thousand pounds. But when, one war year, a good growing season produced an exceptionally large crop from a larger than usual planting, the government bought it all—a whopping 50 *tons* of seed.

Burpee's share of the Lend-Lease business, which stretched over eight years, 1941 through 1948, came close to 4 million dollars. They did not lose money on it, for though the government fixed prices, it did so at levels that permitted acceptable profits.

In World War I there was no Lend-Lease, of course. Far from being a producer of vegetable seeds for the world at that time, the United States was not growing enough even for all its own needs. And its seed sources in Europe dried up in a wink as farm workers were called into military service—and in August, at the height of the harvest season—and the Old World tightened its belt. (Karl Nordgren, now Burpee vice president and business manager, was living in his native Sweden during World War I, and remembers that the country existed practically on rutabagas, even making a kind of coffee from the dried and roasted peelings. Sweet potatoes served a similar purpose in some parts of the Confederate States in this country during the Civil War, and turnips also helped hold body and soul together. Readers of Margaret Mitchell's *Gone with the Wind* may recall a scene in which Scarlett O'Hara on returning to her ruined plantation, scratched out a living on the turnips she found still growing in the kitchen garden.)

As the United States was moving into war in 1917, Burpee's already rushing business doubled "almost overnight," as they told their customers. By then, W. Atlee Burpee, Sr., had been dead a little more than a year, and W. Atlee, Jr., was joining the Navy, so it was up to elder son David, who became twenty-four years old the same month we declared war on Germany, to run the biggest mail-order segment of one of the most stragetic war industries.

To dramatize gardening for victory and to educate the public, Burpee's set up demonstration vegetable gardens in a number of cities. The biggest attention getter was the one in New York, managed by F. F. Rockwell, then the manager of Burpee's Fordhook Farms, and well known since as a garden authority and writer on horticulture. The New York City garden was in Union Square, directly opposite an imitation battleship bristling with wooden guns aimed at the tomatoes and cabbages. The battleship was a recruiting office but the garden was really a garden, despite the rumble of subway trains passing beneath it, and it attracted as many straw-hatted sidewalk superintendents as a skyscraper going up. The official names for these food gardens of World War I were Economy Gardens if small and War Gardens if large.

The Philadelphia *Record* took editorial note of the educational campaign, recalling that it was in the Burpee tradition. "Seedsmen laughed at Burpee 40 years ago," the newspaper observed, "when he said he would help folks in out-of-the-way places grow wholesome and profit-earning vegetables. But they laughed less when they saw the educational publicity that he put out. Burpee's advertising was the first national effort to show how the soil should be cultivated, and the first popular campaign to preach the gospel of intensive farming. It made more people turn to the soil than any other one force. Amateur gardeners became experts by following the advice. . . .

"When Uncle Sam sent out the call last Spring to start 'War Gardens,' Burpee's concentrated their publicity on a 'How to do it' campaign. The results were overwhelming. There was an increased yield of over 200 per cent. alone from vacant lots and home gardens—a crop worth over 300 millions of dollars."

Burpee's had worked a twenty-four-hour day during the busy spring planting seasons of 1917 and 1918, and when World War II came, they did it again. They expanded further by opening a new front—the big Midwest branch in Clinton, Iowa. It started right off on a three-shift basis, to a jubilant blast of publicity from the Clinton *Herald,* which ran an eight-page special edition welcoming the arrival of Burpee prosperity.

In the home office at Philadelphia things were hectic. To help get seed packaged ("papering" in seedsman language) and the orders filled and out, Burpee's had to take any help they could get. This resulted in quite a motley crew at times, especially on the night shift. Now and then fist fights broke out on this owl run and things got so lively that Burpee's had to look up some off-duty Philadelphia policemen to moonlight for them. The sight of the law lurking around put a damper on the high jinks.

This eliminated one headache for Burpee's but it was inevitable that another—the mistakes made by green help—would be with them for the duration, and it was. The surprising thing is that there were so few muffs, considering that each order had to pass through several operations, and that so many orders were—and are—hand-written as if by sputtering candlelight with a rusty Post Office pen. But though the Burpee merry-go-round was slowed, it broke down only in minor ways. Occasionally a customer who had ordered chive seed, say, planted it and found himself charming all the neighborhood cats with a bed of not chives at all, but catnip. One American woman gardener, whose husband was a Greek national fighting for his country, ordered some snapdragon seed from her favorite seedsman to cheer her up. Burpee's did not fail her, except that the snapdragons grew up to be French marigolds, a flower she simply could not abide, as it happened, including its pungent foliage. She put on her garden gloves and pulled all the marigolds out, but forgave Burpee's anyway.

The labor problem was bad enough in the store, but still more rugged out on the seed farms—especially on vital Floradale in California, Burpee's mainstay. There the Japanese workers, who then formed the bulk of the gardening force, were all taken away in a single day—the "protective custody" move stimulated by war jitters along the exposed Pacific coast. The loss of this efficient help was almost disastrous, even though Burpee's catalog department wrung what comfort it could out of the situation by showing a quartet of women field hands in the 1943 catalog, and remarking sagely if a little ambiguously: "Many years ago we were convinced that Germany planned another war for world conquest. To do our part we started in to train women to raise vegetable seeds on Floradale."

The labor problem was partly patched also by employment of some Filipinos, and then with the opening of Camp Cooke (now Vandenberg Air Force Base), Burpee's and the other Lompoc Valley seed companies were able to hire the wives of servicemen. While many of these women were by necessity an itinerant labor force, they made, while there, a lasting reputation with their seedsmen employers as excellent workers. "Those girls could do anything," a Floradale staff man said years after, with the light of admiration still in his eyes. "And how they *loved* to run those tractors!"

A curious side effect of the war was that it forced Burpee's into cracking the Japanese code, so to speak, for breeding all-double petunias. In a nutshell, they found out what the Japanese had discovered years before and kept mum about: that once in a great while a perfect double petunia showed up—that is, one with both male and female parts instead of only male. By in-breeding these perfect doubles, Burpee's purified them for dou-bleness, and since doubleness here is a dominant trait, when these purified double petunias were crossed with single ones, *all* of the first hybrid generation that followed were double-flowered, instead of only half of them as was formerly the case. That is what a plant breeder means by "all-double"—that *all* the flowers of a particular generation will be double.

Petunias, incidentally, were one of the three most popular garden flowers during the war, according to Burpee sales. The other two were zinnias and marigolds.

If war comes again, what can gardeners expect? What can they do to help themselves, and what changes will they probably have to make in their gardening? Here is a thumbnail appraisal by one of the Burpee people, Lyman G. Schermerhorn, Jr., of the vegetable seed department:

If there is another war, many of the home-gardening methods used during World Wars I and II are likely to be of little use. This would be so because of the development of atomic weapons which pollute the air with radioactive material. In World Wars I and II it was sufficient simply to concentrate on producing garden vegetables which would produce the greatest volume and at the same time contain the highest percentages of vitamins and food value. Such vegetables as tomatoes, squash, greenpod beans, lima beans, Swiss chard, lettuce, carrots, onions, and cabbage meet the volume and food value goals required by home gardeners during wartimes in the past.

However, we should face up to the likelihood that another war will be one of atomic weapons and as such will cause a tremendous change in gardening. Actually, it may not be possible to start or tend a garden because of the danger of being outside where radioactive debris would cripple or kill the gardener. If the garden could be started, it might be necessary to plant only those vegetables which grow their edible portion below the surface of the soil. Such vegetables as beets, carrots, salsify, turnips, peanuts, onions, parsnips, and radishes would come under that heading.

Regardless of the type of war conditions we may have to contend with in future gardening, *one of the best preparations is to maintain the garden soil in a high state of fertility and at a lime level (pH) high enough to grow good garden produce with a minimum addition of fertilizer or lime*. This advance preparation is important because even in wartime not involving atomic weapons, fertilizer materials are drastically restricted owing to the priority given to war production and transportation of war materials and equipment.

To summarize:

1. Concentrate on *nutrition* and *volume* in vegetable production.
2. Give increased space to *root crops*.
3. Keep your garden's *fertility* built up.

Since garden seed may be expected to become scarce again if there should be a major war, the question comes up: Can surplus seed be saved for the next season? The answer is a qualified yes; it depends on the life expectancy of the seed and on how you store it.

For most people the simplest and best storage place is the refrigerator. Put the seeds in a dry fruit jar, along with a quarter-cup of silica gel in a cloth sack (about 25 cents' worth at the drugstore, and you can make the sack from the toe of an old stocking), and screw the jar lid on tightly. Like most seed houses, Burpee's does not encourage such seed storage, not caring to get blamed for poor germination caused by things they cannot control. However, this method of refrigerator storage can keep seeds well, and if shortages occur it is well worth while. In that case it would also be useful to know how long seeds can reasonably be expected to live in storage. The majority do better than you might think. Here is the average longevity of the seeds of the vegetables and flowers you are most likely to be concerned with:

| Plant | Average Longevity in Years |
|-------|:--------------------------:|
| Beans | 3 |
| Beet | 5 |
| Chard | 5 |
| Broccoli | 4 |
| Cabbage | 4 |
| Carrot | 3 |
| Cauliflower | 4 |
| Celery | 3 |
| Celeriac | 3 |
| Chicory | 3 |
| Corn | 3 |
| Cucumber | 5 |
| Eggplant | 4 |
| Lettuces | 5 |
| Melons | 4–5 |
| Okra | 4 |
| Onion | 2 |
| Parsley | 1 |
| Parsnip | 1 |
| Peas | 3 |
| Pepper | 2 |
| Pumpkin | 4 |
| Radish | 4 |
| Squash | 4 |
| Salsify | 1 |
| Spinach | 3 |
| Tomato | 6–7 |
| Turnip | 4 |
| | |
| Ageratum | 4 |
| Alyssum | 4 |
| Snapdragon | 4 |

| Plant | Average Longevity in Years |
|-------|----------------------------|
| Aquilegia | 2 |
| Aster | 1–2 |
| Balsam | 5–6 |
| Calendula | 5–6 |
| Calliopsis | 2–3 |
| Candytuft | 2–3 |
| Carnation | 4–5 |
| Celosia | 4 |
| Centaurea | 1–3 |
| Clarkia | 2–3 |
| Coleus | 2 |
| Cosmos | 3–4 |
| Dahlia | 2–3 |
| Delphinium | 1 |
| Dianthus | 4–5 |
| Calif. Poppy | 2 |
| Gaillardia | 4 |
| Geranium | 1 |
| Gypsophila | 2 |
| Hollyhock | 2–3 |
| Impatiens | 2 |
| Morning Glory | 2–3 |
| Larkspur | 1–2 |
| Lobelia | 3–4 |
| Marigold | 2–3 |
| Nasturtium | 6–7 |
| Nicotiana | 3–4 |
| Pansy | 1–2 |
| Petunia | 2–3 |
| Poppy | 3–5 |
| Portulaca | 3 |
| Salvia | 1 |
| Scabiosa | 2 |
| Sweet Peas | 4–5 |

| *Plant* | *Average Longevity in Years* |
|---------|------------------------------|
| Verbena | 1 |
| Viola | 1 |
| Zinnia | 4–5 |

Although the matter of where to get reliable gardening information is not confined to wartime by any means, it assumes a new importance then. Here are four excellent sources:

1. *Garden clubs*

The knowledgeable individuals in the clubs know local gardening conditions. Co-operation of the clubs in victory gardening during World War II not only helped produce thousands of tons of food but also helped to prevent some of the waste that usually goes with first-time gardening efforts.

2. *Commercial sources*

Seed houses such as Burpee's will supply educational literature, and answer garden questions. So will other suppliers such as fertilizer and insecticide companies.

3. *Magazines and newspapers*

There are both national and regional magazines directed solely at gardeners, and a lot of space is given to gardening in many other magazines. Most daily newspapers run a weekly garden feature, and some big ones—notably the New York *Times* and the *Herald-Tribune*—carry highly informative garden sections in their Sunday editions. Also, your public library will have some practical garden books, as do bookstores. See the list of titles at the end of Chapter 15.

4. *Official sources.* These are mainly four:

*The United States Department of Agriculture.* A vast number of publications are on tap here. To start, you can state your needs in a letter to:

U. S. Dept. of Agriculture
Office of Information
Washington 25, D.C.

They will then send you a list of pertinent publications. Many

are free and few are expensive, and while somewhat dry and of-
ficial-sounding, they are up to date and of course authoritative.

*The Agricultural Agent of your county* is a gold mine of
gardening help, and he will also have a good many free bulletins, both federal and state publications. The county agent, as
this overworked man is usually called, has his office at the county
seat.

*Your State Department of Agriculture* has a variety of services available, including bulletins and other publications often
referring to local gardening problems. The department is in the
capital city of your state.

*Your State Agricultural Experiment Station.* This is a source
of technical know-how, with intimate knowledge of such things
as your particular climatic conditions. Address the director. Here
are the locations of all the stations in the United States:

| State | City |
|---|---|
| Alabama | Auburn |
| Alaska | Palmer |
| Arizona | Tucson |
| Arkansas | Fayetteville |
| California | Berkeley |
| Colorado | Fort Collins |
| Connecticut | |
| State Station | New Haven |
| Storrs Station | Storrs |
| Delaware | Newark |
| Florida | Gainesville |
| Georgia | Experiment |
| Hawaii | Honolulu |
| Idaho | Moscow |
| Illinois | Urbana |
| Indiana | Lafayette |
| Iowa | Ames |

| State | City |
|---|---|
| Kansas | Manhattan |
| Kentucky | Lexington |
| Louisiana | University Station, Baton Rouge |
| Maine | Orono |
| Maryland | College Park |
| Massachusetts | Amherst |
| Michigan | East Lansing |
| Minnesota | St. Paul Campus, St. Paul |
| Mississippi | State College |
| Missouri | Columbia |
| Montana | Bozeman |
| Nebraska | Lincoln |
| Nevada | Reno |
| New Hampshire | Durham |
| New Jersey | New Brunswick |
| New Mexico | University Park |
| New York | |
| State Station | Geneva |
| Cornell Station | Ithaca |
| North Carolina | State College Station, Raleigh |
| North Dakota | State College Station, Fargo |
| Ohio | Wooster |
| Oklahoma | Stillwater |
| Oregon | Corvallis |
| Pennsylvania | University Park |
| Puerto Rico | Rio Piedras |
| Rhode Island | Kingston |
| South Carolina | Clemson |
| South Dakota | College Station |
| Tennessee | Knoxville |
| Texas | College Station |
| Utah | Logan |
| Vermont | Burlington |

| *State* | *City* |
| --- | --- |
| Virginia | Blacksburg |
| Washington | Pullman |
| West Virginia | Morgantown |
| Wisconsin | Madison |
| Wyoming | Laramie |

# 13 WHERE IN THE WORLD ARE THE CUSTOMERS?

While on a trip through southern California in the summer of 1961 a Midwestern farmer and his wife took the opportunity to visit the place most of their vegetable seeds came from—Burpee's Santa Paula Farms. The couple felt right at home among the rows of tomatoes, cucumbers, melons, and so on, but while they were winding up their tour in the seed cleaning department their heads snapped around and their jaws dropped as a slight and swarthy bearded man with his head in a blue turban whizzed by. "Who the heck is *that?*" the male visitor exclaimed, but before their guide could tell them, the brown-skinned man turned with a bow and smiled pleasantly. "Please forgive me," he said in perfect English. "I did not intend to startle you." He was, the couple discovered, Karambir Singh of New Delhi, India. A horticulturist with master's degrees from universities in India and Hawaii, he had arrived at Burpee's farms three weeks before. His purpose was to study the commercial end of seed growing, after having concentrated on its scientific aspects till then, and he would be doing this with Burpee's for a year or longer, the visitors learned, before his return to India where he planned to put the knowledge to practical use.

"To grow hybrid vegetable seeds for your countrymen?" the Midwestern man inquired, but Singh shook his head. "I doubt that hybrid seed has any meaning for India in the near future," he said. "It is much too expensive for our people." When the visitor said something about the greater productivity of hybrid plants, Singh shrugged. "Of course hybrid seed is good," he said, "but any money for seed is too much if you haven't got it."

Burpee's do not attempt to solve the situation suggested by the Indian horticulturist's statement. Nor is it a job a private commercial seedsman is even remotely able to cope with. What Burpee's do is to give one, two, or three foreign students each year the chance to learn seed growing, plant breeding, and seed selling as Burpee's do it. This program has been going on for about thirty-five years. Since 1948 it has been on a more planned basis, and had twenty-two participants from then through 1961. They came from eight countries. Most of them—seven—were Danes, and the next largest national group was six West Germans. Of the rest, one or two each came from Norway, Switzerland, Holland, France, Japan, and India. Burpee's have kept no track of a good many other foreign students, many from Latin America, whose main interest was a summer job on one of the farms to help pay for their schooling.

Some of the students have been interested in getting permanent jobs with the Burpee organization, and one of these former students is now in charge of their export business. He is Joaquin Moncrieff, from Guatemala. Moncrieff was one of five or six graduate students in horticulture whom Burpee's helped during the 1930s and 1940s with payment of tuition plus cash grants of $500 or more. These fellowships were confined to Bucknell University and the University of Florida, but in 1945 Burpee's launched a program more ambitious in its geographical scope. This was an offer of $100 each year to a student in each agricultural college in the United States. Fifty of the colleges made use of this offer, awarding the money at their discretion to the students they selected. Through 1961 the program had cost Burpee's almost exactly $30,000. The company does not publicize the program or urge it on the colleges, but it remains in effect and the money is given if asked for.

Over twelve consecutive years through 1962 Burpee's had made varying contributions for a total of $35,750, plus seed, to the National Junior Vegetable Growers Association. Its object is to spur youthful interest in growing and marketing fruits and vegetables. Participants are from fourteen to twenty-one years old, and the board chairman and leading spirit, Professor Grant B. Snyder of the University of Massachusetts, estimated in 1962 that eight to ten thousand young people take part in the program each year.

In 1945 Burpee's staged at Fordhook Farms what they called their symposium on horticulture of China. It took place over three days and was attended by twenty-three Chinese agricultural technicians and teachers, and by several American university, government, and institutional agricultural experts. The object of the gathering was, David Burpee explained in his address of welcome, to gain a better understanding of the problems of horticulture in China. The tone of the discussions was scholarly and there was a considerable exchange of views and information on the vegetables of the Chinese mainland, very many of them unknown to gardeners of the Western world then, and now.

If the international flavor of most of the Burpee assists to education suggests a world-wide trade, that is entirely correct. From 6 to 10 per cent of their sales are export ones—say in the neighborhood of half a million dollars a year. The vast majority, as you might expect, are vegetable seed sales. Most of the sales come through agencies of the foreign governments, and while the business is welcome, Burpee's do not try very hard to extend it through more retail foreign sales. Such sales are not especially profitable, and by not going after them, Burpee's stay on better terms with foreign seed houses. In their catalogs for commercial growers and dealers they head each class of vegetables with the name in five languages besides English. Thus, lettuce is listed as *laitues* in French, *lechuga* in Spanish, *kopfsalat* in German, *lattuga* in Italian, and *alface* in Portuguese.

In 1962 Burpee's had about 6500 foreign retail customers, nearly half of them in Canada. The rest were scattered literally all over the earth. On a March day just chosen at random, seed orders came in from customers in Afghanistan, Brazil, England, Iran, Curaçao, France, Mexico, Nigeria, Peru, Natal, Portugal, Switzerland, Poland, India, Madagascar, and Libya.

The West Coast branch office at Riverside, California, handles the oriental trade, which gives it certain special problems. An example is this letter from a Japanese:

> Dear W. Atlee Burpee Co., Sir:
> I heared your company's name at long time ago, and production seed from your company was stocking indirect than other seed company in Japan. And it is accepting for good result. But my seed company was ratter to few years from start. So I can not transaction for other of outside country, that growing of seeds and adopting of seeds enlarge of those. Then I wish, you remember me to lead. I'm sorry, if you sends to me a catalogue and trial rearing of seeds. I am very glad.
>
> Picture into envelope was carrot, make to very do one's best in my co. I thinking that if you might be send at trial rearing. I play a health of Sir and deverop of company.

Long experience has made Burpee's nimble at interpreting, and Gerald F. Burke, manager at Riverside, had no great trouble understanding what the man wanted. Here is his version of the letter:

> I have heard your company's name a long time ago, and the seed from your company was being stocked by another seed company in Japan and was having very good results. But my seed company is very new and hasn't been started very long, so I haven't been able to make transactions in

other countries. But I do have some plans for the future that will include trade from outside countries; that is, the growing of seeds and adapting them to this area and enlarging upon them. When I start this I hope you will help me out. I do hope you can send me a catalog and some trial samples of seeds for growing, and I will be very glad if you do.

The picture in the envelope is a carrot which grows very well in my country. Perhaps you would be able to send me a trial of this carrot which I can grow. My very best wishes to you, sir, and I hope your company develops.

Burke's favorite foreign customer is a gentleman in Thailand—not because he buys much seed, but because his letters to branch manager Burke always begin: "Dear President."

Burpee's have about half as many foreign commercial, or wholesale, customers as retail ones. Compared to foreign retail sales, foreign wholesale ones fluctuate wildly from year to year. One season Burpee's may sell so many sacks of peas to French growers and dealers that it distorts the year's figures. The next year France may be indifferent to peas but from Egypt will come a passionate desire for watermelon seed by the ton. Shortages on the part of other suppliers have a good deal to do with this see-saw situation.

Fifty or sixty years ago you could sum up nearly all of Burpee's export business in two words: sweet peas. And Great Britain was the customer for almost all the sweet pea seed Burpee's shipped. The British are still good sweet pea customers, but this flower seed is one of only three flowers that Burpee's export in any kind of quantity these days. Marigolds and zinnias are the others.

Incidentally, they export practically no seeds to Communist bloc countries. This is not a matter of principle on their part, but arises from the fact that governments behind the Iron Curtain generally look coolly on requests from their citizens for licenses to import. Yugoslavia is an exception, and some Burpee seeds go there. Since licenses affect only commercial orders, however, individual citizens behind the curtain presumably could order seeds from Burpee. In practice this is fairly rare. It is perhaps suggestive that when our ambassador to Russia, Llewellyn Thompson, ordered seeds from Burpee's last year (including Big Boy tomato, Curlilocks aster, and Whitey marigold), he had them sent not to Moscow but to Helsinki, Finland.

Despite the outlandish places Burpee seeds sometimes light in, they receive some of their best testimonials as a result. A pioneer gardener in Hawaii some years ago, who had to hack a planting spot out of the jungle growing from light volcanic soil, declared he raised a five-pound cucumber so sturdy that he took it along on three inter-island boat trips—apparently to show it off —and found it still good to eat, finally, six months after it was picked.

A couple homesteading in Alaska near Juneau reported with astonishment on the explosive growth of plants during the short, wet summers. Some dwarf border flower bushes grew to the size of washtubs, the delphinium spikes shot up to eleven feet, and the Burpee edible-podded peas, they noted, "were delicious but had to be picked from a stepladder."

An Illinois University agricultural associate discovered, while visiting a missionary friend one summer in the Belgian Congo, a tomato in the mission garden that the missionary and his wife were wild about. Thinking to introduce this equatorial beauty into the United States, the visitor asked if his friend would mind saving some seeds for him.

"Not at all," said the missionary, "though I think you might get faster service if you ordered them from Burpee direct."

The tomato story brings to mind another peculiarity of the seed export business—differences in national tastes. Fairly large tomatoes are most popular in the United States, but in northern

Europe a tomato of two or three ounces is liked, and miniature kinds such as San Marzano, used for making tomato paste, are favored in Italy.

Savoy cabbages are very popular in France, England, and Germany, and red cabbage sells heavily in Germany, Holland, and Denmark. The French and Italians delight in many greens that are little grown in the United States—for example, sorrel, chervil, and roquette. Peas are so well suited to the cool summers of the British Isles that seed catalogs there give three times as much space to them as to tomatoes. In Burpee's catalog it is just the reverse.

As an illustration of a national prejudice at work, a Burpee staff man cites the attitude of the people of Costa Rica toward eggplant when he grew it there while operating a Burpee seed farm once located in that country. "They had no previous experience with eggplant," he said, "and they called them *cochinadas moradas,* literally 'dirty purple things.' After showing them some ways to prepare the vegetable for the table, a more kindly relationship was established between the people and the eggplants."

So well known are Burpee's all over the world as a garden seed supplier that portions of their customer list read like an international *Who's Who.* In his heyday, ex-King Farouk of Egypt was a good account, and the palace gardens shimmered with Burpee blooms. A few years ago the Duke of Windsor attended the New York flower show and was so impressed by Burpee's double petunias that he impulsively bought a great wad of packets on the spot.

A constellation of European princesses and other royalty, both deposed and active, have personally ordered Burpee seeds, and a current and good customer is the King of Sweden, whose 1962 order came to $167.90. It included quite a few of the thrifty collections offered in such flowers as marigolds, snapdragons, and zinnias, and the King ordered three Burpee vegetables: broccoli, a hybrid sweet corn, and zucchini hybrid squash. The squash was so immense an order—twelve pounds, costing $139.20 of the total order and being enough seed to plant nearly eight thousand hills—that it is assumed it was intended for supplying something besides the royal table.

Speaking of Sweden, Burpee's take a quiet satisfaction in the fact that one of their customers there is the Institute of Systematic Botany of the University of Uppsala, where the famed Swedish botanist Carolus Linnaeus taught. It was there in 1753 that he wrote his *Species Plantarum*, the pioneer landmark of scientific classification of plants.

Politically, Burpee's as a business are nonpartisan and so enjoy the trade of both Democrats and Republicans in this country. Mrs. Eleanor Roosevelt bought seed from them, as did former Presidents Herbert Hoover and Dwight D. Eisenhower. Though President Kennedy is not on the books as a customer, his father Joseph Kennedy bought Burpee seed. A few years ago, Mrs. Harry S. Truman seemed to be preparing for horticultural accomplishments, from the order she sent Burpee's. It was for a pair of garden gloves. They mailed the gloves off and waited hopefully for the seed order they assumed was coming. They were whistling in the dark, it turned out, and didn't make another penny on Mrs. Truman.

Last year they were intrigued to get a request for a catalog from Gypsy Rose Lee, writing from Hollywood. Among her talents Miss Lee is a novelist, and a good Burpee customer is another novelist, Marcia Davenport, who does her gardening in Como, Italy. Thanking Burpee's a few years ago for special attention her orders had needed, Mrs. Davenport said her Italian neighbors regarded the yield of her Big Boy Hybrid tomatoes as "fantastic . . . over there where tomatoes are very serious business." Hybrid cucumbers also bore like mad in the friendly Italian climate, she reported, and Burpee's Big 6 pole lima beans were so growthy that "ordinary poles will not hold them," she said. "We use saplings about 12 feet high, with other poles joining them at the top, and the plants make a thing like a grape arbor. We have to use a high painter's ladder to get up in the sky to pick the beans."

Although he sells more seeds overseas than his father ever did, David Burpee has no need to make the annual summer tour of Europe that W. Atlee Burpee made in his constant search for good new varieties. The shoe is now on the other foot, with this country supplying rather than buying seeds abroad, and any trips Burpee makes to other lands are for other purposes. He does not make many, and when he went to Japan in 1960 it was such a novelty to him that he was led to seek out some advice on such things as social decorum, particularly the giving of gifts. Knowing that the son of his Philadelphia tailor had lately served a tour of duty with the Army in Japan, Burpee asked him what sort of gift might be most welcome.

"Anything but silk," said the young man, and added that silver was always nice. Burpee accordingly picked out some silver trays to take along, and before he left, picked up another tip, this one from his neighbor, Pearl Buck, who knew oriental etiquette forward and backward. "When you present them," she said of the trays, "present them with both hands." He did so, and was as big a success with his trays abroad as with his seeds.

# 14 HERE'S HOW—149 GARDENING TIPS FROM BURPEE EXPERTS

What follows is a kind of coast-to-coast panel discussion by assorted Burpee scientists, skilled dirt gardeners on the staff and others, and articulate customers—on the general subject of home gardening. Some of the ideas are offbeat, some are unusual, but all have been tested. Somewhere in here there is something that can save you time and work, or give you more pleasure, or make you money, or add professional polish to some gardening operation. Where a tip is definitely regional, such as the one on posthole tomato planting, this is stated; in other cases, such as saltcellar seeding, the tip will work anywhere. Gardeners being experimenters, the tips are the fruit of experiment, passed along in the same spirit.

These are some of the Burpee people whose tips will be found here. *Philadelphia headquarters:* David Burpee, president; Harry B. Dietrick, comptroller; Louis Frankl, manager of the flower seed department; Jeannette Lowe, customer service and flower breeding; M. H. Kuhn, new products development; Karl E. Nordgren, vice president and business manager; L. G. Schermerhorn, Jr., vegetable department; Lois Stringer, customer service, flower shows, and trials; Carol Whitenack, customer service, flower shows, and trials. *Fordhook Farms:* Lois (Mrs. David) Burpee; Jerome H. Kantor, research assistant to president; Frederic C.

Streland, vegetable breeding; Theodore C. Torrey, farm manager
and director of vegetable research. *Clinton branch:* Margaret
Hendrickson, customer service; Eugene Veit, branch manager.
*Floradale Farms:* Frankie Mae Case, office manager; Andrew W.
Learned, seed production; Phyllis (Mrs. Andrew W.) Learned;
Walter R. Manfrina, farm manager; Myra (Mrs. Walter R.) Manfrina; Ellwood S. Pickering, flower breeding; Ron Sissons, flower
breeding. *Santa Paula Farms:* Dorothy Ammerman, plant breeding department; I. A. Condit, farm manager; James Knowlson,
plant breeding. *Riverside branch:* R. L. Bloy, sales department;
Gerald F. Burke, branch manager.

Not everyone agreed on some practices. A case comes to mind
where one of the dirt gardeners put tea leaves on the soil of her
house plants, another gave them "a drink of tea about once a
month," and one of the plant breeders stated: "Tea leaves are
definitely *not* to be used with house plants." In cases such as
this, where some must be wrong or may have been dealing with
special situations, none of the tips were used. But in other cases
a difference of opinion was illuminating, showing that something
that doesn't work in California, say, may work splendidly in Iowa.
This was a useful fringe benefit of the opinion round-up, and
important for gardeners to keep in mind at all times when swayed
by new ideas.

*Planting*
When in doubt how deep to plant lily bulbs, plant shallowly.
Their roots are contractile—can actually pull the bulbs down to
the right level.

How deep is "4 inches deep"? In measuring the depth a bulb is
to be planted, one should know that the figure given refers to
the distance from ground level to the *neck* of the bulb.

To sterilize potting soil for a flat, bake it in the oven 1½ hours
at 350 degrees, in old coffee cans. Still simpler: fill flat two-thirds

full of unsterilized soil, add a top layer of vermiculite or shredded sphagnum moss. Seeds germinate in sterile top layer, send roots down to nourishing soil.

Most critical period of watering in a plant's life: while the seed is germinating. Drying out for even a few minutes may kill it. To hold moisture, cover soil loosely with polyethylene plastic, burlap, newspapers, or a board; remove at first sign of sprouting. For flats covered with sheets of glass to keep moist, turn glass over daily; stops condensed moisture from dripping.

In cold-winter states of the North and Northeast, seed perennial flowers in June, not fall. This grows plants strong enough to weather their first winter with less protection than fall-seeded ones.

To keep track of successive plantings, write each date on the seed packet until seed is used up.

To make a straight guideline for row: stretch a rope taut and walk on it. Leaves a good indentation in soft earth.

Experienced dirt gardeners and experts agree on the spot or station method of seeding a row. Instead of trying to space each seed, spot them in little groups of two to six, with a few inches between groups. The seeds help each other up. Then gradually thin to the best plant in each group.

For continuous-row planting of fine seed, mix them with sand, shake from an old saltcellar. Another way: fill a soda straw with the mixture, pinch one end almost shut, tap seeds out. Note: if white sand is used, dark seeds stand out clearly.

Parsley—notoriously hard to sprout—may be seeded thickly and allowed to grow without thinning. Also helps control weeds.

A cautious old rule when sowing larger seed (corn, beans, peas . . .) quoted by British-born gardener: "One for the rook, one for the crow, one to rot and one to grow."

Don't even try to cover very fine seed such as petunia or snap-dragon. Just press it gently into moist soil or a planting medium such as vermiculite.

Before filling a clay flowerpot with soil for planting or transplant-ing, immerse it completely in water for a few hours. Keeps the clay from robbing the soil of moisture.

Automatic radishes: Drop radish seeds every few inches when planting rows of other things. Quick sprouters, the radishes give you a guideline for early cultivating, are ready for picking when the other plants in the row need the room.

### Row Markers

All panelists who had anything to say on marking rows agreed it was good garden practice, and most favored the thin wood stakes that come in 4-inch to 12-inch lengths. These range in cost from about two for a cent to two for a nickel, are easy to read, and can often be used more than one season.

Most foolproof row marker: a simple map, or plan, of your gar-den. This is standard Burpee farm practice, and once saved a lot of headaches when some frolicking youngsters uprooted stakes marking half an acre of rows at Floradale.

Best for writing on stakes: soft lead pencil, china marking pencil, or a carbon base ink. Many inks fade in sunlight.

Or instead of writing on stake, slip empty seed packet over it, fasten with paper stapler and it won't blow off.

### Mulches

Mulching—sometimes a controversial subject—was approved by all panelists, though some preferred only a dust mulch as being neat and keeping weeds down.

Western rose gardeners find ground-up lava a good mulch to keep roots cool. Lightweight and porous, it does not deteriorate or affect soil acidity.

Sawdust makes a good mulch and is often available free at saw-mills or lumber yards. Note: Add fertilizer to keep the cellulose bacteria from competing with soil bacteria for nitrogen. Rate: One pound of a 5-10-5 fertilizer to each 4 pounds of sawdust; or about a pound of sodium nitrate per bushel of sawdust.

Most permanent mulch: gravel.

Mulching too early in the year in some areas keeps the ground too wet and cold for tomatoes and vine crops to get a good start.

If mulch packs too hard, work small twigs into it. They will keep it airy.

Warning from southern California gardener: "If you use grass clippings here as a mulch, they may carry Bermuda grass stollens and it becomes a nuisance in the garden."

Mulching may backfire if it provides cover for pests. Most apt to take advantage of mulch: snails, slugs, cutworms, mice, and rats. Best remedy: clean cultivation until pests are eradicated.

Mulch-in-a-hurry: newspapers, held down by stones or clods.

Keep mulch cleared away from bases of woody plants such as blueberries to keep bark tough at soil line.

Pre-soak peat moss before mulching with it. Keeps it from scattering in wind, makes it easier to work with.

### Ties and Stakes

Old nylon stockings were one of the most popular strong ties for plants among the Burpee panelists. Some cut off feet and tops first. Another synthetic—plastic bags—can be cut up and folded into strips.

Pipe cleaners make quick, light ties, easy on tender stems of small plants.

Founder of the company that bears his name. W. Atlee Burpee began selling seed and livestock by mail in 1876, when he was barely eighteen. Less than seventeen years later his was the world's largest mail-order seed house, a position it has kept ever since. Mr. Burpee had run the business almost forty years by the time he died in 1915. This formal photograph was taken in his fifties.

*Sanders Studio, Doylestown, Pa.*

Frequently featured in the forepages of Burpee seed catalogs, the farmhouse at Fordhook Farms, Doylestown, Pennsylvania—the original, and still the showplace, seed farm of the W. Atlee Burpee Company.

Here on a porch at Fordhook Farms in about 1908 W. Atlee Burpee is surrounded by his wife Blanche, sons W. Atlee, Jr., and David (standing), and David's favorite dog Don.

W. Atlee Burpee, Jr., and his elder brother David with one of the Fordhook Farms collies in the summer of 1899. The brothers were then four and a half and six years old.

David Burpee as a young man (c. 1911) at the then new Burpee Floradale Farms near Lompoc, California.

Seedsman David Burpee in a Fordhook Farms greenhouse with his great-nephew W. Atlee Burpee IV, great-grandson of the company's founder. The flowers are Burpee's big Climax marigolds. David Burpee is for the marigold as the national flower of the United States.

Here a caged zinnia is being pollinated by plant breeder Jeannette Lowe on Burpee's Santa Paula Farms in southern California. Hundreds of florets — separate flowers — make up each zinnia blossom. After hand pollination, the cage formed by mesh cloth around the wooden stakes is again assembled, to keep out insects bearing other pollen that would throw the controlled breeding off.

Two members of the team of schoolgirls employed during the summers at Burpee's Santa Paula Farms in southern California. Here, Glenda and Paula Cook emasculate blossoms of the tomato that will produce seed to grow best-selling Big Boy Hybrid.

Formal judging climaxes each year's trials in Burpee's search for a pure-white marigold grown from seeds sent by customers. Looking over a 1961 entry here are David Burpee, president of W. Atlee Burpee Company; Dr. Robert E. Atkinson, horticulturist; and Dr. Vernon T. Stoutemyer of the University of California at Los Angeles.

Horticulturist Karambir Singh of India noting trials of petunias on Burpee's Santa Paula Farms in California in 1962. Singh is one of the many foreign students the big seed house has hired since the late 1920s in a kind of good-will training program on a worldwide level.

Plant breeders' triumph: the tawny giant at the top, colored chocolate and golden, is the highly popular Gloriosa daisy, also available in a "double" form; it traces its ancestry to black-eyed Susans shown here below it.

Here, reading from the top down, are American gardeners' top favorites in flowers and vegetables as indicated by Burpee's seed sales: single and double Gloriosa daisies, together the leaders in perennials; marigold, the leader in annual flowers; and tomato, the most popular vegetable with home gardeners.

In its Garden Number of April 3, 1926, the national humor magazine *Judge* made playful comment on the size of the Burpee garden-seed business in this Gardner Rea cartoon captioned: "Mr. Burpee Sits Down to a Vegetable Dinner."

Save the paper-covered wire twists from stalks of celery at the market, re-use them for garden ties if paper is not worn away so that wire may cut plant stem.

Keep ties loose. Treat them as slings, not tourniquets, to avoid strangling plant.

Stake with a built-in tie: straighten out a wire coat hanger except for the hook. Push other end into ground at base of plant, bend hook over, encircle plant stalk with it. Especially good with bearded iris and delphinium.

Stake plants before they need it. Drive stake while plant is still small, avoid disturbing roots later.

You won't have to stake tall marigolds if you pinch out the center tips early; especially good for hybrid marigolds and zinnias, making sturdier, bushier plants.

## Transplanting

To move bigger plants to new planting spot, ease the root-ball onto blade of spade, then skid plant over the ground, holding it upright. Slide it off blade gently into new hole. With "spreadier" root systems, skid on old plastic drop cloth or burlap sack.

Dig transplanting hole about a third larger in diameter than is needed for snug fit and fill in with topsoil when plant is set. Speeds up new root growth.

For difficult transplanters, drive spade all around plant to prune roots a few days before actual transplanting. Gives plant a chance to recover from some of the shock before lifting.

To get tomatoes earlier, a Burpee customer living in an arid region reported good crops with this method: He made 18-inch-deep holes with a posthole digger at 2-foot intervals, set one small tomato plant in each. On nights frost was still expected, he laid a board over the holes. Water was poured in as needed, and holes were gradually filled with compost as plants grew, encouraging deeper root growth.

Easiest place to harden off indoor-grown seedlings in the spring: a coldframe.

*Don't* transplant larkspur, lupine, nasturtiums, phlox, poppies, portulaca, sweet peas. (Some resent moving, others mature so quickly, seeding is simpler.) Similar cases in the vegetable garden: beans, carrots, peas, radishes, spinach, sweet corn, anise, chervil, dill.

Not-so-weak weak sisters: with double, Giant Fringed, and Giant Ruffled petunias, the weakest-looking seedlings often grow up to have the prettiest flowers.

### Cultivating

For easier hoeing, work close to your toes. It sets the hoe blade at a shaving angle—more efficient than a nearer vertical one.

After seeding carrots and parsnips, throw a slight earth ridge along top of row. Knock it down when the seeds sprout, eliminating any crust and many weeds.

Removing sucker shoots from the base of corn plants to get bigger ears, more ears, and earlier ones doesn't work, tests show. It actually reduces the yield.

### Fertilizing

When adding hydrated lime to soil do it a week or two before applying fertilizer. Average application: 5 pounds per 100 square feet. Sandy soils need less, clay and muck soils more.

Did you know you can overfeed a plant just like a person? For most annual flowers, about ¼ cup of a 5-10-5 fertilizer per plant once or twice a season is plenty. General rule for the vegetable garden: one pound of 5-10-5 for 25 feet of row. Use as side dressing once or twice during season.

Yellowing leaves don't always indicate nitrogen deficiency. Lack of phosphorus can cause yellow margins; potash lack, yellow mottling.

Cracking of root crops and of celery may be due to boron lack. If so, spread ½ pound of borax per 1000 square feet.

To get your soil tested for richness and acidity, ask the country agricultural agent (at your county seat) or state agricultural experiment station (at your state university or state agricultural college; see list in Chapter 12, "Seeds for War . . . and Peace").

*Harvesting*

Try harvesting squash, snap beans, okra while still small. Makes plant bear more, and the flavors of very young vegetables are often delightfully different from mature fruits.

Watermelons are the hardest vegetable to test for ripeness. Some rules:

1. Listen for deep, hollow sound when tapped.
2. Tendril where fruit stem joins vine should be dry.
3. Deep yellow color on belly of dark fruit where it touches earth.
4. Bluish "bloom" on surface of dark fruit.
5. Sound of crunching when pressed with heel of hand (don't overdo—it can bruise fruit).
6. Grasp fruit by fruit stem only—not vine—and shake gently. Ripe fruit will come loose.

Cantaloupes are ripe when the fruit pulls away from the vine easily; it is called "full slip." At this time a yellow color may show through the skin, and there may be a softening around the blossom end.

To tell when vegetables are due to be ripe, check calendar at time of planting and write maturity date on marker stake. (Packets and catalog listings give average number of days to maturity.)

To get more flowers, keep picking them. Going to seed is a plant's hardest job, and it stops blooming to do it.

Try eating very young kohlrabi bulbs raw, like radishes. Or slice them up in a salad.

Sweet corn makes sugar during sunlight hours, so pull ears in late afternoon if possible.

Keep pulled ears of sweet corn cool till cooked. Its sugar changes to starch 8 *times* as fast at 100 degrees as at 40.

Good cook's advice: use only mature, well-filled ears of sweet corn. Shuck completely and cook on broiler rack with steak, turning when slight browning shows. When roasted all around, drench with melted butter.

Later-planted peas actually grow faster—so if you want successive pickings, plant early, midseason, and late varieties all at the same time.

*Poor Soil*

In answer to the question of how to contend with the raw, debris-spotted earth around a new home, many of the panelists had good and sympathetic advice, but one of them took a surprisingly optimistic stand. "Much of the soil may be excellent," he declared. "Furthermore, it hasn't been subjected to overplanting, many soil diseases and insects haven't become established, and there is no competition from shrubs and lawns. The new-home owner has the best chance for a successful vegetable and flower garden." Another suggested writing a no-debris clause into the building contract.

Frame beds are a way to grow some annual flowers or vegetables the first season and without a lot of work on new, raw house grounds. Make a coldframe type of box from four 2- by 12-inch planks (6 feet on the long sides, 3 feet on the others), place it where you want the bed, spade the earth inside it, fill frame with bought topsoil, plant seeds.

Fast way to condition heavy clay soil: spread 2 or 3 inches of sawdust, add lime and fertilizer indicated by testing, plus one extra pound of 5-10-5 fertilizer for each 4 pounds of sawdust (or about one pound of sodium nitrate to each bushel), work into the soil with rented Rototiller set for 8 inches deep. Peat moss is good; more expensive, but needs no fertilizer to offset decomposition loss. Both it and sawdust add organic matter, encourage beneficial soil microbes.

New-house lawn with a two-way punch: white clover (test soil for lime and fertilizer needs first). Makes a pretty cover and adds valuable humus to soil when turned under after two years. Then seed permanent lawn mixture suited to your locality.

If you do plant a vegetable garden in heavy clay soil around new home:
   Avoid root crops (carrots, beets . . .)
   Mulch generously with straw, dig it in that fall.
   Keep garden small and experimental at first.
   Plant seed thickly.

Best bets as first-season flowers for new home are the easy growers: marigolds, petunias, alyssum, Gloriosa daisies, gaillardias, zinnias, sunflowers.

Some plants prefer low-fertility soils. Nasturtiums grown in such soil produce more flowers. So do French marigolds. And herbs develop more flavor, especially if any needed lime is added.

*House Plants*
Most of the panel members felt that house plants were a particularly difficult subject to offer tips about. There is a good deal of variation in growing conditions, and a lot lies in getting to know your plants and anticipating their needs. Burpee's leaflet

on house plants (see list at end of Chapter 4) is handy and includes a bibliography.

A rule of thumb for watering house plants: in summer if in doubt —water. In winter if in doubt—don't. As with outdoor plants, when you do water, water thoroughly.

House plants apt to tolerate scant light are woody ones and broad-leafed evergreens.

The average house plant needs surprisingly little feeding. Once every three or four months is enough. To rejuvenate plant between repottings, remove surface soil (not deeply enough to disturb roots) and replace with fresh potting mixture (equal parts of garden loam, sand, and peat moss, compost, or vermiculite, plus one cup of complete fertilizer per bushel).

Leaf spots may be caused by sun shining on drops of water. To prevent, let plants dry off out of sun after top-watering.

Did you know your house plants radiate heat? On cold winter nights, pull down window shades to prevent house plant at window from chilling by radiating its heat to glass.

Too-cool-natured house plants for living room winter culture: cyclamen, calceolaria, cineraria, primrose. Grow them in a cool room; best: 40 to 50 degrees. Most flowering house plants do better in cool spots during night. Exception: African violets.

Extremely small gas leaks can "asphyxiate" house plants. Cold drafts also hurt them.

African violets hate to be moved. Find the window where they grow best and leave them there.

Some house plants take regular rest periods (stop flowering, or shed their leaves, or stop making new ones). Don't feed them at these times, and water only enough to keep them from wilting.

Parsley and chives aren't the only herbs you can grow inside in a pot. These will do well too (in a cool room—60 to 65 degrees— with plenty of light, and planted in sandy loam): sweet basil, lemon verbena, mint, rosemary, sage, sweet marjoram, tarragon.

## Tools

Best tool for tamping soil in a small garden: your feet.

Broken hoe handle? Before replacing it, try this: Saw it off to a foot or less, then try this shorty tool for close-up cultivating.

A 3-pronged cultivator welded to the top of a hoe blade doubles the hoe's usefulness, adds weight that some gardeners like.

Tool preserver: an old paint brush in a can of half lubricating oil, half kerosene. Coat spade blades, fork tines, etc., with it to keep rust away.

Holder for small tools on garage wall: old shoe bag.

Handy storage for insecticides and garden accessories: a parcel post mailbox mounted on a 5-foot post right in the garden. High enough to keep things out of reach of small children, weather-proof, durable. Paint it green or run a vine up it.

Save old shower curtains; wonderful for toting piles of leaves, prunings, weeds. When transplanting, pile dug earth on curtain to keep lawn neat.

To move potted plants and flats around the garden, borrow your child's wagon. Also saves work when spreading fertilizer if you prop sack in wagon, move it around where needed.

## Windbreaks

Plagued with a persistent, damaging wind in your garden? A planting, or some kind of structure, may curb it and can some-times lengthen your gardening season. Panelists had these sug-gestions for windbreaks:

Quickest: louvred fence of wide boards.

Most permanent: evergreens, garden house, a wall.

Least expensive: corn, castor beans.

Prettiest: flowering shrub hedge; moonvine or morning glories on trellis.

Dual purpose: plant sunflowers, give them a 2-week head start, then seed pole beans at their feet, say Kentucky Wonders. The sunflowers will stay ahead of the beans and support them as they climb.

*Birds*
On the problem of how to attract birds without damage to the garden, the panel split right down the middle. The bird lovers on it were for the birds, damage or no damage. The others wanted the birds to stay out of the garden, holding that they did more harm than good. Depending on which group you agree with, here is their advice.

*To attract birds . . .*
If you have grapes, let some bunches dry on the vine; they provide winter feed for birds. So will crab apples. One panelist plants tall-growing popcorn and sunflowers, and said they "provide feed for the birds even when snow is deep."

Plant a summer garden just for the birds; they like garden peas, for instance; also ranunculus, morning glories, monarda.

For early-nesting birds such as robins and grackles, provide evergreens for nesting places.

Sure-fire attraction: water; a shallow pool, bird bath, spray, fountain, or even a dripping faucet.

*To discourage birds . . .*
Sprinkle commercial crow repellent over seeded rows if crows are a problem. Better than scarecrows.

If birds are eating your peas, stick twiggy branches into the row every few feet and string some black thread back and forth among them. Baffles birds.

Good strawberry protector: cheese cloth. Peg it down on each side of row with old clothespins, nestle mulch up close.

*Frost Protection*
Late spring and early fall frosts are hazards of gardening throughout the Temperate Zone. The object of the tips here is to help you to an extra month or so of garden interest, and to increase your harvest.

When frost is expected, cover plantings the night before, do not remove until mid-morning. Things to use: over beds, use old shower curtains, plastic drop cloths, newspapers, straw; a sheet of plastic can be stretched over four bricks at corners of seedling bed to make an overnight "greenhouse." Don't let plastic touch plants. Over individual plants use bushel baskets, cardboard cartons, paper bags held up by four sticks, light blankets, burlap, plastic bag covers from dry-cleaned clothes punched with air holes.

If frost slips up on you, spray plants with hose early on the frosty morning. It may save them.

Experiment with various planting sites on your property for tender things. Trees, hedges, and buildings sometimes give surprisingly good protection from light frosts.

To protect newly set out annuals from late spring frost, spot upside-down clay flowerpots among them and light a short, fat candle under each pot. These little heaters will keep the air gently warm for hours. Some gardeners use highway road flares instead of candle pots.

Cold storage: Rose buds beginning to show color can be picked just before frost, the stem ends sealed with melted paraffin, the whole thing wrapped in a damp paper towel and then in waxed paper, and put in the salad keeper of refrigerator. They will keep for a month or longer.

Keep frost in mind when choosing planting sites (or buying a home). A spot even slightly higher and with good air drainage may escape frost an entire month longer than low-lying adjoining areas.

Plant late tomatoes close together, and overlapping foliage will help protect fruits from frost.

## Mailing Flowers

You can send fresh flowers from your garden to friends by mail if you do it right. Here are some do's and don'ts from Burpee panelists who have mailed more flowers than they can count.

Choose blooms that are not too mature to stand the trip without wilting or shattering. Best way to tell this is to experiment beforehand, picking blooms at different stages of maturity, then holding them a few days, treated and packed as if for mailing.

Pick blooms in early morning or late dusk, let them stand in water up to their necks in a cool place 8 to 12 hours before packing.

Shipping container: Cardboard box long enough to take the stems straight was the choice of all panel experts.

To pack: Wrap the end of each stem in moist cotton, facial tissue, peat moss or sphagnum moss, and keep in place with wrapping of wax paper or plastic. Don't wrap tightly. Lay gently in box, remembering that "the best packing companion for a flower is another flower."

Position: Some flowers are geotropic, which means they will raise their heads if packed horizontally. Snapdragons and gladiolus are examples. Pack them vertically and write, "This End Up" on box. (Your experimenting beforehand will show you which flowers are geotropic.)

Flowers with large heads, such as Climax marigolds, should have pillows under their necks to avoid crushed petals. Make pillows of shredded newspaper rolled loosely in sheet of newspaper.

Hold them still: flowers must not shift about in box. Use paper pillows fastened to inner box sides to take up space, if any. Then either run two strings or tapes around bottom of box and through holes punched in sides and tie over flower stems, or hold them firm with padded cross-sticks cut to fit box width and secured to box sides with tacks or staples.

Finally: Sprinkle foliage lightly with cool water, close box, punch a few small air holes. Mark box PERISHABLE—CUT FLOWERS. Air mail is usually best. Also special delivery.

Mistake: Never mail flowers in a plastic bag, thinking this will keep them moist and fresh. They almost always quickly go to pieces.

### The Week-end Gardener

What, panelists were asked, can be successfully grown by someone who has only week ends to tend it, such as in a garden at a country vacation house? Few took a discouraging view of such a "garden of neglect" as one called it, and one of the plant breeders said flatly that a garden with only a five-day interval of inattention would be a happy garden compared to most. Here are the tips:

Watering will be the main problem. Best bet: Set up an irrigation ditch gridiron, water thoroughly just before leaving, maintain a heavy mulch.

Transplants: To avoid root check and need for frequent watering, grow these plants in pots, transplant without breaking ball of earth, water and mulch well.

Trellises? Best to avoid them if wind damage is likely, and if plants to grow up them need frequent tying.

Pests: Thorough weekly spraying or dusting with an all-purpose fungicide-insecticide is practical substitute for more frequent inspection.

What to grow: Almost anything you like among annual flowers; some perennials, such as ageratum, asters, hollyhocks, will take neglect. As to vegetables—practically anything.

*Porch Garden*

If you had only a porch to grow things on, panel members were asked, what would you grow? This question brought out the lion in everyone, for some reason. Almost everything but corn was recommended, and nobody said he wouldn't bother to plant anything at all. One panelist mentioned a Burpee customer who learned in a sandy-soiled section of Florida how to grow tomatoes in tubs, and still prefers to grow them that way in fertile Iowa, where he now lives.

While water is always available for a porch garden, enough sun may be a problem. Five to eight hours daily was considered necessary for most plants.

Herbs were recommended for porch pots; not only parsley and chives, but any of the herbs. They yield a lot of useful flavoring for the space they take, and many fresh herbs are impossible to find in markets.

Climbers: Here, too, small space can return a great deal of harvest from vegetables that can be grown up a trellis. Running squash was recommended, if the fruits are gathered when small. Cucumbers also, and tomatoes and beans. A cherry tomato plant is attractive when trained in the espalier shape.

For looks as well as taste, red chard, kale, and rhubarb were mentioned. Also carrots, with their ferny foliage, in a box 14 inches deep.

Flowers especially recommended: balcony petunias, geraniums, alyssum, primula, Gloriosa daisies. If sun is scarce, try impatiens and begonias. For something different, try lagenaria gourds, which are night-flowering.

*Flower Shows*
What helpful hints do you have, panel members were asked, for gardeners ambitious to enter blooms in a flower show—garden club, neighborhood, or bigger one? Here are their suggestions:

For one thing, don't pin all your hopes on one plant. Grow enough to give you a good chance of finding some blooms at the very peak of perfection when you need them. With annuals, make succession plantings two or three weeks apart to compensate for weather differences.

Disbudding: Do it early, when buds are just barely showing, to avoid ugly scars.

Don't water show flowers with a sprinkler; they may spot or water-burn. If rain threatens just before the show, pick the specimen blooms ahead of time.

When gathering the flowers, take along a sharp knife and a bucket brimming with water. Put flowers in water immediately. The first half minute makes a difference.

If possible, pick flowers early in the morning the day of the show, keep in water in a cool place, keep in water en route to the show.

If show blooms must be picked when wilted or soft, place them immediately in warm water (80 to 100 degrees) and put in a cool place.

Note: Booklets to tell you how to organize a flower show are available from the U. S. Department of Agriculture. See your county agricultural agent at the county seat.

*Floral Decoration*

Asked for ideas on how to use flowers for decorating, suggestions from the panel ranged from earring bouquets to parade floats. Because the big new marigolds are spectacular and lasting, they were mentioned more than any other flower. The great range of colors in zinnias made them popular also.

Corsages: Condition flowers as for flower show. Wrap each stem with light wire and floral tape. Use dainty flowers for wearing on light summer dresses. Join stems with wrapping of floral tape.

Marigold nosegay for little girls: Wire and tape about twenty small flowers. Use one for the center, surround it with a row, then put a second row around that one. Add a fringe of ivy leaves, twist all stems into a handle and push it through a slot cut in middle of a cardboard disk covered with lace paper doily just big enough to show around edge of nosegay. Add a ribbon streamer.

For dinner party, make table runner of marigold heads and ivy streamers. They will not wilt quickly. For a garland around a cake, use marigold, double petunia, or double hollyhock heads. Hostess can wear a double hollyhock in her hair and float some more of the same as table decorations.

Earring bouquet: Small zinnias glued to dime-store earring blanks. Other choices: Strawflowers, and some of the others used for dried blooms.

For decorating parade floats à la the all-flowers rule of the Tournament of Roses, a California panel member said she got a complete color range by using marigolds, bachelor buttons, calendulas, and dwarf dahlias. The flower heads are glued to the float framework to make the design.

Marigold *lei:* Here's how to make it, in the words of one lady of the panel. "I use the carnation-flowered American marigolds. I pick them the day before, and soak them in water up to their heads overnight so the *leis* will stay fresh several days. (If you want them for just one day, you can pick them the same day, and they don't need to be in water.) I cut each stem off at the base of the head and pile the blooms in a box. Then I thread a thin, straight upholstery needle (you can use a sack needle, or a strong wire) with a strong, smooth twine and string the flower heads by pushing the needle through each center. I just tie the two ends of the twine together when I finish, using all the same color of flowers or combining orange, golden, and primrose for a more striking effect. You can also make one *lei* of each color and wear the three of them at once.

"You don't have to treat these leis with kid gloves—you can toss them around and they won't crush, brown, or fall apart. And their lasting quality is wonderful."

*Miscellaneous*
The tips that follow are ones that didn't fall under any of the other headings but seemed too potentially useful to pass up.

*Letter Warmers:* A Burpee customer wrote that she says it with flowers, via packets of seeds she tucks into letters. Those of spring flowers—larkspur, petunias, asters—go into Easter notes. A packet of parsley or chives may set an apartment dweller to window-gardening. To tardy correspondents sometimes goes forget-me-not seed, or those of rosemary for remembrance, and Bells of Ireland to Irish friends on St. Patrick's Day. For a get-well card enclosure she finds that almost any seed works: "I could hardly wait to get out of bed and plant them," people sometimes write back. Note: With larger seed it is advisable to write on the envelope: "Seed enclosed—please hand-stamp."

Can't grow something? Before you give up, try a different variety of it. Experience at Burpee's Fordhook Farms in Pennsylvania shows it often pays. Examples: Greenbud broccoli does well there as either a spring or fall crop, but Waltham 29 is no good for spring; onions are fussy about day length, short days being preferred by Crystal White Wax and Yellow Bermuda, and long days by Yellow Sweet Spanish; lettuce is often very particular about growing conditions, so several varieties should be grown; California types of tomatoes (Pearson strains, Early Pak, J. Moran, etc.) defoliate rapidly in the East. Fordhook finds that hybrid vegetables and flowers are usually more tolerant, and grow where regular varieties may sulk.

Garden without spraying? One of the best barriers to insect damage is lusty plant growth.

Sunshine doesn't make tomatoes red—it sunburns them yellow. Encourage leaf growth to shade fruits. One way: When removing suckers, pinch out only the growing tips, letting leaves grow along.

Never use sulfur on most vine crops (cucumber, squash, pumpkins, most melons). It is poison to them.

In wet seasons, a shingle under melons helps keep them from rotting.

When to thin: when leaves of adjoining plants touch.

Handy thinning tool: a pair of scissors. Cutting small plants off at the ground line keeps roots of neighbors undisturbed.

Keep Out: To keep rabbits and other such browsers out of the garden, these things have sometimes worked like charms: moth balls scattered on the ground; hydrated lime dusted lightly on leaves; leaves sprayed with three ounces of Epsom salt dissolved in one gallon of water; leaves sprayed with soapsuds made of strong yellow laundry soap (not detergent).

Squash borer insurance: Mound earth over some vines where leaves join the stem. Roots will form, and plant will be saved even if a borer cuts off nourishment from the original roots.

Coffee grounds regularly put at the base of a shrub in the shade frequently attract earthworms.

A couple of 1 by 8-inch planks are handy garden accessories. Some uses: temporary board walks between rows when ground is soft; protective covers for seeded row during germination; straight-edge guide for row marking; traps for bugs that crawl underneath them; shade for row of small transplants (lean one plank against three short stakes spaced along row, lean the other plank against it so as to form a long low tent over the transplants).

Use for old garden seeds: Broadcast them over garden in early fall for winter cover crop and bird feed.

To keep parsley for winter use, dip it in salted, boiling water, shake well, and dry in 150-degree oven. Store in capped jars. Same procedure for celery tops, mint, dill.

Spring-clip clothespins in bright plastic are handy in the garden, too. Clip them on partly used packets of seed so the rest of the seed won't spill. Also keeps the wind from scattering any packets you lay aside.

# 15 THAT'S A GOOD QUESTION

Every year about ten thousand baffled gardeners turn to the W. Atlee Burpee Company headquarters in Philadelphia for comfort and help with some problem that, to them at least, is a lallapalooza. Most of the questions are about as complex as, "How much fertilizer does a radish need?" or "When is sweet corn ripe?" Some, at the other extreme, find the staff people scratching their heads: "What can I feed my schizanthus to make it smell its best?" Occasionally a question that seems simple enough turns out to be a boomerang. One man asked about the kinds of grasses to sow on acreage in his particular locality and was given some standard pasture recommendations. Presently in came a hot letter announcing that if ever he found himself in Philadelphia he planned to stop in at the Burpee building and personally "punch this Mr. J. Lowe of yours in the nose." The customer had been talking about, it seemed, not a pasture at all but the grounds of his new estate, and what he wanted was a velvet lawn, not the muscular veld that sprang up when he planted what Burpee's had recommended. The J. Lowe he referred to wasn't the beetle-browed gent he apparently envisioned, but a slip of a girl who heads the question-answering department in the Philadelphia headquarters during the winter and spring, then spends the summer and fall on experimental flower breeding at Burpee's Santa Paula Farms in California, where she gets so used to the pedestrian-protection practiced in the Golden State that she nearly gets mowed down the first few days back East each year. Not one to take injustice supinely, this J for Jeannette told the over-grassed customer that she sympathized with his troubles but he had brought them on himself by stating his question wrongly.

A policy of using initials instead of first names results in "Dear Mr. Hendrickson" letters coming to the Clinton, Iowa, Burpee branch office, where Margaret Hendrickson handles Customer Service for midwestern gardeners; and Jeannie Bankey in the Riverside, California, branch, is, inevitably, "J. Bankey, Dear Sir," to western flower and vegetable fanciers with problems.

Here are some of the questions gardeners have asked Burpee's, and the answers given, selected for general interest and usefulness.

*Question:* I have a row of beautiful red zinnias in my garden. One plant is the talk of the neighborhood because in some of the flowers there is a yellow wedge going right into the center of the blossoms. What causes this? If I save seeds from these flowers can I grow the same kind next year?

*Answer:* A change has apparently occurred in some of the bud tissue. In part of the cells there has been a mutation in the genes (carriers of heredity), and the factors necessary for development of red pigmentation have been altered or lost. All those portions of the flowers developing from these altered cells are yellow. This condition is called a vegetative, or somatic, mutation. We see examples of this occasionally in our flower fields. There will be a plant with stripes on some of the leaves, or else there will be a blossom with a wedge of another color.

Such somatic mutations usually do not reappear in the next

generation unless the plant is carrying hereditary factors which cause mutation rather frequently.

If you could protect a bud from cross-pollination by bees and then very carefully self-pollinate the yellow section, and then the red section, the resulting seeds from the yellow portion would probably produce a plant with yellow flowers; from the red section, red flowers.

*Question:* What is this odd-looking zinnia plant I have in my garden? The buds stay green but get bigger and bigger, yet never open up into regular flowers with petals. I don't think there's anything wrong with the way I'm growing the plants, because all the rest are all right.

*Answer:* The unusual-looking zinnia which you describe is a type we nickname a "mule" in our production fields. Even though these mules have a unique appearance we consider them undesirable and are constantly trying to eliminate strains of zinnias that occasionally produce them. They are caused by a recombination of a number of recessive (usually hidden) genes. When pollination occurs between normal plants carrying these hidden genes, occasionally a few seeds develop which carry all the recessive characteristics without any masking dominant normal genes. Plants grown from such seeds are the mules. The blossoms have no petals and look like heads of tight green buds, which never open. There are no functional reproductive parts and mules do not produce seeds. Because they look unique they are sometimes exhibited in flower shows in a separate class.

*Question:* One of my African marigolds has a very thick flat stem with a huge cluster of flowers all blooming together at the top. What causes this, and if I save seeds from this plant will I have the same thing next year?

*Answer:* Your description is a good example of fasciation. In other words, something happened—possibly an injury—to the growing point of the plant, so that all the side branches grew fused with the main stem. Likewise, all the lateral flower buds are fused with the terminal, making one big cluster of blossoms. Fasciation occurs occasionally but is often not hereditary.

*Question:* I have tried some $F_1$ hybrid tomatoes but I can't see that they're a bit better than regular varieties. What's the matter?
*Answer:* You probably are not giving your hybrid plants enough feeding, water, and space. They need more, just as a powerful engine needs more fuel than one less powerful. Even so, many tests have shown that under any conditions in which a regular variety will grow, a hybrid of its species will grow better. You can prove this for yourself by growing them side by side.

*Question:* My neighbor tells me that if I save some seed from my Golden Cross Bantam corn and plant it next year it won't grow. Will it?
*Answer:* Yes. But don't try it if you want the same top performance and uniformity next year. Plants from such seed are weaker, grow unevenly, and produce much less than $F_1$ hybrids. There will be reversion toward the parental strains that went into the cross making the hybrid.

*Question:* I like to soak foliage with the hose before spraying with an insecticide. Is this all right?
*Answer:* No. Insecticide sticks better and more evenly on dry foliage. Furthermore, dripping foliage would dilute insecticide and even cause it to run off the leaves. Dust sticks a little better on slightly damp foliage, as on dew-covered leaves early in the morning, but we don't recommend applying dust to dripping-wet foliage.

*Question:* What kind of weather and what kind of day is best for spraying insecticide?
*Answer:* Calm weather, with little or no wind. The air is usually more apt to be still in early morning, late afternoon, and early

evening. Avoid spraying in the middle of the day in hot, sunny weather; a scorching sun on sprayed leaves may burn them.

*Question:* I never have enough time to garden, so how about my mixing soluble fertilizer into bug spray and doing two jobs at once?

*Answer:* A chemist might be able to do this successfully but it wouldn't work for the average home gardener and in fact could do a great deal of harm, even killing plants. There is the big problem of compatibility between the various chemicals in sprays and the chemical elements in fertilizers. Unless the different chemicals were compatible, very toxic preparations might result. There are some lawn fertilizers which also contain insecticides, but they are not for general garden use.

*Question:* When we go away on a vacation I set big fruit-juice cans with a few holes punched in the bottoms with an ice pick, alongside my tomato plants. Then I fill the cans with water when we leave. Somebody told me this waters only one side of the plant, and someone else says it would be better to use a wick, not punched holes. What *is* best?

*Answer:* Soak the soil thoroughly by letting water trickle in slowly for six or eight hours, then put down a thick mulch of straw or similar material. This should see the plants through several weeks of vacation, and will also keep down weeds.

*Question:* I don't have much room for starting seed indoors, so what are the most important varieties to handle this way?

*Answer:* Concentrate on flowers and vegetables that (1) take a long time to come into bloom, or to produce a crop, or (2) which have very tiny seeds.

Most important such flower varieties include ageratum, asters, dianthus, bedding dahlias, lobelia, petunias, snapdragons, stock, and verbena. Start indoors six to ten weeks before outdoor planting time.

Vegetables include celery, eggplant, peppers, and tomatoes (start these eight to ten weeks before outdoor planting); and broccoli, cabbage, cauliflower (about six weeks before).

*Question:* Can I start marigold and zinnia seed indoors?
*Answer:* Yes, but they do just as well or even better when sown directly in the permanent location in the garden. If you do plant them inside, they grow large enough in just three or four weeks.

*Question:* I'm growing seedlings in my basement. The plants are getting tall and spindly and the leaves look yellow. What's wrong? Can I save these plants?
*Answer:* Your basement is probably too warm and too dark. Seedlings need plenty of light and moderately cool (60 to 70 degrees) temperatures to do well. Move them to a sunny, cooler location. Or give them additional light from incandescent or fluorescent lamps suspended above the containers.

When you transplant your spindly seedlings, set each one lower in the soil then it is now growing.

*Question:* It nearly breaks my heart to throw away nice little plants when I thin the row. Can I transplant them—lettuce, for instance, and radishes?
*Answer:* Lettuce can be transplanted, but not usually any of the vegetables raised for their roots, since damage to tiny roots is likely to result in forking and splitting of tap roots.

*Question:* My soil is clay, which is heavy to spade in the spring, and bakes hard as rock in summer. I use plenty of fertilizer, but things grow poorly. Is the trouble with my soil?
*Answer:* Yes. In hard, heavy, compact ground, plant roots do not have enough space, air, or available moisture for good growth. Chemical elements are not converted to forms plants can use, so they actually starve. Work in lots of organic matter each year to improve heavy (or very sandy) soil. Peat moss or well-rotted manure are excellent. So are composted leaves and garden refuse.

Every gardener should have a compost pile to convert leaves and other garden waste to valuable organic matter.

*Question:* Exactly what do the numbers, such as 5-10-5, on fertilizer bags stand for?

*Answer:* They are formulas, and refer, always in the same order, to the three most important elements of plant nutrition: nitrogen, phosphorus, and potassium. A 5-10-5 preparation contains 5 per cent nitrogen, 10 per cent phosphorus, 5 per cent potassium. Therefore, in a 100-pound sack you would get 20 pounds of these nutriments.

Nitrogen is necessary for the continuous healthy growth of the leaves; phosphorus, or phosphate, is important in flowering, fruit set, and seed production, also in aiding root development and generally healthy growth; potassium, or potash, is a general conditioner, making stems stronger, hastening maturity and seed production, and aiding good root development.

*Question:* I've been wondering if commercial fertilizers are harmful, since organic gardeners use only such plant food as manure, compost, bone meal, dried blood, and straw.

*Answer:* Many experiment station reports based on carefully controlled trials show that the use of organic matter plus commercial (inorganic) fertilizers gives the highest, top quality yields. Organic and inorganic materials complement each other.

*Question:* I used to have a lot of hummingbirds in the garden, but we moved and they don't come here. Could you suggest a few flowers that might attract them?

*Answer:* Columbine, delphinium, phlox, bee balm (bergamot), petunias, larkspur, trumpet vine, honeysuckle, nicotiana, scarlet sage, penstemon, tritoma.

*Question:* My white nicotiana is fragrant, but not the colored one. Is this normal?

*Answer:* White or light pastel colors often seem to be more fragrant than darker colors in the same variety. For instance, the white, cream, light blue, light lavender, and light pink shades in sweet peas are more fragrant than red and dark blues.

*Question:* What are some "weatherproof" flowers I could grow? I don't have much time for gardening, but I'd like a colorful display.
*Answer:* Try alyssum, cleome, gaillardia, Gloriosa daisy, marigold, petunia, phlox, portulaca, salvia, sunflower, verbena, zinnia.

*Question:* I have a shady spot in my yard that needs color. What would thrive there?
*Answer:* Impatiens and Begonias do better in partial shade than in full sun. The following also do fairly well but get lankier: alyssum, aster, coleus, cornflower, nasturtium, nicotiana, petunia, snapdragon, torenia.

*Question:* There is an unsightly view at the back of my new yard. In time I intend to screen it out with trees and shrubs, but what can I grow fast and easily this first season?
*Answer:* Giant sunflower or castor oil plant. Watch out for children around the latter, however; the foliage and seeds are toxic.

*Question:* Will different varieties of tulips in the same bed keep on blooming true, or cross? How about daffodils?
*Answer:* Bulbs cannot cross, and seed pods of these plants rarely mature in most of the United States. There are certain virus diseases of tulips that cause "breaking," or streaking of the colors. Also, sometimes one color of tulip or daffodil increases faster than other kinds, and may eventually take over a planting.

*Question:* My snapdragons are always very spindly and the spikes are short. How can I make them grow better?
*Answer:* In the almost-frost-free sections of the country, sow seeds in the fall. The plants then thrive during cool winter weather, and bloom in spring and early summer. In all other sections, start snapdragons as early in the spring as possible. It is

best to sow seeds indoors in early March. Set the plants out in the garden as soon as the soil can be well worked and the danger of heavy frost is over. Space bedding types at least eight inches apart, and tall types twelve inches or more. Cover the ground around the plants with a mulch of grass clippings, straw, buckwheat hulls, or something similar, to keep the roots cool and moist. In midsummer, after peak of bloom, cut the plants back to encourage fresh shoots for fall bloom.

*Question:* We just bought a place with an old rhubarb bed in the back yard, and I hear I shouldn't cook the tops because they're poisonous. Are they? And if so, are many other ordinary garden things poisonous in any part?

*Answer:* Rhubarb leaves *are* poisonous, and should not be eaten. Other poisonous plants include: monkshood (all parts), jimson weed (all parts), delphinium, larkspur and foxglove (foliage), Christmas rose (root), kalmia-laurel (all parts), oleander (all parts), castor oil plant (foliage and seeds), yew (leaves and fruits), narcissus (bulb), columbine (berry), lily of the valley (all parts), rhododendron (all parts). This is only a partial list. More complete ones can be found in garden encyclopedias.

*Question:* My Climax marigolds grow about twice as tall as the catalog states, but the flowers are just average size. What's wrong?

*Answer:* The plants are probably too crowded. Big marigolds need at least a foot of space between plants, and the Climax varieties do better with eighteen to twenty-four inches between. Shade also may be making the plants tall and spindly. Most annuals, including marigolds, need all-day sun to do their best.

*Question:* My husband recently retired and we moved south to a much warmer climate. I hear I must dig my tulip bulbs each year or they'll peter out. Is this true? (I thought gardening would be easier in a milder climate.)

*Answer:* Northern varieties which need a dormant period during freezing weather do not do well in the South, but of course there are many lovely tropical and semitropical varieties which flourish there. Tulips are really good for only one season in the South—and then best if they are pre-chilled before planting, and set extra deep. The University of Florida recommends chilling at about 40 degrees for four to six weeks before planting, and then setting about twelve inches deep.

*Question:* My cantaloupes taste bitter. Could they have crossed with some cucumbers that are growing near them?
*Answer:* No. Poor growing conditions such as cold wet weather during the ripening period, or diseased vines, cause bad flavor. Melons need fertile well-drained soil, a long growing season, and warm sunny weather during the ripening period, to be sweet and mellow.

*Question:* What causes my tomatoes to rot at the bottom just before they get ripe? Can I prevent it?
*Answer:* This sounds like blossom-end rot, caused by uneven water absorption by the plants. Mulch the ground around them, water thoroughly during prolonged dry weather, and avoid heavy applications of fertilizer high in nitrogen.

*Question:* My lima beans are loaded with blossoms but they fall off before any beans set. What's wrong?
*Answer:* Terrific heat or a cold wet spell often cause blossom drop. An overdose of fertilizer high in nitrogen may do the same thing.

*Question:* Is there any plant I can grow that discourages nematodes, the way castor bean is supposed to discourage moles?
*Answer:* Not that we know of. There is a lima bean variety, Nemagreen, supposed to be somewhat resistant to nematodes.

*Question:* What seeds could my kindergartners grow on a classroom windowsill?

*Answer:* French marigolds, bush beans, corn (just for fast germination), nasturtiums, leaf lettuce.

If a gardener asks for the name of a reference book on some subject or if the Burpee staff feels it would be useful to suggest it, they usually recommend one or more of those on this list:

*The Standard Cyclopedia of Horticulture,* The Macmillan Co., New York City.

*The Complete Book of Annuals,* F. F. Rockwell and Esther C. Grayson, Doubleday & Co., Inc., Garden City, N.Y.

*The Complete Book of Bulbs,* F. F. Rockwell and Esther C. Grayson, Doubleday & Co., Inc., Garden City, N.Y.

*All about the Perennial Garden,* Montague Free, Doubleday & Co., Inc., Garden City, N.Y.

*All about House Plants,* Montague Free, Doubleday & Co., Inc., Garden City, N.Y.

*The Gardener's Bug Book,* Cynthia Westcott, Doubleday & Co., Inc., Garden City, N.Y.

*Plant Disease Handbook,* Cynthia Westcott, Doubleday & Co., Inc., Garden City, N.Y.

*Better Homes & Gardens Garden Book,* Meredith Publishing Co., Des Moines, Iowa.

The Sunset books on gardening (for western gardeners), Lane Book Co., San Francisco, California.

*Landscaping Your Own Home,* Alice L. Dustan, The Macmillan Co., New York City.

*Garden in Your Window,* Jean Hersey, Prentice-Hall, Inc., New York City.

*Greenhouse Gardening for Everyone,* Ernest Chabot, M. Barrows & Co., Inc., New York City.

*Gardening in the Shade,* Helen K. Morse, Charles Scribner's Sons, New York City.

*Pioneering with Wildflowers,* George D. Aiken, Putney, Vermont.

*The New Book of Lilies,* Jan de Graaff, M. Barrows & Co., Inc., New York City.

*10,000 Garden Questions Answered,* F. F. Rockwell, Double-day & Co., Inc., Garden City, N.Y.

*The Pocket Book of Vegetable Gardening,* Charles H. Nissley, Rutgers University Press, New Brunswick, N.J.

# 16  NAMING THE BABY

When David Burpee tells a garden club audience he is always on the lookout for something suggestive, hardly any of the ladies grow nervous. Even if he hasn't already explained his particular use of the word, he looks much too much like a benevolent college professor to be pulling any blue whizzers. What he wants are names for new flowers and vegetables that are suggestive of important qualities they have. It is not for aesthetic reasons that he is on the prowl for such suggestive names. The plain fact is that gardeners are a shifty lot, swayed by the music of syllables. Burpee has a vivid recollection of what happened to his father one time with an onion.

The elder Mr. Burpee found this onion in Italy and was so pleased with its fine big size and flavor, he brought it back to this country and introduced it under its long Italian name. His son no longer can remember what the jawbreaker was, but he has no trouble remembering what happened. The onion was a flop and after a few years it was dropped from the catalog. Then, running across it once more and being impressed all over again, Mr. Burpee impulsively slapped it back into the catalog—but this time he picked a name Americans could dig. He called it Burpee's Gigantic Gibraltar, and with this impressive handle it became a best-seller almost overnight.

Another seed house had a similar experience with a melon they introduced as the Hoodoo. When they changed it to Hearts of Gold, it tasted entirely different to gardeners.

David Burpee has never forgotten these lessons. It hasn't guaranteed that he can always pick a winning name, but it has kept him on a constant lookout for likely prospects and made him a man without shame about grabbing off whatever strikes his fancy. "I nearly always get two or three good ones from any novel I read," he said recently. He did not mean, necessarily, that he lifted the names of characters from the novels, but that certain words struck his fancy. This also takes place during ordinary conversations. During a chat, someone used the word "zest," for instance, causing Burpee to whip a scrap of paper from his coat pocket and jot it down. Eventually it may appear in the catalog. He is also a billboard watcher for the sake of name possibilities.

By zealously noting down every such candidate, he has accumulated a reserve of, he estimates, about a thousand names. He treats this asset in much the same way the Victorians treated capital, preferring not to touch it. One time while pondering what to name some fine new asters just developed, he was invited by staff people to a picnic at one of his California farms. Since Burpee outdoes the natives in outdoor living whenever he comes to California, picnic lunches are a frequent thing during his visits, and at his orders, patios with ten-foot-high board fences to keep the winds gentled are as standard equipment on the farms as the greenhouses. This particular picnic was a larger affair, including the families of the staff men, and to Burpee the opportunity was irresistible. After finding something nice to say to each of the wives, as is his habit, he took charge of things along toward the latter part of the meal. Handing paper and pencils around to his captive audience, he asked them to observe closely what he was about to show them, and write down the first word that popped into their heads. He then whisked from

under cover, one at a time, the new asters, waving them hyp-
notically before the picnickers.

The hair-trigger suggestions the session produced are the kind
that have coined names oftener than other approaches. Aside
from the satisfaction of seeing his idea ripen into print in the
catalog, a Burpee employee's winning name bears fruit in the
form of a $10 prize to him, and occasionally this has been hiked
to $25.

Sometimes, as a mark of esteem, a new plant is named for a
person, just as Burpee named one of his carnation-flowered
marigolds Mary Helen for the wife of William H. Ayres, member
of Congress from Ohio who had been so swayed by the seedsman's devotion to the marigold for our national floral emblem
that he told Burpee he intended to support that cause.

There is a built-in drawback, however, in naming plants for
persons: it may crop up when the namer describes the plant in
his catalog. Years ago a good friend of W. Atlee Burpee's in England, a noted sweet-pea grower named Henry Eckford, graciously named one of his creations for Mrs. Burpee. "Blanche
Burpee," he then announced to the world, "is pure white, of
broad, expanded form on stout stems." Two years later the luckless man decided to try again, this time picking for the honor
Mr. Burpee's sister, a maiden who happened to be on the scrawny
side in an era of fashionable plumpness. With uncommonly bad
luck, Mr. Eckford came flourishing forth with the tidings that
Sadie Burpee was a beautiful sweet pea on long slender stems,
after which he stopped trying.

As far as that goes, Mr. Burpee didn't do much better in working out a heading for an 1891 listing of a new sweet pea. "Improved Painted Lady, or Miss Blanche Ferry," was the way he
put it. Incidentally, Burpee's no longer list any vegetables named
to honor persons, perhaps to sidestep the explosive possibilities
of some such description as "Betty Jones is a pretty smooth

tomato." One time a good old beet that had been bettered by selection came out sounding queer in the catalog. Known originally as the Blood Turnip beet for its color and shape, it was called in the upgraded version simply Burpee's Improved Blood. It seems probable that the name may not have caused even a ripple, since gardeners of the period did not seem to find Blond Blockhead an odd name for a lettuce. There was also one called Thickhead, and another known as Burpee's Hardhead.

Several years ago a couple of birds helped rename a flower for Burpee's. A pair of linnets took a notion to build a nest from the little golden-yellow flowers of a bush on the house grounds of the manager at Burpee's Floradale Farms. The plant was *Helipterum Sanfordii,* but it instantly became Bird's Nest Flower when David Burpee was taken by the hand to see the secret by its discoverer, the manager's little daughter. Burpee, who is as fond of children as he is of flowers, was entranced. By rare luck the Bird's Nest Flower was one of the everlasting group, as flower people call those that are easily dried for long-lasting bouquets, so when the birds were through with the nest it was still in good shape. Burpee thereupon borrowed it and skipped off East, where he displayed it at the next New York flower show. It was the hit of his exhibit, and appeared in color, complete with four speckled bird's eggs, in the 1938 catalog.

One pretty good way to get a name, experience at Burpee's has shown, is to stand around looking at the candidate and talking about it. Thus, plant breeder Jeannette Lowe recalls that she remarked of a brand-new phlox variety as she and Burpee were viewing it, "See how it twinkles," and the name Twinkles was born. Looking back, Jeannette thinks she was probably talking about a dewdrop on one of the petals.

This naming method has also produced at least one name through a kind of verbal typographical error. Once again standing with the boss over a new flower, this time a hybrid Supreme snapdragon, Jeannette, a girl seldom at a loss for conversation, said: "Notice that highlight?" Burpee's face took on the animated look it gets when an idea clicks into place. "That's the name," he cried. "High Life."

Burpee's French marigold Naughty Marietta got its name because a hotel dining room orchestra happened to play a selection from that light opera just as Burpee was racking his brain for a good name while having dinner.

In the early days of the business, new things were often named by the originator who sold his rights in the novelty to Burpee's. The house could then use or discard the name, or change it a bit as they did with a 1905 potato. Rights to this seedling were sold to them by Gideon T. Safford of North Bennington, Vermont, one of the country's outstanding potato experts and then a man of eighty. Mr. Safford's new potato was so early, producing useful tubers in less than two months, that he named it Quick Lunch. Burpee's followed through by calling it Uncle Gideon's Quick Lunch, and featuring it for fifteen years.

A sweet corn called Howling Mob was also named by its originator, a market gardener. He wrote W. Atlee Burpee: "I send you by mail a trial package of a variety of sweet corn which I have gotten by about ten years' selection. It has short fodder, large ears, white cob, and follows White Cory within one to five days. I call it 'HOWLING-MOB,' for when I take the first to market the grocers collect about my stall *in a mob,* each endeavoring to secure at least a few dozen of the first large corn."

In keeping with his kind of goldfish-bowl operation of the business, the original Burpee seedsman frequently asked his customers to try their luck at naming some new pip he had found. He usually offered a few small cash prizes, and merchandise for a lot of runners-up. His son tried this in 1940 with a new tomato, and found himself in a bind when five different contestants came up with precisely the same name and the exact one that most took his eye—Table Talk. Unlike his canny father, who always specified that the prize money would be split among contestants who suggested the same winning name, David Burpee had no choice but to pay the first prize five times over. This experience cost him $500. However, one of the happy winners wrote him later on that she had used her pile as down payment on a snug cottage she had longed for, and was planting the whole yard with nothing but Burpee seeds.

Another tomato, Big Boy, cost nothing at all for its name. The name was the nickname the tomato's developer, Dr. Ovid Shifriss, gave to Burpee's son Jonathan when the boy was four years old. Dr. Shifriss, then in charge of vegetable breeding at Fordhook Farms, was working on the tomato project at the time, and nobody could deny that "Big Boy" fit like a glove, for the fruits of the hybrid ran up to a pound or more each.

Jonathan Burpee's honor is pretty incognito, but David Burpee, as previously noted, sells a zinnia named David Burpee. It should be added that this has always embarrassed him a little. He did not choose the name himself, but gave in to the demand of his Floradale manager at the time, Bill Hoag, who considered that it was the zinnia, not Burpee, that ought to feel flattered. It was the second time in Burpee's life that he had had a flower named after him. The first occurred when he was sixteen years old, a Dutch seedsman friend of his father's naming a new nasturtium for him. The seed cost 25 cents a packet, a pretty fancy price for nasturtium seed in those days.

Burpee thinks his name on the zinnia probably helped a little in selling it. The house has found that flowers and vegetables which have as part of their names Burpee, Burpeeana, Fordhook, or Floradale, usually sell more than those that don't. The only conclusion they can draw is that gardeners identify such varieties more closely with the W. Atlee Burpee Company—a comforting conclusion, since it implies a sturdy customer loyalty. To a disinterested observer it may seem inconceivable that Burpee's would knowingly identify themselves so closely with anything but a sure winner, and this with the build-up a long series of successes brings is perhaps another reason for such popularity of varieties carrying one of the house names.

This house name point came under the scrutiny of a conscientious Department of Agriculture official in 1947. Itemizing twenty vegetables the firm listed with the prefix Burpee's or Burpee in each case, he asked in effect that they show cause why it should not be ordered dropped, since the very same varieties were listed by other seed houses without the prefix. With painstaking care, David Burpee explained that each and every item had been exclusively introduced by his seed house and that though, in the accepted ethic of the trade, other seedsmen had then helped themselves to it without identifying it as Burpee's, this did not make it any the less a Burpee original. All of the twenty vegetables not superseded by newer varieties since are still proudly carrying the Burpee prefix.

Burpee's relations with the government are ordinarily as harmonious as those between a threadbare nephew and his rich uncle. If there is a villain in seedsmen's lives it is apt to be nature when she stops co-operating. This happened to W. Atlee Burpee with a dwarf sweet pea he was so proud of that he announced it by name a year in advance, in 1895. The little thing grow only five inches high, so he called it Cupid. Cupid looked wonderful until it rained. Then mud spattered all over him. Consequently, Cupid was a failure. David Burpee is hoping to avenge this old defeat with a brand-new dwarf variety he won an award on in 1961 from the Scottish National Sweet Pea Society. This one blooms earlier than the early varieties, and for a longer time, and it grows only fourteen inches high, so it is above the spatter, yet needs no stakes. Not caring to tempt fate by using the name

Cupid again, Burpee decided on Bijou, defined by the dictionary as "a jewel." But when he tried it on some of his employees, all they could think of was a burlesque house. Burpee still likes "bijou" even if he has to translate it.

Sometimes a flower name is chosen with an eye toward a commercial tie-in which will advertise the flower and the seed house that originated it. This one-hand-washing-the-other arrangement is usually premeditated, but in the case of a Supreme snapdragon Burpee's call the Super-Jet, it was the other way around. A few months after the name popped into the flower seed department manager Lou Frankl's head and out of his mouth during a typical name hunt, TWA dreamed up the same thing all by itself for a new plane. Jumping happily on this coincidence bandwagon, the Burpee organization with its president's then twenty-year-old son Jonathan acting as front man, hurried a bouquet of Super-Jet snapdragons to the Los Angeles airport, where Jonathan presented them to a pretty stewardess in front of a SuperJet airplane, cameras clicking.

Another type of commercial tie-in is the premium offer—for which a name may be deliberately chosen. "Spring is new every year," David Burpee says, when speaking of the value of seeds as premiums. Suppose that a coffee firm has a brand of coffee it calls, God forbid, "Dimples." Suppose further that Burpee's have a new and unnamed French marigold the name Dimples seems somehow to fit. This, then, is a made-to-order situation for a premium tie-in. The procedure is to request permission of the coffee people to use their copyrighted name for the marigold (a piece of business etiquette in any case, and also insurance against legal squabbles). Then, if the coffee people are interested, Burpee's will be delighted to sell them packets of the coffee's marigold namesake (or any other, naturally) to give away with cans of coffee. This presumably helps the coffee sales, the seed business *certainly,* and the housewives buying coffee get something for nothing.

# 17 NO SHRINKING VIOLETS

Soon after David Burpee was flushed with success by his development of odorless-leafed marigolds, he happened to walk into the diner of a San Francisco-bound train and sit down at a table opposite Clare Boothe Luce. He recognized the attractive author and soon-to-be Congresswoman but she didn't know him from Adam, and remained buried in a book. Burpee restlessly ordered himself a cocktail, and presently when Mrs. Luce emerged from her reading he greeted her with fellow-traveler camaraderie: "I'm Burpee," he announced, whereupon she looked casually concerned.

"Martinis do that to some people," she murmured. "Now, they make *me* sneeze." By the time she got things straight, they were well acquainted, and Burpee spent the dinner hour telling her about the seed business. He ended up by promising to name a sweet pea after her, and did so. It is listed as one of the Burpee's Giant sweet peas, described as "a beautiful deep salmon-pink color."

The "I'm Burpee" part of the meeting was picked up by the *Reader's Digest*, and Burpee, who has an abounding respect and admiration for this phenomenally successful magazine, was charmed by its interest and not in the least sensitive about its telling a few million readers of the pun on his name. He feels about publicity as some optimists are said to feel about the weather—that all of it is good, only some of it is better.

The *Digest* again elated him, in its issue of June 1960, by reprinting another Burpee story—this time one that Burpee had told about his father. It had appeared as part of a requested write-up from Burpee on his company in a book, *Ideas That Became Big Business* (Founders, Inc., Baltimore, Md.). It was a story of how the elder Burpee had apologized to his customers for picturing on the cover of the 1914 catalog a Matchless tomato larger than any Mr. Burpee had seen, despite a last-minute $5 reward he had offered to any Fordhook Farms employee who could find him one in the forty acres of Matchless growing there. In a footnote in the catalog Mr. Burpee then resignedly said:

"We are surprised, as doubtless our friends will be, at the size of THE MATCHLESS TOMATO appearing on front cover. While MATCHLESS *is 'the largest and best'* of all large-fruited, smooth, bright red tomatoes, yet it cannot be expected to come *quite so large as painted*. It is difficult to understand how the original proof, shown us last April, could have been marked O.K. The only explanation we can offer is that when looking at the finished design, the writer, impressed with the known solidity and extra large size of his favorite tomato, must have forgotten to compare the painting with the actual photographs furnished as copy. Not until today (September 25, 1913) did the *'artistic license'* become apparent. We aim always to tell the exact truth, both by pen and picture, and regret extremely that it is now too late to make correction, as more than four hundred thousand covers are already partly printed. Will YOU accept our apology?"

The customers not only accepted the apology—they sprang to the defense of Mr. Burpee's pet tomato. David Burpee was able to write, years after: "Gardeners everywhere just loved it and took up the challenge. During that summer tomatoes were shipped to father's home from all parts of the country with letters from customers bragging that they had grown Matchless as large as the picture on the catalog cover. They had, of course, taken extra care in growing them and had really produced big toma-toes."

Although hard pressed by newer varieties, including some superb hybrids, old Matchless is still carried in the catalog. "Heavy cropper," the blurb says. "Large, meaty, rich scarlet-red, perfectly smooth, firm, long-keeping fruits."

David Burpee's historical hero is Napoleon, but whether this stems from the seedsman's Culver Military Academy training is debatable. What he seems to admire most about the Little Corporal are traits typical of a business executive, and somehow of Phineas T. Barnum. "Napoleon," he has said, "taught me how to give a flower show."

The teaching in this case was Napoleon's technique to whip up public interest in Italian art treasures being shipped as repara-tions to Paris. Instead of getting them there with the least fuss, as Burpee tells it, Napoleon invented all sorts of delays en route, and every time one happened he banged off a news flash on it until he had every soul in Paris chewing his nails, waiting for the great day of arrival. Burpee's adaptation of this teaser tech-nique to flower shows has taken the form of concealing some new and splendid novelty until he has everyone in the audience drooling over his story of its creation. Not until then does he flick aside the curtain and reward them with the McCoy in all its glory.

He may be giving Napoleon too much credit for educating him to the sweet uses of publicity. Years before he started being such a flower showman, he had been following his father's ex-ample in urging one and all to come visit Fordhook Farms, and he printed a road map in the 1929 catalog so nobody would get lost. The official visitors' day was traditionally Wednesday, and for years Burpee omnibuses met every passenger train arriving at Doylestown on that day. At length, however, and with easy transportation by private automobile, the thing got out of hand.

After having to hoe thousands and thousands of footprints out of trial beds, and soothing greenhouse men who had begun to dream bad dreams about mobs of strangers breathing down their necks, Burpee finally yanked in the welcome mat. Visitors today are not sent packing, of course, but they are no longer solicited en masse and come what may. Visiting is now apt to be done by groups and to be carefully timed and dramatically staged. This is more to Burpee's liking and talents. In the busy midst of being host one recent summer's day to a hundred or so East Coast journalists, he found time to escort a New York newspaper woman into the library of his Fordhook manor house. Brushing aside the display there of gold and silver trophies won for horticultural prowess, Burpee pounced on a couple of skimpy little old cups. "Now *this* is what I wanted to show you," he cried. "I won these for running—back in 1910. First time I'd ever raced on a cinder track in my life."

Like his father, who also knew well the publicity value of a famous name, David Burpee has from time to time associated his seed business with the mention of a public figure. The device got a little out of hand once when a picture of the author and naturalist, John Burroughs, appeared for two successive years in the Burpee catalog, in 1927 and 1928, showing him bending over the same squash in a garden. On the first appearance, six years after the naturalist's death, the caption identified him as having been a satisfied user of Burpee seeds, and stated:

"Here he is in his garden patch inspecting one of his Hubbard squashes. He sent this squash, which weighed 23 pounds, to Thomas Edison. . . ."

In the 1928 catalog the picture appeared again, with the following information: "The photo to the left shows Mr. Burroughs lifting a squash growing in his garden. He was so proud of this squash grown from Burpee's Seeds that he sent it on to his friend, Henry Ford. . . ." Anyway, it was a lovely squash, whoever got it, and Mr. Burroughs was undoubtedly a fine judge of seeds.

Now and then so juicy a big-name publicity plum has fallen, all unguided, into Burpee's lap that it almost argues for clean living and constant hope. One such time was during World War II. As reported by the factual St. Louis *Post-Dispatch*, Maj. Gen. Leslie R. Groves, anxious to present to Army Chief of Staff George C. Marshall his arguments for needing another hundred million dollars for the atomic bomb development, was kept waiting while General Marshall worked over a little list before him, then signed a check. After seeing Groves and agreeing to his request, General Marshall explained why he had had to keep him waiting. "I was ordering some garden seeds," the chief of staff was reported as saying. "You get the hundred million and Burpee's get the $3.45."

Most of the time, the seedsman has had to work diligently in order to associate the name of Burpee with one that is more an intimate of headlines. Success came to him in this wise in 1939 in connection with the start of commercial airline service across the Atlantic Ocean. It coincided, by chance, with Burpee's production of his Red and Gold Hybrid marigolds, and in discussing with his then director of public relations, Clare Ogden Davis, ways to publicize this accomplishment, the idea of sending a marigold bouquet to Dowager Queen Mary of England came up. The flowers, which fortunately could stand up under rigorous conditions if necessary, were flown over in three boxes, each costing $18.75 for postage. To get around any sordid commercial taint that might have knocked the whole scheme in the head, the Burpee blooms were ostensibly sent by the National Council of State Garden Clubs, with their enthusiastic consent.

At the last minute the elaborate preparations tottered and nearly fell apart when the Dowager Queen was hurt in an automobile accident, and Ambassador Joseph Kennedy, who had been scheduled to present the gift, decided against it. Not one to be thwarted at the very lip of success, however, the girl P.R.

whiz—she had raced the lumbering plane across the ocean on a ship and was in there punching—buttonholed both the royal florist and a co-operative lady-in-waiting to the Dowager Queen, and the Burpee marigolds were finally borne triumphantly into the presence of Her Majesty. The London newspapers played the story, Mrs. Davis went on the British airways and told the wireless audience how the Red and Gold Hybrid marigolds came to be, the Dowager Queen sent a thank-you autographed photograph to the National Council of State Garden Clubs, and later the marigolds won the Award of Merit from the Royal Horticultural Society of Great Britain. David Burpee picked up the tab for the expensive stunt, feeling it was money well spent. So did Mrs. Davis, now garden editor of the Austin, Texas, *American-Statesman*.

Burpee was, in fact, so pleased with the flying flowers that he did it all over again in 1960, sending a couple of boxes of big marigolds ("known as friendship flowers," he noted) to Japan for the Emperor and Empress, via Ambassador Douglas MacArthur II. This time everything went easy as pie. The ambassador was glad to co-operate in a gesture of friendship on the heels of the demonstrations that had canceled President Eisenhower's proposed visit to Japan; this time Burpee didn't bother to hide behind the skirts of the garden clubs; and the Emperor sent his thanks and appreciation through the Grand Master of Ceremonies at the Imperial Palace.

By the time the flowers went to Japan, shipments by air were old hat and the attention given Burpee's action by newspapers was mild. He has small cause for complaint, though, all in all. His file of press clippings over the years is fat. As head of the world's biggest business of its kind, he is a natural news source and he lives up to the role. As far back as 1926 the old humorous magazine *Judge* in its garden number had a full-page cartoon by Gardner Rea titled: "Mr. Burpee Sits Down to a Vegetable

Dinner." No further identification was needed for readers to understand the logic—for big Burpee's—of an ear of corn as long as a limousine, a stalk of celery like a tree, asparagus spears as substantial as telephone poles, and so on. In 1931 *Time* wrote up Burpee's acquisition of Luther Burbank's trunk of seeds, and picked him up again in its business department of the magazine in 1960 as "The Gardener's Gardener." In 1946 *Life* ran a feature on him, in which it remarked: "The Frank Buck of seedsmen, he gives the story of the creation of a sweet pea the breathless excitement of a tiger hunt." *Life* was referring to Burpee's then annual posh flower debut at New York's Waldorf-Astoria, where he unveiled his newest triumphs and told the big (up to four thousand persons) audience all the thrills and terrors of the breeding. In the May 1961 issue of *Holiday,* Burpee, shown leaning comfortably on a stack of his catalogs and surrounded by his marigolds and a constellation of "Burpee Seeds Grow" signs, was the only seedsman or nurseryman to grace a well-illustrated article on garden flowers.

Burpee has appeared four times in the *Saturday Evening Post,* twice in as-told-to feature articles written by Frank J. Taylor in 1938, again in 1939, and under Taylor's own lone by-line in 1951. Burpee was so pleased with the 1951 article, titled "They've Grown Some New Posies for the Ladies," that he had thousands of reprints made up into little booklets that he still hands out to those in need of enlightenment. When the original *Post* article appeared, the magazine still cost a nickel, and to make sure the populace learned about the piece on his seed house, Burpee had a few thousand cards printed up ahead of time, glued a nickel to each, and zinged them off to everyone he thought proper.

One excellent reason for David Burpee's success at publicity is that he is, in newspaper language, good copy. This is due partly to his willingness to co-operate, partly to his own highly tuned sense of the dramatic, and partly to the fact he is one of those people that things happen to. This may be because he is an agreeable-looking man who appears to be a good listener and who isn't overly concerned with his appearance. If he were concerned, he certainly would not have continued to flout fashion and wear the same strictly functional steel-rimmed spectacles, as round as headlights, year after year ("I have five pairs," he once told an acquaintance happily), nor would he frequently yank his breast pocket handkerchief out, to hang from his coat like a blowsy pennant, as a reminder to himself to do something. His voice, slightly nasal, sounds like that of a man much younger, and his hands are the slender, long-fingered hands of an artist.

If he does have an artistic talent it is not a manual one, but he is handy with his hands in other ways. Once when he was peacefully reading the newspaper in the lobby of a small hotel in Ventura, California, one of the things that happen to him happened. Another guest, an indignant man, came storming down the stairs to see the manager. "Nobody home but me," Burpee told him. "Manager's gone to a party. Be back in an hour or two." This was literally true, the good-natured Burpee having been pressed into minding the shop for a while.

"Well, see here, you," said the other guest, "my bed isn't made up."

"Let's have a look," said Burpee, following the other back to his room without bothering to say that he wasn't there to make up beds. Sure enough, the bed was stripped. Burpee ransacked the closet and dresser for sheets but there weren't any there.

"This is some dump," said the sheetless guest sourly, but Burpee, to whom difficulties are but a challenge, streaked for the hotel dining room. Whisking tablecloths from four tables, he returned, calmly made up the bed with them, and had no further complaints from his customer.

Another occasion that brought out the best in him was the time he couldn't find any restaurant open for breakfast during a stop in a resort region after the season was over. Discovering a crossroads grocery store, Burpee sent a wave of prosperity through it by buying eggs, milk, instant coffee, cornflakes, tomato juice, sugar, sweet rolls, a set of picnic spoons, and an 88-cent special consisting of two glass mugs and two bowls. He needed two of each because his research assistant, Jerome Kantor, was along. Returning to the motel where they were staying, Burpee served the tomato juice and cornflakes while he was cooking the eggs in the way he remembered doing fifty years before as a student at Culver—by running hot water from the wash basin faucet over them for twenty minutes. Finishing off with coffee and rolls, he proceeded to a good day's work, untroubled by inconveniences or indigestion.

During his trip to Japan in 1960 Burpee showed himself equally adaptable at the table, sitting on the floor and chopping away with chopsticks. He handled them like a veteran until a seventeen-year-old geisha girl complimented his skill, whereupon he went to pieces and dropped a piece of fish in a cup of warm saki. Ordinarily it is Burpee who is the one doing the complimenting to the fair sex (never "women" to him but always "the ladies," in the same automatic way that he is "D.B." to his staff). To an attractive matron in her late forties who remarked that when young she had felt life would no longer be worth while after age thirty, Burpee instantly replied, "Oh, I'm sure you won't think so when you get there."

While he is insatiable in his taste for publicity for his business, Burpee does not seek out attention to himself as a private individual and does not make capital of such acts as providing, at Fordhook, office quarters for Welcome House, an organization sponsored by his Bucks County neighbor, author Pearl Buck, to provide foster homes in the United States for Eurasian orphan children. Burpee also serves on the board of Welcome House, and on a number of others, and is a trustee of Bucknell University, which made him an honorary doctor of science in 1959.

In 1957 he was thrilled to appear as the star of one of Edward

R. Murrow's Person-to-Person series on television. It took place with Murrow seated in New York, and Burpee dodging around Fordhook among thirty-five television henchmen who had begun setting up shop at 1 P.M. the day of the show. Burpee was on the air for thirteen minutes, and though he seemed to the television audience to be as cool and collected as one of his cucumbers, he had to rush madly between shots, from room to room of the big house, and from there to a greenhouse, leaping into a car waiting with the engine running, as in a gangster movie. Highly conscious of his opportunity, he unveiled to what he considered a bated-breath waiting world, two of his brand-new babies for that year—the first Gloriosa daisy, and Burpeeana lettuce, now called Burpee Bibb.

The show made quite a hit, even though one viewer got a little confused about the new lettuce and wrote Burpee she had been so glad to see it again because it was exactly the same as her father used to grow thirty years before. Another fan letter, however, was a model of brevity with punch. It merely said: "Dear Mr. Burpee: We seen you Friday night on the TV and you was a doll."

# *18* "DEAR MR. BURPEE"

"Dear Mr. Burpee: I am not so very pleased with your Enkhuizen Glory cabbage," a customer wrote W. Atlee Burpee some fifty years ago. "The heads are solid enough but not even one came to as much as ten pound." The letter was routed to the Complaints Department, then run by a feisty old Scotchman. Buzzing and foaming, the Scot banged off an answer saying in effect that if the customer didn't have sense enough to read the description in the catalog, he needn't come crying to Burpee's, since it was distinctly set forth that the cabbage was of medium size, the heads weighing from six to eight pounds trimmed.

This correspondence happened to come under the eye of young David Burpee, who was almost old enough to vote and was just then trying to decide in which department to start learning his father's seed business. Horrified at such blunt handling of a customer, weak-eyed or not, the youthful Burpee took over the Complaints Department and immediately changed its name to something politer. From that time forth, he announced, it would be known as the Adjustments Department and would be a joy to deal with.

Today the department is called Customer Service. In addition to handling complaints it takes care of pleasanter forms of correspondence, the whole coming to about twenty-five thousand items a year (not counting requests for gardening information) in the main office at Philadelphia, plus a few thousand more at the branches.

Actually, complaints form a minority of the letters, most of them being more nearly like notes from chatty friends, or sometimes like the letters young people write home when they are surprised at how sensible the old folks were about something. One such came in years ago, bemusing everybody who saw it. The customer wrote: "I can honestly say that Burpee seed have Made a Man of Me, and so great a confidence that I scarcely Plant any other seed."

Had he written this brave testimonial a few years earlier, when W. Atlee Burpee was alive, the customer would possibly have landed in the next year's catalog. The elder seedsman printed so many letters it sometimes seemed as if the customers were writing the catalog for him. Most of these letters were hard-headed reports on the performance of vegetable novelties the writers had tried out with the free seeds Mr. Burpee broadcast by the thousands of packets every year. This type of sampling is still done by Burpee's, though any seeds they give away now are already proved performers, and the sampling is usually for sales promotion.

Not always, though. In 1959, out of the goodness of their hearts, Burpee's answered a query about hybrid tomato seeds from the master of a British school by sending him free samples of some. He was so touched that he sent a lengthy report at the end of the season. Big Boy tomato, Burpee's best seller, was his and the British schoolboys' favorite, it turned out. The ties of one of his plants had broken under the weight of twelve pounds of fruit, but the vine "grew without check after being hauled up again," he wrote. "My wife found it the perfect tomato for bottling and we have 20 or so jars stored away for frying with our breakfast this winter."

While the British gardener was new to Burpee seeds, some of

the long-time customers have occasionally gone overboard in praise, though few so unconditionally as one gentleman who wrote that he had been buying Burpee seeds "every year for 65 years and had never had a loss." This is considerably more than Burpee's can claim for themselves, having quite a few times had to confess, as they once did about a new cabbage: "Unfortunately, the crop of seed was a total failure." The name of this embarrassing plant was Burpee's World-Beater.

In 1924 a joky customer declared he had planted some seed of the Mammoth Whale squash that had grown so fast and immense it finally ended up three farms away, where one of the fruits was sawed in two and the halves used for a barn and a stable. This squash variety, no longer offered, did grow to about three feet long and often exceeded a hundred pounds. A more credible, though still impressive, report came from a gardener whose zinnias were caught in a flood from the Delaware River and after a day and a night under ten feet of water, survived and later bloomed in the muddy wastes.

Some letter writers could be sued for the insults they hurl by mail at Burpee's, though these are a small minority of the correspondents. They are answered impersonally and briefly as a rule unless they have earned a name in the office as incurable cranks who are best ignored.

Along with other sizable businesses Burpee's receives quite a few requests for donations. They are more likely to give free seeds than money to a worthy cause, though the number of fake claims for help makes them wary all around. Not all these requests come from organizations, by any means. From the looks of the mailbag, there are a smart number of adventurers who specialize in brash requests for money from business houses. The needs they cite range all over the lot—auto repair bills and mortgage payments, a new graduation dress or a bicycle for the children, a hearing aid or new television set for senior citizens.

On the other hand, one elderly woman wrote Burpee's Clinton, Iowa, branch a friendly letter every year, enclosing $5.00. Her handwriting, however, was so difficult that they were never able to read more than a scattered word here and there. Writing back to ask what the $5.00 was for did no good at all, merely producing another pleasant set of hen tracks, so they just picked out $5.00 worth of flower seeds they thought she'd like, threw in the usual free marigolds, and sent them off. The Tower-of-Babel correspondence continued for years, with the customer apparently enchanted over her annual grab bag.

Other customers write not only when ordering seed but in between times. A lawyer in a small midwestern town used to write Burpee's every Thursday. He wrote about his garden, amiable, essayish letters. Some older correspondents fill several pages with their life histories and it seems sad that the drama and feelings of eighty or ninety years summed up in such letters may have no other audience than the busy employees of a corporation.

Once in a while a Burpee correspondent is very young for a gardener. One, aged six, sent in an order for his first garden, asking for "one apple seed, two tomato seeds," and so on. The order was filled exactly as specified. Recently a small veteran gardener in New York State wrote Burpee's as follows, showing how much ground can be covered in a few words if you try:

> I am only 11 years old and I started planting when I was 5 years old. I have a garden already and I would like to improve it. I would appreciate if you would send me information on improving it.
>
> Yours truly,<br>Charles Frisch
> P.S. Also send me information on Killing disease.

Brides, for some reason, seem prone to write Burpee's about their gardens. One astounded girl who dropped a few zinnia and marigold seeds into a bit of ground her man prepared for her, reported: "The results were fantastic . . . zinnias six feet tall. And the marigolds grew like trees." They bloomed like flowers, nonetheless, yielding a final, end-of-the-season bouquet of 160 blooms just as the first snow fell. Another bride was not so fortunate. She had nearly finished planting a wedding present bushel of tulip bulbs all over the yard when her bridegroom happened by and callously told her she was planting them upside down. She burst into tears, and then wrote Burpee's, pointing out that nowhere in the cultural instructions did it tell you which end was up. A third bride, Burpee's swears and declares, wrote them thusly: "All my mother told me when I got married was to plant Burpee seeds and everything would turn out all right."

Not everyone has been so sure of Burpee's and their seeds. Years ago David Burpee remarked wryly on "the 'brickbats' that come with the introduction of every new variety." He was thinking at the time of some remarks on a new celery from disgruntled planters such as one who said: "I was completely carried away with it last fall but I have lost most of this enthusiasm. . . . It is badly mixed and a poor keeper."

A woman gardener thought, for some reason, that Burpee's would like to know that her neighbor wouldn't buy a thing from them, claiming "that you specialize in seeds that are guaranteed to do nothing at all."

A lady got so exercised over David Burpee's promotion of the marigold for the national flower that she wrote, calling his pets gaudy near-weeds that smelled bad and asking him to abandon the campaign "because I feel sure the influence of your company will be very great." Burpee, who isn't nearly that sure about his company's influence, thanked her for writing and sent her some free marigold seed.

Advice in one form or another is always coming to Burpee's from the gardening public. Some years ago a male customer passed along this toothsome suggestion, headed "Roasting Ears & Pancakes":

"When the Golden Bantam has been boiled 10 minutes in water to which has been added a heaping tablespoonful of sugar and a good pinch of salt, pour the water off, and while the corn is steaming in the pot under cover, proceed as follows: To a pint of flour add two rounding teaspoonfuls of baking powder and a pinch of salt; bring to a batter through the medium of an egg, two-thirds of a cup of cream and a cup of water beaten together; when griddled to a fluffy brown, seat yourself at the table with Golden Bantam to your left, pancakes to your right, and a copious hunk of good country butter in the center. After liberally doping both pancake and corn with butter, add a sprinkling of salt to the corn, bite one glorious nipping of the Golden Bantam, immediately add a wedge of pancake, close your eyes and forget all mundane things. . . ."

Burpee's, especially in their earlier years, when the customer-seller relationship was more personal, occasionally passed out some fatherly advice of their own, such as an 1894 observation that Spanish peanuts were "splendid to fatten hogs and children." In the same helpful vein the elder Mr. Burpee lectured his clients about eggplant, saying it "should be grown in every garden as it is one of the most delicious vegetables known. Sliced and fried in batter, served with raw tomatoes, it can well take the place of meat for supper in the summer or fall."

Though the founder's successors have not in recent years given out medical advice, the 1917 catalog confided that a "Dr. Finck," whom they said was a food authority, "highly recommends *Escarolle* (Southern name for Endive) as a food for persons suffering from indigestion." The following year, with the nation still at war and diet an important topic of conversation, Burpee's leaped into the discussion with the declaration to their customers: "World-famous scientists have discovered by actual laboratory tests that many diseases like rheumatism, gout, nervous troubles, etc., originate from the collection of poisonous germs in the intestines." The world-famous scientists advised salads to avoid getting into such a fix, Burpee's said, adding for proof that the French called spinach "the broom of the stomach."

One of their customers preferred beans for health. Writing from Mexico to praise Burpee Golden pole bean, he urged them to try his recipe: "Boil the bean in clear unsalted water only until it is crisp done. Drain it into a collander, sprinkle it with salt. Return to a dish, pour over it olive oil and add lemon juice and eat it with your fingers. Or make a cream of bean soup. Boil the Golden pole bean until it is very tender, and it doesn't take long to do it. Press it through an ordinary potato ricer and make cream soup, and if you desire an additional wrinkle, dice some salt pork in small cubes, fry it brown, and sprinkle a little into each plate of soup."

Besides culinary advice, Burpee's are often told by customers how to run their business. Writing that her vegetable garden had come through a hard season with flying colors, a customer suggested that this would make a good slogan for them. Another, after seeing David Burpee and his wife on Edward R. Murrow's Person-to-Person television program mentioned in Chapter 17, ordered him to name a flower for Mrs. Burpee's eyes because they looked kind and understanding. At least one other customer of record tossed out a piece of advice that Burpee's have never quite made up their minds to recommend unconditionally. "I have got rid of my liver troubles," he wrote, "entirely through Burpee's seeds. Try my cure."

As Burpee's have been in business since 1876 and many customers have grown old along with them, some of the childhood reminiscences in their letters have the mellow glow of old and yellowed lithographs. An eighty-nine-year-old customer recalled that when he was a boy on an Ohio farm the family literature was the Bible, his mother's church paper, his father's county weekly,

*The Youth's Companion, Farm Journal,* and Burpee's catalog. His father once ordered a clutch of Barred Plymouth Rock eggs (13 for $2.00) from Burpee's, and when they hatched, sent a complaint that the chicks—a new breed to him—were not barred at all, but black. "Keep your shirt on," Mr. Burpee calmly advised him, "and wait till they feather out." They soon did so in what the confident Mr. Burpee called in his catalog "their plain Quaker-like attire, a suitable every-day work dress."

Sometimes the memory of an old customer for minor details astonishes Burpee's. A woman mentioned that her son was a third-generation customer, and added that the first-generation one, her father, had ordered "about 58 or 60 years ago your bush limas, and had a most excellent crop." It had been exactly fifty-seven years before, as the writer accidentally verified by remembering the catalog her father had ordered from. "The cover was decorated with chestnut burrs and pods of peas," she wrote. It certainly was, this being a rebus readers were invited to solve. Literally thousands of triumphant "Burr-Peas" poured into the mail chute that year, each winning for its solver a free packet of balsam seeds and one of fancy little peppers.

The ages of the older correspondents lend some weight to the claim that gardening makes you live longer. "If I live until October 4 I shall be 94," said one—rather cautiously, since his letter was dated September 9. Another, in his ninety-fifth year, had lately retired from professional gardening and was busying himself in his own backyard plot. A woman of ninety-nine wrote to thank Burpee's for their many catalogs she had enjoyed, then bade them good-by and said cheerfully: "Sincerely hope to see you on the other shore."

Some are handicapped, but undismayed. "I am nearly blind," one wrote, "—perhaps 25 percent vision with the inner corner of the left eye." But: "Gardening is my hobby. Plants are like children to me. I talk to them, praise and scold them." At the end of her letter one customer whom paralysis had compelled to be-

come an armchair gardener, added matter-of-factly: "Please ex-
cuse the many mistakes. I type with a stick in my mouth and
can't erase."

If age and adversity make few distinctions between gardeners, neither does place of residence. Burpee's sell millions of
packets to city gardeners, including apartment dwellers. Others,
contending with the subsoil grounds of housing developments,
sometimes write progress reports to Burpee's in the vein of one
woman who said: "The ground here was so hard I had to plant
the seeds by sticking an ice pick in the ground." Her reward, however, was a traffic-stopping garden of zinnias. Proving that admiration is where you find it, though, another city gardener reported
on her vegetable patch in this pithy summary: "All our neighbors
watched with amazement, and even the garbage collector remarked what beautiful big tomatoes."

Considering everything, perhaps the most curious aspect of a
seedsman's letters from customers is the poetry they write. No
one has tried to explain why seeds bring out the bard in people.
Children (usually little girls) have dashed off many such tributes
to Burpee's as this one:

> Burpee's seeds are the all of all,
> And the cost of them is very small.

The adult poets tend to be inspired by the catalog itself, or, as
one woman gardener shrewdly noted:

> Cultivation is sheer joy
> When from a chair it's done.

Another gardener, who should have qualified for some kind
of meritorious customer award, wrote Burpee's a long letter in
verse singing the praises of its catalog, merely as a request for the
current edition, which somehow had not been sent her:

Now look what I've thought with an old book from you—
Then think what I might do if I had a new '62!

One customer last year wrote so gentle a complaint in verse
(about some rhubarb roots he had received and considered stone-
cold dead) that three girls in the Philadelphia Customer Service
Department were each and every one inspired to respond in
poetry, in addition to new rhubarb roots. One answer per customer is considered par, and when the rhubarb man got three
(titled jointly, "Odes to a Sad Customer," from Margaret Huff-
nagle, Sarah M. Johnson, and Lois Stringer), he wound up all
over again and thanked them in another five stanzas. Without
pausing for breath, he then wrote them a whole new eulogy in
verse on "The Life of an Office Girl," leaving everyone feeling
fine and mellow.

For a kind of poetic succinctness in prose, however, Burpee's
staff cherishes a beautifully penned letter that came in one day
from a gentleman who was as direct with words as he was open-
handed with hospitality. He wrote:

Dear Mr. Burpee:
Am ordering some beans that I don't see in cat. But U will
know what to send and I leave it to you to send me your
selection. What time shall I plant these seed. Am in State of
Va., northern part.? When you come to Va. come to see me.
Cost U nothing. Thank you for advice.

# *19*  THE WINNERS

Simply by being in business a seedsman conducts a constant poll among the gardening public on the most and least popular flowers and vegetables grown from seed. Since Burpee's are the number one mail-order seed house, and overwhelmingly a home gardener supplier, their discoveries of American preferences carry a particular ring of authority. Here is what they find:

The most popular vegetable on the American table today is the tomato. Runner-up: beans.

The most popular annual flower in American gardens is the marigold. Runner-up: zinnia.

The least popular vegetable? Probably celeriac. And this is not because people necessarily dislike it, but because not many seem to know what to do with it. (Burpee's do their best. Their catalog description says: "It has a flavor similar to celery and is highly valued boiled or used in vegetable soup, stews, and other dishes. May be grated and eaten raw. Flesh is pure white.")

Strictly speaking, there is no "least popular" flower in the same sense as vegetables. Compared with marigold sales, nepeta, for example, is a dismal failure. But nepeta, or catamint, fills a specialized little role as a rock garden plant, and in that role it is a success. Celtuce, on the other hand, a general-type vegetable

greatly esteemed in its native China, has never made much of a
dent in the United States. Another only slightly favored vegetable is chicory, and among the herbs, caraway and sorrel have
small sales.

A reasonable question here, since Burpee's specialize—if that
is the word—in the things most gardeners want, is, Why do they
carry the unpopular items at all? They do so for two reasons: At
a big seed house even an unpopular item sells thousands of
packets; and in many cases the item is a delicacy, and Burpee's
don't want to send their gardening gourmet customers off to play
footsie with rival seed houses.

Another kind of unpopular vegetable is any variety that was
outdated years ago by others better in every way, but which
keeps a loyal core of die-hard friends. "This is the most difficult
type of offering to consider eliminating," Burpee's admit. "We
know we are not offering the best quality, but—" And at this
point all a seedsman can do is to shake his head. An example is
Dry Weather cauliflower. In the opinion of Theodore C. Torrey,
director of vegetable research at Fordhook Farms, this variety
keeps its following largely because of its name. There are better
cauliflowers, and some that tolerate dry weather better than Dry
Weather does. Another example of a vegetable too well named
for gardeners' good is Improved Long Green cucumber, Burpee
people say. There are much better cucumbers, but apparently
Improved Long Green sounds so good its devotees can't give it
up.

It might be added that there are certain vegetables of indifferent quality that keep on selling well to some gardeners because
they are at least dependable producers under tricky local growing conditions.

Here, in order of popularity according to the money home
gardeners spend for seeds, are the dozen top flowers and vegetables from seed in American gardens today:

| Annual Flowers | *Perennial Flowers | Vegetables |
|---|---|---|
| 1. Marigold | 1. Gloriosa daisies | 1. Tomato |
| 2. Zinnia | 2. Delphinium | 2. Beans |
| 3. Petunia | 3. Carnation | 3. Corn |
| 4. Aster | 4. Sweet William | 4. Cucumber |
| 5. Snapdragon | 5. Columbine | 5. Peas |
| 6. Sweet Pea | 6. Poppies | 6. Lettuce |
| 7. Alyssum | 7. Hollyhock | 7. Cantaloupe |
| 8. Pansy | 8. Day lilies | 8. Radish |
| 9. Delphinium | 9. Foxglove | 9. Beet |
| 10. Salvia | 10. Dianthus | 10. Carrot |
| 11. Portulaca | 11. Violas | 11. Squash |
| 12. Dahlia | 12. Lupine | 12. Cabbage |

A generation ago sweet peas led the list of popular annuals. Burpee's were virtually the U.S. headquarters as suppliers of sweet pea seed, endeavoring to carry every useful variety known to man, and even shipping seed to England, a country that considers the sweet pea as British as Yorkshire pudding. England, in fact, is still one of Burpee's biggest customers for sweet pea seed. During the 1930s, however, it looked for a while as if sweet peas were doomed as an American flower. A root disease threatened to wipe them out, and it was in an effort to find a replacement that David Burpee pinned his hopes on the marigold as most likely to win. Since then, thanks to the breeding of varieties resistant to the root disease, sweet peas have made a strong comeback—as their respectable sixth place in the table shows.

A popular vegetable is popular, as nobody will deny, because it is good to eat. In the same way, a popular flower gets that way

*Some of these perennials are listed as annuals by Burpee's because they bloom the first season if seeded early. And there are also annual varieties of some in this list.

because it is pretty to look at. And it must also, like the popular vegetable, be easy to grow. Marigolds, Burpee's darlings, are so easy to grow that a farm wife in Missouri got a vigorous yardful of them a few years ago merely by throwing a discarded bouquet out the kitchen window. While this wouldn't have very satisfactory results with an F$_1$ hybrid, such as the big Climax marigold, it does suggest how eager marigolds are to show what they can do.

For home gardeners seeking willing growers, the All-America Selections offer some annual guidance. There are five "All-America" organizations which test new varieties of plants each year in locations spotted so as to show plant performance under various climatic conditions. The five organizations are All-America Camellia Selections, All-America Gladiolus Selections, All-America Mum Selections, All-America Rose Selections, and All-American Selections. Burpee's and their fellow seedsmen are concerned almost entirely with the last-named, which tries out new vegetables in twenty-three of the regular trial grounds set up by the seed industry, and new flowers in twenty-five. It lists as sponsors the American Seed Trade Association, Southern Seedsmen's Association, Pacific Seedsmen's Association, and Western Seedsmen's Association, embracing what it calls the garden seed industry of the United States and Canada. The activity is financed for the most part through contributions from within the trade. The machinery of selection is this:

A seedsman who develops a new variety of something may enter it for testing by paying a small fee and furnishing sufficient seed to plant a row in each of the trial grounds. (So may a private plant breeder, or one working for a public agency in the field.) The one entering his variety for trial must also agree to offer, if it should be a winner, at least half his market seed—setting his own price for it—to other seedsmen for selling to their customers, but he is also assured against their growing their own market seed for three years. His candidate is then grown on the appointed trial grounds and appraised by the judges in residence by comparing the newcomer with standard varieties.

The trouble with this system, some seedsmen say, is that the judges of a man's entry are also, frequently, his competitors. They feel this is something like a boxer being matched with the referee. All is not always sweetness and light among all the other All-America Selections groups either, judging from occasional *sub rosa* rumblings. This, however, is an in-the-club kind of dissension and seldom attracts any public attention.

In Burpee's case, perhaps partly because they are big enough to toot their own horn loudly, they sometimes decide against entering for All-America trials an especially good new thing they have brought along. This, of course, reserves to them the exclusive sale of it for at least the introductory year. Now and then they have been less than pleased by what they considered short-sightedness by the All-America Selections, such as the rejection a few years ago of Yellow Climax marigold—the first hybrid African marigold ever offered—that Burpee's considered better than another of theirs chosen an All-America winner later. Consequently, they would hardly subscribe to the All-America Selections' flat statement that their choices are "the results of the only authentic pre-introductory testing and comparative rating of new flower and vegetable seed varieties for North America."

Among the Burpee-bred flowers that have been All-America selections are the marigolds Glitters, Crown of Gold, and Toreador; Silver Medal petunia; Glamour phlox; Vanguard snapdragon; Gloriosa double daisy; and the zinnias Blaze and Red Man.

Burpee vegetables have won fewer All-America awards than their flowers, very possibly because they have neither entered as many vegetables in the judging nor ever entered what they considered their best things—their hybrid vegetables. Altogether, eight Burpee vegetables have received All-America awards.

Among them are the Tender Pod bean, Early Pimento pepper, Fordhook Zucchini squash, and Jubilee tomato.

David Burpee as an individual was honored by the All-America Selections a few years ago when he was chosen to receive its Achievement in Horticulture award. It was given him in recognition of his direction of plant breeding work by his firm and for his effective promotion of new varieties.

Burpee's own trials, as mentioned in some previous chapters, are very extensive and were going on for a good many years before the All-America Selections were even dreamed up. Each row of a plant under test in their trial grounds has its own record sheet each year in a book for that year. At Floradale Farms, for example, these books occupy more than a hundred feet of shelf space in a back office known as the Observation and Research Room. In the books are recorded, among other things, what are called Specialty Comparison Trials, in which Burpee's get together all the varieties of a class of flower they can lay their hands on, and plant them at one fell swoop. This is a time-honored custom among reputable seedsmen. Thus, the 1936 book reveals that asters were being tested that year, and that 2550 packets of them from seed houses all over the world were obtained and the seeds planted. To see what was being done in other places on sweet peas, a similar test was run in 1932, the books show. Such testing as this permits a seedsman to see for himself how the varieties he is offering the public compare with the best from his competitors and from around the globe. In 1962 tests were run on thirteen classes of flowers at Floradale. These included asters, geraniums, marigolds, petunias, and sweet peas, and the total number of test rows was 2253. It was a light year, as the average number of tests is about three thousand.

It may be of interest here to note that each year Burpee's make up to eight hundred or more tomato trials, since this is one of the most important vegetables. Theodore C. Torrey has said: "We test all strains of commercial varieties we are offering to the public; new varieties, including hybrids, that have been released or are nearly ready for release by experiment stations and competitors; and our own breeding lines and experimental hybrids. . . . Each year, also, customers send us samples of their 'pet' tomatoes, and some years we may have nearly 50 such samples."

Among the appointments of Floradale's Observation and Research Room are a lot of old water glasses and a few dozen Coke bottles painted green. They serve as vases for continual testing of cut flowers. "Opening tests," for one, are conducted on buds to see which varieties sulk in water and which will open. "Keeping tests" are those in which cut flowers are timed to see whether their usefulness in bouquets can be mentioned in the catalog. Plain water is used for some of the flowers and others have commercial preparations added to the water—products said to lengthen the life of bouquets. Marigolds, the tests show, can take the stuff or let it alone, but some of the additives have a bracing effect on some other flowers—carnations, for instance.

In addition to these businesslike tests, Burpee employees are expected to do their bit too, by trying things out on their own. This is a pretty pleasant chore, everything considered. "I get scolded all the time," one man said cheerily, "for never taking enough flowers home." He didn't say who did most of the scolding—his boss or his wife.

# 20 PRETTY AS A PICTURE

Most businesses take publicity pictures of their products, but Burpee's are different. They have discovered over the years that a pretty girl admiring a mangel-wurzel seed lacks the oomph of a babe of any age caressing a big bouquet of flowers. Consequently, except for catalog shots of certain edible seeds such as lima beans, they deal in much the same kind of photographs the average home gardener-photographer does.

If you think this qualifies them to hand out some sound advice on the subject, you are right. They know a good deal about picture taking, including how to make a dunce of yourself at it. Take the case of the collapsing background. This took place at Burpee's Santa Paula Farms, where acres and acres of Red Man zinnias were being grown, so that a nice publicity shot of this big red zowie seemed in order. Instead of just sauntering out into the field and shooting away, however, the Burpee people doing the photographing wanted something that would show Red Man in a cozy homelike atmosphere. This called for setting up a glass-topped table outdoors, putting a vase of the zinnias on it, and then nailing together a background that would fool everybody into thinking it was a genuine inside house wall. So far, so good, and then somebody got the idea of putting a window in the wall. That did it. Just as everything was set and the photographer was about to trip his shutter, up came a howling breeze and over went the fake wall—on top of zinnias, glass table, cameraman, and all. Jeannette Lowe, who was plant breeding at Santa Paula at the time and who is also a kind of roving expert on flower photography for Burpee's, recalled later that her first remark to the dazed photographer as they hauled him out of the shattered-window wreckage was, "I certainly hope your camera's all right."

Another time, also at Santa Paula, she and farm manager Al Condit were preparing to photograph a bed of tulips. To pretty things up he built a section of brick wall as a background, and wouldn't you know—down it came on the innocent tulips like a brick wall.

Undaunted by disaster, Miss Lowe has drawn on her experience for the following suggestions on taking portraits of cut flowers:

Pick the flowers in late afternoon or early evening. Take a bucket of room-temperature water to the garden and plunge the cut stems into it. Use a sharp knife or scissors and cut stems cleanly and on a slant. Condition the flowers by keeping the stems in water several hours, preferably overnight, before arranging them. Bloom-Life or one of the other chemical preparations on the market will help keep the flowers fresh. Varieties that exude a milky juice should have the cut stem ends singed or plunged into hot water before conditioning. (Examples: poppies, poinsettias, Gloriosa daisies.)

The easiest way to take a picture of an arrangement is to set it outdoors on a table in the sunlight or in diffused light shade. Choose a wind-free spot; nothing is more aggravating than to have a sudden gust tip over the flowers just as the shutter clicks. Putting the camera on a tripod is best, and essential if you use a shutter speed of slower than $\frac{1}{25}$ of a second. Slow speeds are not advisable if there *is* any wind to jostle the flowers. To stop movement you need a $\frac{1}{100}$ of a second exposure or faster.

*Background:* For a background you can use a large sheet of cardboard in a color contrasting with the bouquet. A mid-blue or soft green is usually satisfactory, in a flat finish. A sheet or cloth or a blanket will often work well, too. Cloth with a strong texture may add a dramatic effect. You may wish to match the background to the picture in some way—such as using a Mexican serape for background if you are photographing a pottery container of zinnias or marigolds, flowers originally found by Europeans in Mexico. A picture that "speaks" in this way helps create a mood.

*Direction of light:* It is usually best to have the light coming over your shoulder onto the subject. However, slight side lighting is an interesting alternative and makes the flowers look somewhat rounder and fuller. If there are too-heavy shadows, you can lessen them with reflectors; just have someone hold a sheet of white cloth, a light-colored cardboard, or a newspaper out of view of the camera but at an angle reflecting light onto the dark places. Backlighting, in which the main source of light comes from behind the subject, can give a dramatic effect; the light should not shine directly into the camera lens, and a lens hood is the best way to avoid this. With backlighting you can often get a more delicate effect, some of the light coming through the translucent petals.

*Film:* The foregoing suggestions apply to either black-and-white or color film. The outdoor type of color film would be called for and it can also be used indoors if the walls are light-colored, if there is good daylight coming in through big windows, and if you use a tripod to hold the camera steady for longer exposures. Flash attachments or floodlights will also handle indoor lighting problems, and come with directions for use.

*Lenses:* These differ with every make of camera, and questions of choice for special effects are of chief interest to the professional or advanced amateur—who are usually familiar with special equipment available. The practical way for anyone else to get the thing most likely to be of interest here—a very close-up shot, because otherwise you may show so much background in certain cases that the flower itself becomes incidental—is to take the picture as near the subject as the indicator mark on the camera lens shows it can be taken, and then have an enlargement made of only the interesting portion. Do so by drawing guidelines on a smaller print, for the enlarger to follow. When taking the picture, use as small a lens opening as conditions permit; this will give you a sharper negative, and consequently a better enlargement. Owing to the higher cost of color-film enlargements, these suggestions are, for practical purposes, limited to black-and-white film.

*Posing the subject:* To make the flowers stay where you want them in the arrangement about to be photographed, stab the stems into a boxful of moist sand. It often helps to wire stems onto sharp-pointed sticks, like big skewers. If you want to bend the head of a zinnia or marigold at some particular angle, push a four-inch length of copper wire right down through its center and on down through the stem. The petals will hide the upper end of the wire, and when you bend the stems they won't break and they will hold the pose. Flowers look more interesting when facing in different directions instead of all staring into the camera. Make sure, of course, that none of the props show in the picture; you can control this by the camera placement or by adding some concealing greenery here and there.

It is a good idea to work fast when photographing cut flowers, especially the thinner-textured ones such as petunias, which may droop quickly under the conditions needed to take a good picture. Bring them onto the scene at the last minute, after everything else is in place.

The other sort of pictures a garden offers are those of the growing plants. Here, less manipulation is possible than with photographs of cut flowers, but there is a good deal more variety of subject.

For close-ups of specimen plants or blooms, most of the rules for photographing cut flowers apply except where they are not practical. Backgrounds, for example, must often be accepted as they are in nature. If you are working with a fast lens, however, you may be able to blur a poor background by using a wide lens opening; this throws the background out of focus, and also requires a shutter speed fast enough to keep the exposure right.

There is much variation in lens speeds and camera gear generally, but good garden pictures can also be taken with simple equipment. It has less latitude than the more expensive kind but is easier to use. In any case, the most basic rule in photography applies to all equipment equally. It is: Learn to use it well. From Burpee garden photographers come these additional pointers for better pictures of your living plants:

*Set the stage:* One thing to remember in garden photography is that the camera emphasizes defects more than your eyes do. Be sure, before taking a picture, that you have removed faded flowers or imperfect foliage. If there are bare spots in a border, you may want to hide them, for the sake of a picture, by filling in with some freshly picked flowers in a concealed container.

Be sure trash cans or other such eyesores are removed from the scene before you take the picture. Things that can't be moved, such as utility poles, can be handled by moving the camera to a spot where the pole is hidden by trees or is not in the camera's angle of view.

*Camera angle:* If there are any buildings in the picture, it is important to avoid tilting the camera upward, as this warps vertical lines and gives distracting, tipsy effects. With flowers alone this is not apparent, and shooting upward from a low angle at them can sometimes result in excellent pictures, especially when you want to use the sky as background, or are after some particular lighting that requires such a camera placement.

*Shadows:* Be careful, too, of shadows that fall in the wrong places. The eye accepts shadows as natural but in a photograph they may jump out and distract attention or even spoil the picture by blotting out an important part of it. Shadows in the right places add interest and a feeling of depth to a picture, but those that interfere with the scene should be eliminated or softened. Some ways to do this are: Choose a different time of day for taking the picture; take the picture from a different angle; if possible, move the thing casting the bad shadow; lighten the shadow area with a reflector.

In most cases shadows will be least useful in the middle of the day—say from 11 A.M. to 1 P.M. The sun is then too directly overhead for interesting patterns, though there are always exceptions.

*Exposure:* Correct exposure of film is vital for good work, and an exposure meter activated by a photoelectric cell is standard equipment for many photographers. While that is the surest guide to exposures—provided the meter is operating right, the photographer knows how to aim it and to translate its reading, and then how to apply it to the film he is using—still, there are a few alternatives which can work nicely. You will find an exposure chart packed with the film you buy, and it will give you a working idea of lens settings and shutter speeds to use under typical conditions. For insurance, you can then take three exposures—one at the recommended settings, one at half that speed, and one at twice the speed. This adaptation of the familiar laboratory control test will have the added advantage of giving you a measure of experience with the film more quickly. There is nothing more valuable to good photography than such experience. Once you are familiar with a make and type of film that give you the kind of pictures you want, it is a good idea to stay with it. Changing to a new film may be desirable later on, when you know what you want, but much sampling around before that time makes you master of none.

*Composition:* Good composition is one of the more neglected phases of most amateur photography. Perhaps those intimately familiar with the subject of a photograph find it interesting enough, no matter how hodge-podge the arrangement of things shown. Still, since there seems no reason not to do a thing well while you are at it, a few basic points might be made here, especially as they apply to garden photography:

1. Avoid clutter. Keep it out of your picture by concentrating on just a few elements (plants, flowers, beds . . .) at one time. The eye gets lost if there are things scattered all over the field of view.
2. Generally speaking, try to emphasize one dominant thing in the picture. Make it the star of the show, featuring it in the foreground, perhaps, or letting it loom up above others, or focusing directly on it.
3. Place this dominant element to left or right of the picture's center, and enough so that it doesn't look as if you may have tried to center it and did not quite succeed.
4. Don't cut a picture exactly in half with a horizon line.
5. Don't jam one side of the picture and starve the other. Spread the points of interest, and remember that a small area of intense color (or of darker shade, in black-and-white film), such as a zinnia the color of Red Man, can balance a much larger area of less intense color on the other side of the picture.
6. Framing the scene by including, say, a tree limb or foliage overhead, or a planting or tree trunk on one or both sides, can keep it from seeming to fly apart. This is especially true with pictures that lack a very dominant element. Taking a picture through a garden gate, an arbor, a natural arch, and so on, will do the same service.
7. A diagonal line is usually more interesting in a picture than a horizontal or vertical one. A curving line is usually more interesting than a straight one.

8. No rules are right all the time. All these have been successfully broken. The important thing is not that one should never break them, but that he should know when he is doing so, and knows why.

*To tell a story:* As a part of garden pictures, persons or animals add interest—too much, sometimes, if you want to concentrate on the garden—and are almost indispensable for the picture that tells a story, as the phrase goes. To tell a story, the person must be doing something, not just standing there. In this connection a Burpee customer offered an excellent suggestion for an annual program of story-telling pictures. "We keep the camera loaded with color film," she said, "and try to take a few pictures every couple of weeks or oftener. That way, we always have something new to send along in letters, and when we get ready to pick something for our Christmas card we have a wonderful selection and none of the last-minute rush and posing. One year we caught a good picture of our two boys starting their first garden. I recall another, of our daughter with a basketful of flowers she had just picked, as she came up the garden walk. I think the most popular of all was one of those spur-of-the-moment pictures; it showed the back of the station wagon full of bumper pumpkins, red apples, and creamy white chrysanthemums the children were helping load to take to the county fair. It looked like a Harvest Home, and made a wonderful Christmas card. Everybody loved it."

*Series pictures:* As a garden goes through the seasons, your camera can follow it by selecting the significant details. A little girl picking lilies says "Easter," a boy eating watermelon means summer. Children carving a jack-o'-lantern speak of fall, and bare branches silhouetted against the sky, a garden bird feeder sprinkled with cracked corn, tell it is wintertime.

Another sort of seasonal picture taking is a series taken to show the garden going through the four seasons. Such a series will pick up a surprising lot of added interest if you are careful to take each seasonal picture from the same spot. Mark it with a stake and point the camera in exactly the same direction each time.

A growth series is also a lively item for the family photo file and can be done with prints, slides, or with motion pictures. The first shots of the series might show a youngster planting popcorn. The second one could show him examining the young shoots, the third might show him cultivating the half-grown stalks, the fourth could be a harvest scene, and a fifth could be a party picture—popping the corn at the fireplace. One of the discoveries that picture-taking gardeners keep making about a camera, in fact, is that it gives their gardens the extra dimension of time-span. The growth of plants is gradual; it creeps up on you. It is a rare gardener who remembers just how things looked a year ago, five years ago. . . . The camera remembers: this bush was then a cutting, this tree a sprout. No pictures are more useful to a gardening education than those showing how your own good —and bad—plantings have changed things by their growth. A camera won't keep a gardener from making mistakes but it can keep him from making a lot of them over.

Among the services Burpee's offer gardeners is the loan of sets of 35-millimeter color slides for garden club programs, or for any other interested group. A request addressed to "Burpee" at whichever of the three addresses is nearest you—Philadelphia, Clinton, Iowa, or Riverside, California—will bring your choice of the following:

*The Story behind the Seed Packet*
There are two sets, A and B, each containing sixty slides. They show some of the steps in the development of new varieties of flowers and vegetables, and take viewers on a tour of the production fields. A script comes with each set, as with each of the other sets also.

*New Flower Varieties*
A set of fifteen slides.

*California Seed Production*
Flower fields and production methods, shown in thirty-four slides.

*How to Root Cuttings*
A set of six slides on rooting soft-wood slips (petunias, geraniums, etc.,) in vermiculite.

# 21 HAVE YOUR CAKE AND EAT IT TOO

The story is told of a faithful Burpee customer, part of whose annual flower order got mysteriously foofed one year, and in place of dwarf nasturtiums she received a packet of beet seed. After pondering this for a spell, the good lady decided to go along with the foolishness and plant the beets where she had intended to put the nasturtiums. Her reward for this open-mindedness was a lush and handsome red-and-green border, the surprise of her franker friends at her sudden brilliance, and fourteen meals of the best beets her family ever ate.

As it happens, the customer was not blazing a terribly new trail. Away back in 1889 W. Atlee Burpee listed three varieties of beets among his flower seeds and advised his customers: "The last year or two Ornamental Foliage Beets have sprung into popularity for decorative purposes, and have been used with striking effect, grown in pots, in some of the most extensive floral decorations in New York City. . . ."

The ornamental foliage beets made more of a thing of their leaves than do regular beets, but anybody who looks at any beet plant with unprejudiced eyes will see a beautiful pattern of growth and color. This is true of many vegetables, so many that there is a temptation to say non-beautiful vegetables don't exist. Just like the lady who got beet seed by mistake, a number of flower gardeners deliberately plant certain vegetables among their ornamentals. In almost every case they have two reasons for doing so: They can add distinctive texture, form, or color with the vegetable plantings; and they have discovered a culinary secret. The secret is that a mere handful of really garden-fresh vegetables is the essential ingredient for a good deal of connoisseur cooking.

Okra is an example of this. An attractive vegetable with hollyhock-like blooms, half-a-dozen plants in a flower border will produce the handful of fresh pods which when added to soup or stew give it an authority. And it takes only a cupful of okra for that best of uses for a stewing hen:

### Chicken Gumbo

Cut up and dredge with flour:

One stewing chicken.

Brown in:

4 tablespoons bacon drippings.

Then pour over it:

1 quart of boiling water.

Simmer until tender. Remove meat from bones and set aside.

Put into soup kettle and simmer until tender:

2 cups fresh, peeled tomatoes

1 cup sliced okra

½ cup chopped green onions

¼ cup rice

½ teaspoon salt

2 quarts water

Add chicken, season to taste with pepper and more salt if wished (plus 1 teaspoon filé powder for a Creole touch).

In the same way, it takes only a few freshly picked green beans —half a dozen of the attractive bushes or vines will ensure plenty —plus little bits of six or eight other ornamental vegetables, to add the touch to that rich and filling soup:

## Minestrone

Soak overnight:

> 2 cups dried beans (pinto, navy, or cranberry) in water to cover.

Next morning, simmer until beans are tender, adding *boiling* water if more water is needed. Set beans aside, put pot back on stove. Put in:

> 2 tablespoons olive oil
> 2 large onions, chopped
> 1 clove garlic, chopped

Cook slowly without browning, until tender. Add:

> 2 large fresh tomatoes, cut up
> 3 tablespoons parsley, chopped
> 1 teaspoon fresh sweet basil, chopped
> (Optional: 2 cups hamburger, or 1 cup chopped ham)

Cook 10 minutes (20 minutes if hamburger is added).
Add beans. Stir well. Add the following vegetables, minced:

> 5 green onions, including tops
> 1 cup cabbage, preferably savoy
> 1 dozen green beans
> 2 zucchini squash
> 1 carrot
> 1 large potato
> 1 handful fresh peas

Add water to cover vegetables (2 or 3 quarts). Simmer until vegetables are tender (about 2 hours).
Cook separately in salted boiling water until tender:

> 1 cup pasta (in small shell form or other attractive ones).

Drain and add to soup just before serving. Top bowls with grated cheese (Parmesan or something similar).

If asked to name at least one thing that could leave the vegetable garden and associate with flowers, most gardeners would probably name parsley. It is a popular choice among Burpee people for this purpose too. Harvest only the outside leaves and the plant will go on producing and looking good all season. Though often thought of as primarily a garnish, parsley is a valuable source of vitamins. Among the dishes where it forms an important ingredient along with small amounts of other fresh vegetables that double nicely as ornamentals too, is:

### Rice Pilaf

Put in a large skillet:

1 stick (½ cup) butter or margarine.

Heat till sizzling. Add:

2 cups uncooked long-grain rice.

Stir till rice is well coated with butter and lightly browned —about 5 minutes. Have ready a large hot casserole, heated in a 375-degree oven, also, bubbling hot:

4 cups of stock (chicken, beef, or fish).

Take casserole from oven, add rice, pour the hot stock over it. Place it in the 375-degree oven for 30 minutes. Then add the following, chopped, stirring well with a fork:

1 cup carrots

1 cup parsley

¾ cup green onions

1 cup nuts

Return to oven for another 30 minutes.

Served with French fried eggplant and a salad of tomatoes and cucumbers, this makes a satisfying and delicious vegetable meal, much of it from your edible-ornamental garden. Rice pilaf stores well, so you can make it ahead of time. Just be sure to stir it well with a fork before reheating.

Perhaps the all-around-easiest little vegetable to grow as a useful ornamental is the radish. A row edging a flower bed gives it a neat and thrifty look; the foliage forms a kind of rosette. Quickly grown radishes served fresh are a crisp delicacy it is impossible to buy. Burpee's Red Giant is a fine red variety and

Burpee White a fine white kind. Both stay delicious and buttery an unusually long time while growing, so that you can pick every other one in the row and keep the border looking attractive while using it.

For a filip of added garden interest, let a few radish plants stay all season and go to flower. Their blooms are plain little things—but watch the hummingbirds. They will neglect many a fancy flower to get at the unassuming radish blossoms.

For unusual and striking foliage, these vegetables are well worth considering, in addition to the beets already mentioned:

*Chard* is often used, both the regular white-stalked, and the rhubarb chard, which has crimson stalks and veining. Both have heavily crumpled, textured leaves.

*Kale* includes the Blue Curled Scotch, which grows 1 or 1½ feet tall, and has bluish green leaves as tightly curled as curly parsley; and Dwarf Siberian kale, about the same height as the other, has grayish-green leaves held like plumes. Kale will take freezing weather without harm, after some other plants in the flower bed are dead and gone. The color of its foliage is quite effective when grouped in the bed with tawny colors of chrysanthemums, whose season matches that of the kale's until hard freezes.

*Carrots* are often used as flower bed borders, for their luxuriant lacy foliage, and may be sown thickly for this purpose.

*Green Curled endive* forms a cushion of beautifully lacinated leaves, shading out darker from a light green center.

*Curled mustard greens* have a sprightly medium-green color, and grow about as tall as kale. Burpee's Fordhook Fancy has a darker green leaf curving backward like an ostrich plume.

*Rhubarb* makes a large handsome leaf—which is nonedible, only the stalk being used—and comes in both red and green stalks. It can be grown from seed or from roots.

*Asparagus* can also be grown from seed or from roots, and its ferny foliage makes a delicate tracery against a house wall.

*Scarlet Runner bean* has such showy red flowers borne in sprays that it is often planted just for its looks. It does its best in cool weather.

Anyone searching out things for raw finger foods on a low-calorie canapé tray can make particularly good use of an edible-ornamental garden. Radishes are obvious choices, as are carrots for carrot sticks—and carrots fresh from the garden are so tender and sweet they are like a different vegetable. Other vegetables of which only a few are needed per serving for this purpose are the miniature tomatoes, Red Cherry and Yellow Plum and Pear, cucumbers cut into sticks, broccoli buds, sweet pepper rings, beets cut in shoestring-potato strips, turnip slices and kohlrabi cut into wedges. French dressing makes a good dip, though it does increase the calorie count. Horse-radish is also good as a dip, and is an excellent appetite stimulant.

Those interested in Chinese cooking can make good use of the added piquancy some home-grown ornamental vegetables will give, especially since this school of taste calls for a minimum of cooking and a maximum of flavor and texture. Sugar or edible-podded peas, for example, are a frequent ingredient in Chinese dishes but are hard to find in markets. The Dwarf Gray is a good variety and of a convenient growth habit for flower beds, getting to only about two feet tall.

Chinese cabbage is also at home in decorative plantings, forming close-wrapped, vase-shaped heads, the leaves attractively ribbed. Savoy cabbage takes a little more space but is beautiful as a border planting and is also excellent for Chinese cooking. Flower arrangers sometimes use it for its beauty of leaf and color. (Red cabbage, while not especially associated with the Chinese cuisine, is also worth considering as an ornamental; the purplish-red heads are solid, and look right at home as border plantings.)

Two other members of the cabbage family handsome enough to look comfortable among the flowers are Brussels sprouts and broccoli. Both enjoy cool weather and can be harvested a bit at a time while continuing to look good. You pick the lowest sprouts of Brussels sprouts, others then continuing to form above them on the stalk, and after the main center heads of broccoli are harvested, side shoots grow strongly for repeated harvesting.

A Midwest gardener who grew a great many bulb flowers hit upon a way of hiding their foliage while it was yellow and unsightly after the blooming period. She named her system the "Will-Call Department," and it consisted of flats of eggplant and pepper plants, which she seeded well ahead of time. After her bulbs finished blooming she put the plants from the flats in the bulb beds, and they soon screened the tired, maturing bulb foliage. Both peppers and eggplants are handsome in bush and in fruit. Peppers are of neat and sturdy upright growth, with glossy green leaves, and the fruit of most turn red when allowed to stay on the plant until fully mature. An exception is the Oshkosh, which turns canary yellow; a hot pepper, Hungarian Wax, starts out yellow and changes to red. Peppers add vitamins as well as flavor and appearance to salads. Eggplants, too, produce fruits attractive enough to appear in decorative groups—and are effective in the garden setting. Plants grow about two feet tall and the foliage is a grayed green. The oval, deeply purple fruits have a natural high gloss. They may weigh several pounds apiece, and a big one will serve a family. Here is a good way to prepare it:

Cut eggplant into strips like large French fried potatoes. Dip the strips into beaten egg yolk, then into flour, then into slightly beaten egg white, and finally into fine bread crumbs. Fry in hot, deep fat until lightly browned.

Of all kitchen-garden possibilities for the flower beds, herbs usually seem the most likely. Parsley has been mentioned. Of the others, the only real limit to one's choice is that of preference. Not everyone cares about the flavor of dill, for instance, so that even its delicate, lovely foliage and dainty seeds may not persuade dill dislikers to plant it. Some of these, however, may be converted if they try the following pickle recipe. In addition to dill it requires green tomatoes—those still on the vine at the end of the season just before the first frost—and little tabasco peppers. These peppers are such pretty things that some gardeners plant a few bushes just for their looks, picking the fruits in the autumn and stringing them on cords as decorations, even though the peppers may be too hot for their taste as a seasoning. Here is the recipe:

### Dilly Green Tomatoes

Put into a Mason jar:

    1 sprig of dill

    1 tiny red tabasco pepper

    Small green tomatoes (with stems left on) to fill jar.

Pour in to cover:

    Boiling white vinegar, slightly salted.

Screw on lid and store. Zesty on a canapé tray, the tomatoes can also be added to some salads. A jar of them is so attractive it makes a nice small Christmas remembrance.

Some of the other herbs most apt to be useful are these:

*Sweet basil.* About two feet tall, this light green plant is so aromatic some gardeners try to place it where they are most apt to be working, so they can smell its fragrance. Fresh or dry, the leaves are good in tomato dishes; it combines well with many beans, and with omelets. A new bronze-leaved variety called Dark Opal grows only fifteen inches high.

*Rosemary.* A half-hardy perennial, it has leaves that look like spruce needles, and little blue flowers that attract bees as well as basil does. Rosemary is good in a marinade for lamb —and if you are charcoal-broiling the meat, drop some sprigs of rosemary on the glowing coals for an appetizing aroma.

*Sage.* Even though you don't need much of this pungent herb to flavor poultry stuffing, sauces, or stews, the plant is a pretty perennial with neat gray-green leaves and violet-colored flowers that hummingbirds love. It grows one to two feet tall and makes a good foundation planting; effective as a backdrop for French marigolds.

*Thyme.* This low-growing perennial herb, good with beef stews and with some sauces, is sometimes used to edge stepping-stones for the sake of the fragrance released when a little of the foliage is trod on. Thyme bears small lavender flowers, and like many herbs, a few rooted pieces can be potted in the fall and grown indoors during the winter.

*Chives.* Also one of the most popular herbs for growing in pots indoors, chives are perennials and make a tidy border planting along flower beds. They can be grown from seed and are useful in the kitchen for their very mild onion flavor —so delicate that they are usually used raw, chopped over cottage cheese and many other dishes as a tasty garnish.

*Summer savory* and *sweet marjoram.* These are two useful annual herbs, good either fresh or dried. Try a few leaves of either in a salad, and with meat and bean dishes. Neither plant is such a lusty grower as sage.

*Borage.* An annual that grows about 1½ feet high, borage is highly popular with bees and so helps to increase the pollination of other plants growing near it. The little borage flowers are an unusually fine blue, and so dainty they are sometimes floated in a pitcher of lemonade, or used for cake decorations—dipped in beaten egg white and then in granulated sugar. Young borage leaves can be added to salads for their slight cucumber taste, and can also be cooked like spinach, combining well with other greens—chard, mustard, tampala, and so on. Borage makes a strong bushy growth, and an effective grouping can be made by using it in a bed as the middle planting, with tall double nasturtiums in back, and in front, Bibb lettuce, its little heads forming prim green rosettes.

Burpee's no longer offer globe artichokes; they are grown commercially largely along a coastal section of northern California, which seems ideal for them. However, they have been grown elsewhere in the United States, and are one of those vegetables almost worth planting for the sake of their appearance. The large, thistlelike leaves, light grayish-green, are an ornament in any garden; they are effective in bouquets, and the artichoke fruits are beautiful in themselves—so much so that they are favorites of professional flower arrangers and still-life artists, and are reproduced in ceramic form.

One word of caution should be added for gardeners planting among their flowers some of the attractive vegetables such as those mentioned in this chapter. You must use extra care in your choice of insecticides and in the spray schedule. Read the label on the insecticide for specific information as to the safe interval from spraying to picking for the table. Some insecticides are not toxic to humans. Organic gardeners who eschew the use of poisonous sprays have an advantage here, obviously.

As a final word, it can be said once again that every vegetable is a beauty in its own right when looked at without prejudice. A few years ago a doctor living in a St. Louis suburb surveyed the yard of his home, almost monopolized by ornamental shrubs and the children's jungle gym, and decided to beautify in his own way a tiny overlooked oblong behind the garage. The plot measured 10 feet by 12, and being a Midwesterner, he made up his mind to raise himself some beautiful sweet corn.

Despite the advice of experts that this was an uneconomic use of his squib of ground, he sowed a high-yielding hybrid in sardine-like closeness, gave it plenty of fertilizer and water, and reaped a bountiful harvest of ears. Since his field was about $\frac{1}{366}$ of an acre, with a little arithmetic he was able to speak with authority on his per-acre production. One hundred bushels is considered an excellent return, but his came to, he estimated, a dizzy 920, and everyone who saw his corn patch thought it as good looking as any flower in the neighborhood.

# 22 BE YOUR OWN PLANT BREEDER

A high school botany student one summer shook pollen from a corn tassel over some miniature Red Cherry tomato blossoms in his family's garden, intending to amaze the old folks with tomatoes you could eat off the cob. The tomatoes paid no attention, but the lad had a good idea even if his science was bad. Corn and tomatoes won't cross, being of different plant families, but by crossing, or hybridizing, man has produced some of the best vegetables—and flowers—we know.

Though professional plant breeding is a job for professionals, there is no reason you can't dabble in a little amateur plant breeding. At worst, you'll have something new to talk about, and at best, you may do millions of your fellow men a lasting good deed by helping to give the world a useful new plant—and that is a thing worth doing.

You don't have to have a headful of science to experiment a bit. You may want to learn more later on, for your own satisfaction, but with what you can learn here in a few minutes, you can go out in the garden and actually breed a new tomato, say, or possibly some time discover a new one nature has made but which would be lost without someone to notice it.

We will deal here with five techniques of getting new plants:

1. Selection
2. Mutations
3. Hybrids
4. Polyploids
5. Seedlings

## 1. *Selection*

This is both a technique and a fundamental procedure in all other techniques. As a fundamental procedure it is, simply and obviously, the constant exercise of judgment in weeding out less desirable plants in favor of those nearer your breeding objective. As a separate breeding technique, selection can be used in this way by the home gardener:

Although a bed of plants of the same variety may seem at a glance to be exactly alike, they are not. This, in fact, was one of the discoveries Charles Darwin made in the course of careful observations of plant behavior. Usually the differences between plants of the same variety are so minor that you cannot notice them. Sometimes, though, a small difference may show up and it may happen that it is a useful difference, such as a slightly better habit of growth. If so, mark the plant, save some of its seeds, and plant them the next season to see if the good character persists. In time you may establish a good new strain in this way.

If the plant is a modern hybrid, its seeds will not breed true. However, you can plant them anyway, just to see what happens. In the assortment of plants that will result, you may find some you like, and then by reselecting for several generations you can get them to breed true. Though they will not be as good as the original hybrid, you may like them quite well.

If you want to take more pains and keep a new strain of plants purer, you can isolate the plant you select by dropping a screen-wire or cheesecloth cage over it to keep insects from cross-pollinating it with the other plants. Then, so that it will set seed, you may have to self-pollinate it by hand, as described under "Hybrids," further on. Some plants will "self," as breeders say, without help. A few examples of these are: sweet peas, larkspur, asters, beans, peas, tomatoes.

Some examples of plants which will *not* self-pollinate, and which depend entirely on insects or wind, mainly (or, in this case, on you), are these: cosmos, cucumber, squash.

The other, non-caging, method, while less exact in some cases, is an old way of plant improvement that has many successes to its credit.

### 2. *Mutations*

This is a further use of the method just discussed—selection. The difference is that what usually is called a mutation is a more striking change. You will probably notice it more easily, and it is pretty apt to be persistent in future generations.

Mutations are mysterious things. All of a sudden one plant out of thousands will bear its fruit earlier, perhaps, or be a bush instead of a vine, or differ in some other important respect. This comes about through some change in the make-up of the genes, the minute bodies that transmit inherited characters. We know some of the things that induce these changes, and plant breeders use some of them in laboratory work to increase mutation rates —exposing seeds to X rays is one—but just why or how such things work is but dimly understood.

We do know that most mutations are not only harmful to the plant but also useless to man, so you are not very likely to find anything worth while in this way. On the average, it takes about a million plants in any one generation to produce among them a single good mutation. However, that single one may be intensely good—a new and lovely color in a flower, a better-flavored vegetable or one better shaped. Therefore it is well worth while to know that mutations do occur, and to keep an eye out for them. Few things equal the thrill of discovery when a thing is worth discovering. If you do find such a mutation, save some of the seeds for trial the following season. A seed house such as Burpee's would quite possibly be interested in testing the seeds. Burpee Bibb lettuce, an improved Bibb variety, was discovered by a home gardener. So was the petunia Salmon Supreme.

Among the possible mutations Burpee's would be overjoyed for some eagle-eyed home gardeners to find and pounce upon are: a Kentucky Wonder green bean with nice straight pods. Also, one that grows in a bush form like Tender Pod and has straight pods, but still tastes like Kentucky Wonder. Another prize would be a mutant of a good heading lettuce such as Big Boston that, instead of bolting (forming a seed head) like the others in the bed when the weather turns warm, remains in usable condition. The lettuce Great Lakes is, in fact, such a selection, and owes its popularity to this heat-tolerance. A vegetable that ripens ahead of its fellows is a possible mutation and worth your close attention. A dividend of early maturity is that bugs, disease, and bad weather get less chance at the harvest. In the same way, quick germination is good. Keep an eye on the plant that gets a head start on its brother and sister plants. If its seeds breed true to this characteristic, you will have discovered an advantage.

Watch also for a plant that resists troubles better than those of its same variety. This is a valuable thing. At their Floradale Farms Burpee's have for years been planting asters over and over in the same ground, though this is against the rules of aster culture, just so they can select the ones that live through the wilt that asters are subject to. Yet, you may find in your garden such a resistant aster at a single swoop as the result of a mutation. Not likely? No, but not impossible.

### 3. *Hybrids*

Most hybrids are plants whose parents are of different varieties. Sometimes the parents are of different species, which is a bigger difference. A modern hybrid is the offspring of a controlled cross (short for cross-pollination) between two highly purified (by inbreeding) parents. The cross is made anew each year to get the hybrid seeds, since planting the seeds the hybrid plants produce would not get you the same hybrids ($F_1$'s or first-generation) the next year.

Years ago, plant breeders used to call any mixture a hybrid, which was technically correct but became confusing when modern plant breeding provided a control over the process. These hybrids of the old plant breeders resulted from crosses made by bees, for instance, as they incidentally dusted pollen from Variety X onto Variety Y as they flew from flower to flower. The seeds that Variety Y then matured grew a hybrid; Variety X was its pollen parent (father) and Variety Y its seed parent (mother). This YX hybrid was really a new variety, and the first generation of that variety. It had hybrid vigor, the usual result of a cross, and it might be a lot better than its parents. If bees go from one variety of a flower or vegetable to another in your garden, you may be able to save some of the seeds, plant them, and grow such hybrids yourself. Note the "may be able to"; there are all sorts of exceptions, and you may bump into such things as incompatible varieties that won't cross. If you would rather read up on the subject more deeply before doing any experimenting, see the list of books at the end of this chapter; they are the ones recommended by Burpee scientists as authoritative without being overly technical.

If you do get some hybrid seeds, and they grow hybrid plants, you can then try another experiment, the same procedure that was once standard plant breeding practice. Save the seeds your hybrid plants produce, and sow them the next season. If they grow (some hybrids are sterile and have no offspring), they will produce the second (or $F_2$, meaning second filial) generation. The first was the $F_1$. This $F_2$ generation should be an interesting mixture, not all alike the way the $F_1$ plants were if the parents were pure varieties, but with various new traits in certain plants.

This is caused by the recessive genes being uncovered in these plants. These genes now get their chance, because in the heredity shake-up that the original cross started, some dominant genes are missing in some of the second-generation offspring. The interesting thing is that a character caused by a recessive gene will breed true to begin with, and will then keep on appearing in successive generations if the line is kept pure. Consequently, if among this $F_2$ generation there are some plants with especially good traits, plant their seeds the next season. You may have to keep on selecting for two or more generations to purify the wanted trait.

A question may occur to you at this point: But if the bees cross-pollinate these plants with others, will the seeds still grow the same kind of plant? Well, you may get some mixing if there are other nearby varieties that will cross easily with the one you want to purify. It depends on what you are working with. Breeders often isolate a planting perhaps half a mile away from others that could cross with it. This is impractical for home gardeners, but as an alternative you can cage some of the desired plants as described in "Selection," to keep insects out. If necessary, you can then pollinate by hand, using pollen from a flower on the same plant or from a same-generation one having the traits you want to continue. You get a smaller quantity of seeds but can save the bother of caging by simply hand-pollinating a few flowers and tagging them. A properly pollinated flower will not be contaminated by other pollen afterwards, so you would be safe there. To be extra sure, you can tie a little wax-paper bag over a bud until it opens, then hand-pollinate, and then replace the bag until the flower fades. If it then sets seed, your choice of pollen was the one responsible.

How do you get the pollen to do this job? The easiest way is to shake it from one flower onto another, making sure some of it lands on the tip of the seed-parent flower's pistil. The pistil is the female organ, and often looks something like a slender-necked vase in the center of the flower. Its tip end, called the stigma, is sticky so that pollen will cling to it. The stamens, a flower's male organs, are a group of little stems arranged around the pistil. Their tip ends, bearing the pollen, are called anthers. When a grain of pollen, by growing down the neck (known as the style) of the pistil, fertilizes an egg waiting at the bottom in the ovary, a seed begins to grow.

Before you start any hand-pollinating, get acquainted with the flower you're working with by pulling the petals off a sample bloom and examining its seed-forming parts under a magnifying glass. We have been talking just now about pollinations using the plant's own pollen, or at least where its own pollen will not throw the experiment out. If, however, you make a pollination in which none of the flower's own pollen must be used (that is, a cross-pollination), you must start by emasculating this seed-parent flower. Take a pair of tweezers and gently pull out each of its stamens. Remove the petals first, to make it easier, and do the job when the flower is young and its pollen not yet matured. It will be ready for pollinating at about the time other flowers at the same stage on the plant are maturing their pollen, so that a little of it dusts off on your fingertip if you touch the stamens. Incidentally, removing the petals will not harm the flower's ability to make seed; surprising as it sometimes seems, a flower's petals are some of its least important parts—to nature, that is— and are merely there to entice insects and get on with the task of continuing the species.

It may happen that you want to cross two plants, but find that one is finishing blooming before the other has started. Try this: Tap some pollen from the early bloomer into a clean, dry plastic pill bottle after drying the pollen out for about twenty-four hours at about 90 degrees, say under an electric light. Then cap the bottle well, and store it in your food freezer until the late bloomer blooms. Pollen is a living substance, as lovely under the microscope as snowflakes, though it looks like yellow dust, and some of it can survive for weeks in a freezer. This is a chancy experiment but particularly interesting, introducing a new element of time into breeding.

Some plants, such as squash, have separate male and female flowers, which makes it easier to hybridize them because if you pull off all the male flowers on a squash plant, its female flowers (the ones with a little "squash," or swelling, at the base) will be fertilized by pollen that bees carry from a neighboring squash plant, and this can be the variety you want to cross with the other. The fruit formed will look and taste the same as usual, but the seeds will grow $F_1$ hybrids—and the fruit from them will be different in some ways. If you like your hybrid squashes you can repeat the original cross and get the same result. Or try using the seed parent as the pollen parent next time. Or grow an $F_2$ generation from seeds of the $F_1$, and so on.

To keep track of any hybridizing you do, make a record something like this on a file card:

Class:   tomato, for instance
Cross:   name of seed parent x pollen parent
Objective:   to get a dwarfer plant, for instance
Date:   that cross was made

Number of seeds obtained:——. Date:————.

Date seeds were planted:——
Results:

If you keep this record simple it will be easier to keep it up to date, and it will give more point and direction to an unusual and useful hobby.

Incidentally, peas and beans are self-pollinating, as mentioned, and while they can be crossed, it is delicate and tedious work. Marigolds and zinnias are composite flowers, made up of hundreds of tiny, separate flowers, called florets, clustered together, so are not the easiest things to hand-pollinate and keep track of afterwards, either. A more satisfactory flower to learn on is a single one with pistil and stamens clearly seen, such as a petunia, hollyhock, or such vegetable blossoms as tomato.

### 4. *Polyploids*

As mentioned before, minute bodies called genes are the things that pass along from one generation to the next the traits or characters that identify a species of plants (or animals, insects, etc.). These genes come in groups called chromosomes, as though genes were hundreds of tiny pills and chromosomes were bottles that held them. Polyploidy is a method of breeding new kinds of plants by increasing the number of chromosome sets from a normal two sets per cell to three or more.

This is commonly done by applying a chemical—usually colchicine today, an extract of the autumn crocus—to young plants. Frankly, this is not recommended for the home-garden experimenter. Colchicine is a poison, and it also causes some persons to break out in a skin rash. The only reason for mentioning polyploidy here at all is to help round out the picture, and to alert you to some possible accidental polyploid plants you may happen on in the future. "Accidental" because plants have sometimes been shocked into becoming polyploids by such things as a concentrated dose of nicotine sulfate, the contact bug killer; by a chance spraying with the herbicide 2, 4-D in a weak solution; by sudden extreme cold or heat; by fumes of naphthalene, the moth repellent; and by simple mutilation such as a blow from a stick. In the latter case, the callused tissues may form polyploid cells, and at one period of experimentation, breeders deliberately damaged plants in order to discover the effects on them.

A plant that becomes polyploid from one of such causes and manages to keep on growing, will be changed some way, often deformed. It may be dwarfed, or bent, or start growing out from one side instead of from the tip end. It may develop strange swellings, or its buds may never open. If, however, it lives on and produces some seeds, plant them to continue the experiment. The second generation will perhaps be just a curiosity, but if a polyploid plant is going anywhere, this will begin showing up in about the third generation. If so, you may have something unique and perhaps valuable.

## 5. *Seedlings*

Certain plants are seldom grown from seed, usually either because they do not ordinarily produce much or any seed or because they do not come true to variety from their seed. Sometimes both reasons apply, as with Irish potatoes. If you plant a row of potatoes, perhaps one plant may bloom and mature some seeds. If you then plant these seeds and they grow, you will probably produce as peculiar looking a collection of potatoes as you ever saw, most of them runty and ill-shaped. Yet this was what Luther Burbank did to get the famous Burbank potato—for not every seedling potato is a failure. So if you have a taste for long shots, watch for seed balls on your potato plants (they look like tiny green tomatoes), protect them from birds by tying a little paper bag over the balls, let them ripen, and plant them the next spring.

Among other things that are vegetatively propagated—meaning by using tubers or cuttings, for instance, instead of seeds—are fruit trees. Nevertheless, you can plant a peach seed, say, and get a tree that will bear fruit. It will not be the same variety of peach, but it will probably be good to eat, if a little slow to bear, and there is something especially interesting about bringing a tree along from a seed to a harvest. Remember, too, that if it didn't work, nobody would ever have heard of Johnny Appleseed, who was no myth, but a real man whose real name was John Chapman.

Another seedling experiment can be made with roses. The ripe hips contain several seeds. Before planting, they should be chilled in the refrigerator for a few weeks. Then you can plant them in the fall, to germinate the next spring. Seed from uncrossed roses such as the multiflora used as a living fence will come true, but those from grafted or hybrid plants will not.

Here follow some references if you want to learn more about plant breeding. Also, see such other chapters in this book as "The Search," "Why Hybrids?" "Polyploiding and Such," and "What You'll be Planting X Years from Now."

*Encyclopaedia Britannica.* See the articles on Botany, Heredity, Horticulture, Hybridism, Mendelism, Plants, and Variation and Selection.

*Yearbook of Agriculture, 1937, Better Plants and Animals II,* and *Yearbook of Agriculture, 1961, Seeds,* United States Department of Agriculture, Government Printing Office, Washington 25, D.C.

*Plant Breeding and Cytogenetics,* Fred C. Elliott, 1958, McGraw-Hill Book Co., Inc., New York.

*Methods of Plant Breeding,* Hayes, Immer, and Smith, 1955, McGraw-Hill Book Co., Inc., New York.

*Genetics of Garden Plants,* M. B. Crane and W. J. C. Lawrence, 1938, The Macmillan Co., London.

*Principles of Plant Breeding,* R. W. Allard, 1960, John Wiley & Sons, Inc., New York.

*Practical Plant Breeding,* W. J. C. Lawrence, 1951, Allen and Unwin, London.

*Elements of Genetics,* C. D. Darlington and K. Mather, 1949, The Macmillan Co., New York.

*Botany for Gardeners,* H. W. Rickett, 1957, The Macmillan Co., New York.

*Textbook of General Botany,* R. M. Holman and W. W. Robbins, 1938, John Wiley & Sons, Inc., New York.

*Introductory Botany,* Arthur Cronquist, 1961, Harper & Brothers, New York.

# 23 HELP!

Toward his blunders and fumbles David Burpee has the frank confessional ease of a man who has been successful enough to afford to be a boob now and then. Not that the mistakes have always been his personally, but this seems to make no difference to him, since his company's personality is an extension of his. Thus he tells freely and happily of such boners as the case of the Ugly Duckling sweet pea.

The sweet pea's name, almost prophetically, was Blue Swan. It is a cool ice-blue in tone and you can find it in the Burpee catalog, featured as one of the Galaxy group of many-flowered giant sweet peas. Blue Swan, in fact, is the only one illustrated, having waltzed off with a 1962 award of merit from the National Sweet Pea Society of Great Britain. Now, you might think a sweet pea that good would have been the pet of its originator right from the start. The humiliating truth is nobody at Burpee's cared much about it.

They cared so little about it that the field where it was growing, at Floradale Farms, was being neglected. Weeds were thick in it, and of course nobody was bothering to rogue out the off-type sweet peas springing up here and there in the rows. And then in from England came the news that Blue Swan had just triumphed.

"By then the block was all mixed up," Walter Manfrina, manager of Floradale, recalled later, meaning that various other colors of sweet peas were growing among the Blue Swans. Worse yet, it was toward the end of the season, making it hard to be sure which color was which any more. The sharpest-eyed staff men were instantly set to sorting through the thousands of faded blossoms, pitching out the ones that didn't look enough like Blue Swan to take a chance on, and so at length the day was saved.

Peculiarly enough, the same thing had happened to Burpee's once before. Again it was a sweet pea, and again nobody thought it worth bothering with—and then to complete the coincidence, along came a cablegram from England gaily announcing it had won an award. But this time, alack, the field had already been plowed up, and all seemed lost. With the vim of despair, everybody set to pawing the disked earth like a pack of terriers, and fate relented; they found a few pods of the prize winner still intact, enough to put them in business again. The same lucky-unlucky timing had happened one time when a misguided worker had accidentally chopped up a stock-seed block of cauliflower. If it hadn't been that the cauliflower was at the mature stage and had set seed, so that some was found in time to save it, that particular variety would have disappeared forever.

Now and then a bit of pure Burpee luck has come along in the nick of time to save the seedsman from himself. Two instances come to mind, one concerning a sweet pea (Burpee's do seem to be constantly getting in hot water over sweet peas), and the other a snap bean.

The sweet pea was one called Fluffy Ruffles. As the name suggests, it had ruffled petals—a characteristic Burpee's dearly wanted in a sweet pea variety—and it had come to them like manna, a mutation in the fields, after they had striven fruitlessly for the same thing in other ways, never being able to get and keep it. Fluffy Ruffles was the same color as Ringdove, the variety of which it was a mutation, and this color sameness was nearly its undoing. Just by chance, an enthusiastic woman gardener-visitor came skipping into Floradale Farms to admire the sweet peas toward the end of the season, and she started carrying on over Fluffy Ruffles. Burpee, who was squiring her around, consulted the "finder," the book identifying all the trial-row plants, to tell her the name of the beauty. To his mystification he found it was marked for extinction, with the notation, "Same color as Ringdove," and not one word about the beautiful, exclusive ruffling. Every last one of the experts, too close to the fields to see the flowers, had completely overlooked the important difference in the rush of the end-of-season business. Thanks to the alert visitor, Fluffy Ruffles was snatched back to safety and survived to become the ancestor of all Burpee's Giant Ruffled sweet peas.

The luck of the snap bean again involved the public in an eagle-eyed role. The bean was Burpee's Tender Pod, introduced in 1941 and an All-America bronze medal winner. "Most tender and best flavored of all green snap beans," Burpee's called it, and they still consider it unbeatable. But, at first, it had one tiny little flaw, they thought—a little tail; they could see no earthly use for a tail on a bean, and they rolled up their sleeves to breed it off. But before they could do so, and to their astonishment, they discovered that people actually *liked* the tail on Tender Pod. It was, said the public, a positive mark of identification. When you saw the tail, you *knew*. Needless to say, the trimming was called off, and Tender Pod still sports its little tail to this day.

Such cliff-hanger episodes might make some men superstitious but not Burpee. He is so unsuperstitious that a few years ago when he was in Europe and was having trouble lining up an early return flight, he was perfectly agreeable to the airline's suggestion he go on a Friday the thirteenth—a day they always had trouble booking. "As a matter of fact," he said later, "it turned out there were exactly thirteen of us on the plane, too, and it was one of the most delightful flights I've ever made."

Once in a while Burpee's get in Dutch by accidentally short-changing a customer on the seed count. The accident is always a mechanical one, since packet-filling is done by machinery. This is true even of high-priced seed with only a few in the packet, such as hybrid tomatoes; they are picked up by a vacuum plate, one seed clinging by suction to each of several holes in the plate. But though almost foolproof, this system is not perfect, and some of the customers ponying up 50 or 75 cents for 30 little seeds sit right down and count them to make sure there really are 30 seeds there. One such skeptic caught Burpee's vacuum plate trying to fob off a mere 18 seeds on him, and he fired the light packet right back to Philadelphia so the seed people could see for themselves. They sent him a replacement, but just out of curiosity, a girl in the office planted the 18 seeds in a window box. Nobody expects every seed in a packet to sprout, not even the government watch dogs of seed germination percentages, but these 18 seeds grew 18 fine little plants. The girl experimenter, emotionally unable to dump them at this point, bore all 18 tenderly across town to her mother, who had a garden, and that summer had so many tomatoes she could hardly stand to look at one by September.

Another time, Burpee's made a mistake in order-filling that chilled them to the marrow. For some unfathomable reason they sent a customer an enormous eight ounces of hybrid Big Boy tomato seeds, a heap worth about $175 wholesale. The customer had ordered only a couple of dollars' worth of assorted seeds. He turned out to be a sterling character, who promptly returned the great package of Big Boy seeds, mildly remarking that there must have been a slip-up somewhere or other. Breathing hard, Burpee's thanked him from the bottoms of their hearts and showered him with some free marigold seed.

To the seedsman, the unkindest mistake of all occurs when some plant he has lavished loving care on doesn't behave itself when it appears in public. This happened one time with a red marigold that looked so good to David Burpee he decided to honor it with a name he particularly admired—Firestone. Accordingly, he got in touch with Harvey S. Firestone, Jr., to ask permission to use the family name. The industrialist was glad to consent, and suggested that Burpee might wish to personalize the thing a bit more by calling the marigold Idabelle Firestone, after his mother. This was done and everybody should have been happy about it ever after. Unfortunately, the marigold itself spoiled everything; a nice, low-growing plant in California, it became lanky and awkward in the East, and finally had to be given up as a bad job. The Firestone people, Burpee was grateful to find, forgave him completely and even became good customers for Burpee seeds, for gifts to their own customers.

The treasonous behavior of the marigold when it changed climates was, at least, nothing new in Burpee company experience. Away back in 1912 W. Atlee Burpee had to confess ruefully that some plants appear more glamorous in California than they do anywhere else, just like some movie stars. Referring to a new lettuce, Black-Seeded Big Boston, he said: "Last June when looking over the crop in California we made the following note: 'A beautiful lettuce; leaves a trifle smaller and rather lighter shade of green with less color on edges.' Comparing the same variety with our selected strain of Big Boston in the trials at Fordhook Farms we had to admit, however, that it was impossible to pick out rows without the finder. Therefore, all that we would say now of the Black-Seeded Big Boston is that it is a beautiful straight stock of Big Boston Lettuce."

Most of the foregoing embarrassments, it will be observed, struck Burpee's in the manner of lightning, not requiring much effort on their part. At times, however, they seem almost to have gone out looking for tight spots to get themselves into. Probably the most fascinating example of this concerned two ventures with, of all things, talking birds.

The first was with parrots, and David Burpee bought a flock of five because it suddenly occurred to him one day what a marvelous gimmick a talking parrot would be in the Burpee booth at the annual New York flower show. It had always made Burpee restive to see crowds of people thronging around his exhibit, and yet to be unable to speak up and recommend his seeds, because any such pitch was strictly against the rules of the show. However, the rules didn't say anything about a parrot, so forthwith the seedsman bought his five. He needed only one, but the other four were spare tires. Having got the birds, the next question was, how could he teach them to say, "Hello! Burpee seeds grow."

"Nothing to it," said a helpful friend. "Farm the job out to some of the prisoners at the Eastern Penitentiary. They have plenty of spare time, and the parrots will be company for them, too." But Burpee shied off; he had a feeling the theft-insurance rates at his plant would skyrocket if "Burpee" became such a household word around the pokey.

The helpful friend then got another idea. He was a director, it seemed, of the Old Working Man's Home in West Philadelphia, and he suggested training the parrots there. Burpee had no qualms about honest old working men, and out went the five parrots in five cages to five selected residents, with an offer of $500 to him who trained his parrot best, with $100 each for place and show.

But though the five competitors, carrying their birds about in the cages wherever they went, roared, "Hello! Burpee seeds grow," at them till they were hoarse and residents in the neighborhood began tapping their foreheads significantly, the parrots had no interest in the project at all. Only one learned to say anything, and all he said was "Is zat so?" with a dubious leer.

Disgusted, Burpee made gifts of the birds to their trainers, who had grown fond of them, and he would gladly have forgotten the whole episode had not somebody spoken up just then and said, "Oh, well, the trouble was, you were working with the wrong breed of birds. What you need is a myna bird, and I know an ornithologist who can fix you up."

Sure enough, the ornithologist could and did fix him up, and also trained the myna bird, with a professional assist from one of Burpee's Bucks County neighbors at the time, the late librettist Oscar Hammerstein II. Hammerstein suggested that for more pleasing cadence the phrase be "Hello, hello—Burpee seeds grow."

A quick study, the myna bird (named Burp) charmed Burpee by rapidly becoming letter-perfect at speaking his piece in human tones that anybody within a hundred yards could understand, and at the next New York flower show he simply loved his job. In fact, Burp wowed the crowds so constantly and well that the show manager finally had to beg Burpee as a personal favor to kill the act and restore the flower show to the flowers. Burpee graciously bowed to this plea—but the fact was he was terribly relieved to do so. The Burpee bird, he had been discovering to his dismay, was pure ham, and such an attraction to his public that nobody paid the slightest attention to the Burpee exhibit. Whereupon he gave old Burp away, free, to a potato merchant who had become hopelessly infatuated with him and was a very good listener.

MR. BURPEE'S NATIONAL FLOWER

When David Burpee heard that his old foes, the rose people, were going to throw a love feast in Washington for senators, representatives, and other big wheels, it caught him at an awkward time. It was July 1961, and as usual he was as busy with summer business as a bee in a greenhouse. The nominal reason for the rose party was the convention of the All-America Rose Selections, and the thing that bothered Burpee was the good impression they might make in the perennial drive to get Congress to name a national flower. His own candidate was, and is, the marigold.

The party was to be held at the swank Sheraton-Carlton Hotel, and besides red and yellow roses galore, the 1961 Rose Queen and plenty of party fixings were to be on hand. Also speeches, resolutions, and a flag made of roses. "Salute to the Rose" this powwow was to be called.

Not until some days had passed and he was in a plane winging his way to his California seed farms did Burpee have a spare minute to try and noodle up any counterstrategy. His brain then zigzagged off on a course roughly like this:

No time for anything elaborate. . . . Salute to the Rose. . . . Hmmm. . . . Somebody said how about handing out marigolds? . . . No, no—the place will be so loaded with

roses, anything else will look sick. . . . Salute to the Rose.
. . . Salute to . . . *Salute!* A gesture of respect, admiration,
etc. . . . AHA—GOT IT!"

As soon as the plane landed, Burpee, chuckling hoarsely,
scuttled for a telephone and phoned back East to tell his nephew
Bill (W. Atlee Burpee III) of the fiendish plan he had hatched,
and to get humping with some typesetting. With just a scrap of
time to get it done, Bill cannily grabbed a printer who had been
trying for years to spring a little business out of the seed company
and told the man this was his chance to make his reputation.

By the time the rose guests were beginning to enter the
Sheraton-Carlton the day and hour of the party, a pair of beau-
teous cover-girls loitering in the lobby suddenly turned out to be
Burpee under-cover girls, their handbags loaded with postcard-
sized cards that they instantly began passing out to the party
guests. On the up side the cards read, in bold black type:

SALUTE THE ROSE!
The National Floral Emblem
of England

And on the other side as the guests turned them over:

SALUTE THE MARIGOLD!
For the National Floral Emblem of the
United States of America.
The Marigold is a native of The American
Continent and of No where else in the world.
The American Marigold is not the National
Flower of any other country.

This piece of scheming paid off for Burpee by embarrassing
the rose people at their own party and by neatly swiping the
headline of the story the Washington *Post* ran the next day:

ROSE PARTY HAS ONE THORN—
MARIGOLD MARS ROSY GLOW

It was not the first time the seedsman had scored in the nation's capital in his marigold crusade. Two years before, he had taken part in a debate on which should be chosen as the country's official flower—the rose, corn tassel, carnation, grass, or marigold. (There were plenty of other contenders, including the daisy, mountain laurel, trailing arbutus, mistletoe, cactus, goldenrod, columbine, and poppy, but the Falls Church, Virginia, Garden Club, which was sponsoring the debate, didn't have all night to listen.)

Burpee's opponents in the debate were professionals at persuasion by oratory—Senator Paul Douglas of Illinois for the corn tassel, Senator Thruston Morton of Kentucky for grass, Senator Hugh Scott of Pennsylvania for the rose, and Representative William Ayres of Ohio for the carnation. Senator Douglas turned out to be the most diligent showman, plying the audience with popcorn, and dressing up several of his office aides to represent notable personalities associated with corn in some way, but when the talking was done and a vote taken, the audience elected the marigold winner.

Though he was the only nonprofessional orator in the debate, Burpee was the only real professional there on the subject of flowers, and he is at his best when talking of marigolds. "Most serious of the debaters," the Washington *Post* called him (not too difficult an achievement, since members of the Congress, understandably, always are more relaxed and often playful in national flower discussions than in such pressing ones as national defense and the country's economic health), and the Washington *Evening Star*, calling Burpee a dark horse who looked "modest and strangely out of place," seemed intrigued with his frankness in introducing himself to the audience as "a registered lobbyist for marigolds."

He is, indeed, a registered lobbyist for his favorite flower, the one he has worked on and talked about so diligently and well since the 1920s that American gardeners now buy more of its seed from him than that of any other flower. Burpee did not have to register as a lobbyist in order to urge the marigold on the Congress as our national flower, though he says he thinks this proper, and he sometimes wonders out loud if he ought not to sic the law on the rose supporters for not registering.

In singling out the rose people, he pays them the compliment of his qualms. The rose, as he well knows, is much the biggest threat to the marigold's chances of becoming the national flower. In fact, should David Burpee succeed in this marigold campaign of his, it would be an astounding feat, something like a baseball pitcher playing the New York Yankees all by himself and winning the game. Even one of his prime arguments against the rose—that it is already the national flower of nine other countries—is a testament to its appeal. The real question, however, is not why he is against the rose, but why he is for the marigold—or, rather, why he chose it in the first place.

The answer is that he chose it with cool and impersonal logic as the flower most likely to rescue his business when, in the mid-twenties, the sweet pea began falling prey to a root disease. At that time the sweet pea was America's favorite annual, and the house of Burpee was the home of the sweet pea, harvesting each year a huge seed crop from about two hundred acres, and regularly introducing new varieties of their own. When the root trouble began discouraging U.S. gardeners with planting sweet peas, Burpee did some heavy thinking. Sweet peas were doomed, he saw, until varieties resistant to the root disease could be found and the resistance bred into many others—and this would be a long, hard job. He determined to pick a successor to the sweet pea, and to pick it scientifically. Accordingly, he outlined a kind of blueprint of the ideal flower for American gardens.

It must be easy to grow (easier than sweet peas, which took some pampering); it should be pretty; it should be widely adaptable and tolerant of the hot summers in most of the United States (which sweet peas could not take); it should flower over a long period, last a good while in bouquets, and have long stems for cutting.

It seemed to Burpee that the one flower which came closest to this ideal was the marigold of that period, even though it fell quite a bit short. Having made up his mind about it, Burpee swiftly set about making the marigold over into a glamour girl, as calculatingly as a Hollywood mother grooming her pig-tailed moppet to be ready for the big chance. He began by combing the world for marigold seeds, to find out what was being grown in other places. His sources mainly were foreign seed houses, botanical gardens, and collectors. The seeds were then planted in trial rows at Fordhook and the resulting blooms studied for faults. The worst ones were lateness in flowering, small flowers, short stems, and limited range of color. "But I was encouraged," Burpee says now. "Those were faults we could cure." He was right—these faults were gradually cured by his plant breeders, and as the marigold steadily grew more popular, helped by vigorous Burpee promotion, another fault that some persons objected to more than any other was also cured in certain varieties— the pungent odor of marigold leaves, as told in Chapter 7, "The Search."

In the course of his guiding the marigold toward its destiny, Burpee did some inquiring into its social background. One of the investigators was Miss Lois Torrance, who became Mrs. David Burpee later, in 1938, but was then working for the company after having studied horticulture. She reported the marigold historical trail murky, finding no conclusive proof that Hernando Cortez, Spanish conqueror of Mexico, did or did not introduce the flower into Europe. To a plan by Burpee to trace the etymology of "marigold" as formed from "the Virgin Mary" plus "gold" (which is corroborated by lexicographers—even though it originally referred to calendulas, called pot marigolds—and is assigned to the Middle English period, 1100 to 1500), Miss Torrance said it was all right for an English story but not a Spanish one, the Spanish for gold being *oro* and the Spanish name for marigolds being Clavel de Indias, and for the African ones, Clavelon.

After meditating on the known and the unknown, Burpee made up his mind and acted with executive decision. "When Cortez conquered Mexico," his catalog states, "he found Marigolds growing in the gardens there. Marigolds are native to southwestern United States and Mexico.

"Cortez took seed to Europe and they rapidly became the favorite flower for the devout to place at the altar of the Virgin Mary. This is how they got the name 'Mary's Gold,' and then 'Marigold.'"

Having disposed of historical vagueness, Burpee went a step further after he began seriously to advocate the marigold as the national flower. "The big ones (*Tagetes erecta*)," he told catalog readers, "used to be called African Marigolds, but now we call them American, which they are. The little ones (*Tagetes patula*) are called French marigolds, although they also are natives of the American continent and nowhere else in the world." Since 1959 the Burpee catalog has steadfastly called African marigolds American marigolds. Taking advantage of his two-million-plus catalog circulation, Burpee also now tells readers of his desire that the Congress name the marigold our national flower, but he also gives some of the opposition free publicity:

". . . Others have suggested the Rose, Carnation, Corn Tassel and Grass. But for hundreds of years the Rose has been the floral emblem of England, and it is the floral emblem of eight other countries, four of which have fallen behind the Iron Curtain since selecting the Rose as their emblem. The Carnation is the national floral emblem of Spain. The Corn Tassel is not a perfect flower and is not grown especially for its beauty. As for grass, who would want to walk on the National Floral Emblem?

"The American Marigold has much in its favor—it is easy to grow from seed and does well in every state of the Union, even as far north as Alaska and in the tropical clime of Hawaii. [To help clinch the point, Burpee named new marigolds for each of these states.] The Marigold can be an ambassador of good will for the United States to every civilized country in the world for it is popular in all of them. It is called by some 'Flower of Good Luck' or 'The Friendship Flower.'"

Approximately the same sentiments are expressed on a Christmas card Burpee sends out each year, with which he encloses a few packets of seeds of his choicest new marigolds.

Everybody in the Burpee ranks is sedulous in eliminating the negative and accenting the positive, avoiding like the plague the term "African marigolds," and gently saying, "American marigolds, please," to misguided customers and anybody else. And so conscious has the employee body become of its chief's national-flower ambitions for the marigold that there is no longer the slightest possibility anybody will be so thoughtless as one farm manager was some years ago. To pretty up the office doorway he planted a climbing rose on each side and then wondered why the boss turned so growly every time he came and went. Finally catching on, the manager yanked the floral emblem of England out by its roots.

Some outside critics have been violently outspoken about Burpee's choice for the national flower. One wrote him: "It appears to me that your efforts are strictly of a commercial nature. You've sold a lot of marigold seed and stand to sell a lot more if your campaign is a success. . . . I'm sure this country has any number of better choices for a national flower."

To such blasts, Burpee returns a soft answer, personally or by proxy, usually enclosing some complimentary marigold seeds to show there are no hard feelings. In the case just cited, he did not try to defend himself against the charge of self-interest, though it would have been easy to point out that rival seedsmen, including big Ferry-Morse, Northrup, King, & Company, and Asgrow, not to mention hundreds of smaller seed houses and allied businesses such as nurseries and florists by the thousands, would all share in any marigold boom. Burpee is, admittedly, big on marigolds and would, if there were any justice, get a good deal of prestige and glory out of it if the marigold were to stand beside the bald eagle as a national symbol. People do, however, often feel strongly about marigolds, though not many threaten, as did the previous critic, to write their congressman to stop Burpee's crusade. Quite a few of the letter writers pay Burpee the left-handed compliment of admitting they have come to like marigolds against their better judgment, so willing is the flower to do its best.

At any rate, whatever complaints David Burpee may have in connection with his efforts toward greater recognition of marigold merits, he certainly cannot, as did England's King Charles I, it is related, link it with public neglect. While in prison awaiting trial, Charles is said to have written the melancholy lines:

> The Marigold observes the Sun
> More than my subjects me have done.

# 25 YOU, TOO, MAY WIN $10,000

A spoonful of marigold seeds arrived by mail in Burpee's Philadelphia office recently, the envelope containing them marked: "For the White Marigold Contest." Inside the envelope was a note from the customer who had sent them. It said: "If anything should happen to me before I win the money, I want it to go to the Soldiers' Home, not to my son."

Another customer wrote in, sending no seeds but saying darkly: "If you get some white marigold seeds from somebody here in my town, they will be my seeds. I had the plant marked, and my neighbor stole the seeds because they are all gone."

Such delicate legal questions are part of the king-sized headache David Burpee concocted for himself when he dreamed up the great white marigold contest he announced in 1954. His object was set forth clearly: He didn't have a white marigold, and he wanted one. He dearly loves marigolds and what they do for his business, and the more colors of marigolds he has, the wider their appeal. He wanted more than white, but it was a good one to start with and seemed more likely to lead to other colors. Asking the public to help find a marigold "as big as Man-in-the-Moon Marigold [3 to 3½ inches across] and as white as Snowstorm Petunia" was not a radical step. Burpee and his father before him consistently welcomed and occasionally asked for help in finding new varieties of plants; it was a way of widening the use of the basic tool of plant breeding, selection. The only thing different about the white marigold contest, in fact, was the money. If Burpee had offered a hundred dollars for a white marigold he would have got a great many entries but not much excitement or publicity. By offering $10,000, he hit a dramatic whack that snatched the public imagination—and certainly $10,-000 for a flower is pretty steep.

The first contest entries were tested in 1955, and though Burpee and his plant breeders did not expect to get their white marigold the very first season, none of them realized that this contest thing was going to be like shaking hands with a hungry gorilla. Seven years later, in 1962, they had:

> Received and painstakingly tested 2290 separate samples of seed from customers in all 50 states. . . .

> Spent a good deal more than twice as much as the prize money in this testing (they estimate each sample costs them $10 to test). . . .

> Found the great majority of the test marigolds no nearer white than a crate of ripe oranges. . . .

> Begun to fear they themselves, with acres full of marigolds, were the ones most likely to find the big white one, putting them in the awkward position of a bridge party hostess who cops her own prize.

The number of contestants each year has varied considerably, going up and down without apparent reason. The first year, 204 entries were received. Instead of more coming in the following year, as everybody at Burpee's expected, the number sank to 114. But it zoomed up to 352 the year after, and as the staff braced itself for the deluge, the entries perversely then skidded to 170, and next to 154. But the year following, 1960, they jumped to 429, and to 536 in 1961, causing David Burpee to anticipate a couple of thousand in 1962 and to work out a system of appraising the entries while still very small by planting seeds in flats instead of beds, thus cutting out some of the expense on the plainly hopeless ones. This could be done because marigolds start blooming when still tiny. The flat system was put into use, but the entry figures crossed Burpee up once more—the 1962 total dropped to less than 300 instead of soaring up.

Judging of the entries is done each year by Burpee and two or three outside experts, usually from the academic horticultural field. The only thing the judges have had to decide so far is which entries are near enough to white to deserve A's for effort, in the form of $100 prizes.

On the other hand, the white marigold hunt has been a stunning publicity coup for Burpee. Even those who doubt his motives or don't agree with him ("All this blather about a white marigold," said a retired government plant scientist, speaking of Burpee) do know about the search. A Burpee staff man traveling by automobile from the West Coast to the East on a business trip found that when filling station attendants saw the company name on his credit card, they almost invariably asked the same question: "Have you found that white marigold yet?"

Back in 1949, speculating on his burning desire for more colors in marigolds, Burpee said: "It seems to us that there are two possible ways to do it. One is to make a cross between cultivated marigolds and a wild species of *Tagetes* that has the desired color. The other possibility is that some gardener will find a marigold of the desired color as a mutation in his garden. It is hoped that a pure glistening white marigold will be found some day."

In speaking of changing the colors of flowers, Luther Burbank was once quoted as saying: "I am disposed to think that all shades of all colors can be produced in our flowers if the work is gone at systematically and persisted in long enough. This may seem extravagant to you, who see certain genera producing only red flowers, or blue, or yellow, and it may be difficult to imagine a yellow delphinium, for instance, or a blue marigold. But these are flowers that have been carefully bred to retain and deepen their accepted color; when you turn to flowers on the other hand that men have patiently sought to change, results have almost always been obtained."

One of the sidelights of the white marigold contest of particular interest to Burpee plant breeders has been the number of contestants who have gone about the thing in a thoroughly sound scientific fashion, inquiring into the genetic background of the close-to-white marigolds that Burpee call their Miracle marigolds (a hard question, as the Miracles have been crossed right and left, and also hopped up with X-ray shots). Burpee's try to give useful answers to such queries (the bookkeeping and correspondence are two of the big cost factors in the white marigold trials, in fact), but they have no doubts that not man but nature will have the most to do with producing the white marigold, when it is produced.

One contestant, quite as aware as were Burpee's that a mutation was the most likely answer by far, wrote for information on the proper X-ray dosage to jolt seedling marigolds with. On the other side of the experiment coin, a gardener sent in some seeds with the information she had used laundry bleach on the marigold seed she had planted, and hoped it would show up in the next generation as pure white flowers.

The Miracle marigolds are the ones Burpee's think will throw the winning mutation, and this is the basis on which they recommend them to gardeners. To supply the demand, their 1961 planting covered five acres at Floradale Farms, which yielded about 1500 pounds of seed. Since there are about 10,000 to the ounce, a little arithmetic will show that the five acres produced

seed enough to grow about 240 million plants. When David
Burpee makes his regular summer inspection tours of Floradale
he keeps an eye out for the possible prize-winning white one in
this planting. He would far prefer, for the publicity value alone,
that one of his customers be the one to grow the winning flower,
but he earnestly desires a white marigold and he cannot afford
to ignore it, wherever it appears. If it does pop up on his own
farm, he will still pay the promised $10,000, probably as a grant
to some university for horticultural research. This, incidentally,
answers a question one anti-white-marigold-contest man raised
in a letter to Burpee. "What if you grow the white marigold yourself?" he demanded. "Won't your own geneticists deserve the
prize money?"

Regardless of who grows the first truly white marigold, Burpee
confidently expects to have it by 1968—as he states in his predictions of flowers of the future in Chapter 28, "What You'll be
Planting X Years from Now." Since he is predicting that market
seed will be available by 1968, and since this crop of seed would
be grown in 1967, he obviously expects to find his white marigold
no later than 1966, and probably a year or two sooner, unless he
manages to telescope time again as with his all-double nasturtium
scoop during the 1930s.

He then goes a little further and predicts that "undated, but
somewhere following the big white," he will be offering gardeners
a big pink marigold and a big red. For each of these mutations
it is likely that Burpee will again offer gardeners a $10,000 dis-
covery prize.

With a white marigold and then a red one, nobody familiar
with the seedsman's national floral emblem crusade on behalf of
the marigold needs more than one guess at what color Burpee
would be aiming for next. Although, as Luther Burbank said, it
may be difficult to imagine a blue marigold, the chances are that
Burpee has not only imagined it, but already in his mind, spread

out in glowing colors, he sees somewhere in the future a huge
flower bed in the neighborhood of Capitol Hill in Washington,
D.C., the bed consisting entirely of red, white, and blue marigolds planted in a faithful replica of Old Glory.

# 26   GOURMET IN THE GARDEN

Except when they are asked to step forward and address some group, most Burpee staff people blend themselves anonymously into the company character so far as the public is concerned. This chapter, "Gourmet in the Garden," makes an exception. Its author is forty-five-year-old Jerome H. Kantor, a top geneticist, research assistant to David Burpee, and father of a sizable family. Kantor was reluctant to speak out here, and agreed to do so only after lengthy insistence by both the writer and his wife, who realized how happily this man combined all the qualities needed. This is not to say Kantor is the only gourmet in the Burpee garden. Of course he isn't. One Fordhook Farms man, for instance, was such a vegetable connoisseur that he never once had to buy lunch—he dined daily on things he plucked, shelled, or yanked out of the earth as he nibbled his way through the trial rows.

Kantor, who prefers most of his food cooked, is speaking here for himself, but he may be considered as also striking a blow for freedom on behalf of all gourmets of the home garden—both in Burpee's and out. He is, indeed, in perfect harmony with the sentiment of Nicholas Roosevelt in the latter's stimulating *Creative Cooking* (Harper & Brothers, New York City, 1956). Roosevelt, whose father and President Theodore Roosevelt were first cousins and who himself has been a gourmet of note in the course of a distinguished career as diplomat, editorial writer, and contemporary historian, summed up the home-garden point handily in a couple of sentences: "Fresh vegetables are, of course, preferable, if you can get them truly fresh. There is no substitute for your own vegetable garden—not even the garden of a generous friend." And Adelle Davis in her *Let's Cook it Right* (Harcourt, Brace & Co., New York City, 1947) put it this way: ". . . I have suggested the frequent use of fresh pimentos and paprika peppers, although they are not sold in many markets. However, when people find how delicious and sweet these peppers are—the Hungarians serve them for dessert—and come to appreciate their outstanding nutritive value, I hope that these peppers will be grown in every home garden."

Here, then, is how a man who knows vegetables professionally as a plant breeder feels about them in their ultimate culinary role. There is gold in these lines, and discovery, for those who want to . . .

## LIVE DELICIOUSLY OUT OF A GARDEN
### by
### *Jerome H. Kantor*

Despite newer and better commercial methods of growing vegetables and preparing them for consumer use, one fact cannot be altered: Because of the trade's demands, commercial varieties can never equal in quality those developed exclusively for the home gardener. Some try to strike a compromise—and they remind me of many other multi-purpose things in that they often are not really suitable for any of their purposes. So let's not pull punches: The first step toward exceptional eating quality in vegetables is to choose varieties *developed for home gardener use.*

And since a variety that's a few points better often has some little idiosyncrasy, pamper it a bit for best results. Even more important, don't throw away all you've gained, by such last-minute mistakes as harvesting too early or late or (in some cases) too long before cooking, or by overcooking.

Many vegetables naturally spread their harvest over a long period, an ideal home-garden arrangement. In other cases you can spread the harvest period by succession plantings. Another way is to plant several varieties that mature at different times. This harvesting spread is especially important where the crop all seems to come in at once, as with lettuce, cabbage, corn, radishes, and "greens"—especially if the vegetable cannot be stored.

Now, not in any particular order, a few remarks on vegetable varieties we've liked growing. We've gardened in the East, on the West Coast, and, during some of the World War II years, south of the border.

## Beans

There are so many varieties of beans it is becoming difficult to choose one or two best for all areas. To me, Tender Pod is the finest flavored and most tender of all, though production is not likely to be as great as with some less flavorful varieties. With our family of seven, we put gobs of vegetables in the freezer, and Tender Pod is just as delightful frozen as fresh—but beans must be picked young, almost before there is any swelling of the bean within the pod. Average soil is adequate, but weed removal is a must for beans. A heavy mulch is good, and cultivation if practical should not be so close to the plants as to risk damaging the roots.

My favorite way to prepare Tender Pod is just briefly cooked, buttered, and lightly salted. For a change, we enjoy:

### Snap Bean Fritters

The batter here may be used either for deep-fat cooking or for sautéeing. If deep-fried, vegetable fats work better. Butter may be used for sautéeing. In any case, drain the fritters well on paper towels after frying.

2 eggs, separated
1 tablespoon oil or melted butter
¼ teaspoon salt
⅔ cup milk, or water, or equal parts of each
1 cup sifted flour
1 or 2 tablespoons sugar
1 tablespoon lemon juice

Beat egg yolks well and add the oil or butter, salt, and the liquid alternately with the flour to make a smooth batter. Wine may be substituted for the lemon juice or the lemon juice may be left out entirely. Sugar is also optional. If making one-bean fritters for finger food with drinks, sugar is probably best left out.

Beat egg white with ⅛ teaspoon of salt until stiff. Fold into batter. Coat bean spoonfuls, or single beans, and fry.

For deep-frying, have fat at 360 to 380 degrees. If using raw beans, 6 to 8 minutes will be ample. Remove when a delicate brown—don't overfry. (We sometimes use tiny flowerlets of broccoli or cauliflower in place of snap beans; spear with toothpick and serve as a hot canapé.) If using leftovers (cooked beans), 3 or 4 minutes of frying will be sufficient.

For a wax bean, Brittle Wax is our favorite, but we use far more Tender Pod than we do wax beans.

The one pole bean we still grow is Kentucky Wonder. It does so well under so many varied conditions that it is highly recommended as a stand-by. Can be used as dry or shell beans, though Tender Pod is still better for drying.

Many of the lima beans are temperamental. On the West Coast we always included two or three varieties of bush and pole limas in our garden: Fordhook, Burpee's Big 6, and Baby Fordhook. Limas are a little touchy as to growing conditions. Soil should be quite warm when planting limas, as with cool, wet weather there is danger of seeds rotting. Fordhook has a more meaty or nutty flavor than Big 6. But—and this is where one of the small touches comes in—while not highly publicized in present seed catalogs, Baby Fordhook is the most tender. Yields are lower, though, and more work is required to produce a sizable harvest for table use or freezing.

For the most nutlike flavor of all we like edible soy beans. These have much to commend them. With only two or three beans to the pod, they become almost a delicacy. They need full sun, and even slight shading, as by weed competition, will reduce the yield. An easy way to shell the green beans is to plunge them briefly in hot water, then into cold water. Though not the equal of limas, soy beans have a distinctive flavor. If you cannot grow limas, by all means try them.

### Beets

I like Crosby's Egyptian and Burpee Redhart. Both of these are somewhat more zoned than dark reds, but the zoning disappears on cooking, and they are unexcelled for sweetness in a "red" beet. Use the thinnings—the whole, very young beet root, and also the tops—as greens.

### Broccoli

The green sprouting is the most popular. De Cicco and Greenbud are excellent. Broccoli should be grown cool, and cut while buds are still rather tight.

### Cabbage

Another of the vegetables that should be grown cool. I seem to be a "raw salad" addict, and except for corned beef and cabbage, we grow cabbage for raw use—salads, slaws, mixed with other greens or alone. We do not store cabbage for winter use, so restrict the varieties to those of good quality when eaten fresh.

For a "white" cabbage we like Golden Acre. Its smaller size makes it more generally adaptable than the larger Copenhagen Market. For a medium green we pick Early Jersey Wakefield. But Perfection Drumhead, a savoy type and dark green, is of far better quality than any of the above.

No garden should be without a red cabbage. It adds much to the table and at no sacrifice in flavor. Not many varieties are available, but Mammoth Red Rock is good.

## Chinese Cabbage

This is not an easy vegetable to grow, and as with most green salad vegetables, it should be grown cool. It is well worth the extra effort. For best results in most parts of the country, plant in July and August.

## Cantaloupes

As far as I am concerned most gardens don't have room for cantaloupes, but for those that do, Burpee Hybrid is the only one to grow. I find that vine crops seem to do better with the old system of a shovelful of manure under the hill. Cantaloupes should be classed as a luxury item, and there isn't much the gardener can do to ensure a good crop. Even if properly planted and cared for, cantaloupes may often be of poor flavor, especially in areas of heavy rainfall. We grow them each year anyway.

We freeze any surplus, either in balls or cubed. For best results they should be served when still icy and not quite thawed. Really delectable in mid-winter when served as a cocktail with mint sauce. (To make the sauce, boil ½ cup sugar with ½ cup water for 5 minutes; pour over 3 or 4 tablespoons of chopped mint leaves; when cool, strain and add juice of one lemon and one orange.)

## Carrots

Here we take exception to the bull's-eye varieties and grow Tendersweet only. We use them only in season, the younger the better, although they can be stored and kept well. We have grown Oxheart, which will do in heavy soils where Tendersweet is unsatisfactory. As a change we like candied or glazed carrots, and use young to half-grown roots for the purpose. Wonderful to relieve the monotony of starchy vegetables with chicken or ham.

When using thinnings, it is well to loosen the soil on both sides of the row with a spade, pull desired thinnings, and tamp the earth back in place to prevent drying out of the roots left.

### Cauliflower

We don't try to grow white cauliflower each year. This is a difficult one for most gardeners. The Purple Head is worth doing; it is easier to grow and it freezes very well. Cauliflower should be grown cool. In this case, as with all other vegetables that require cool weather, this means getting started early, and I mean early. Part of this start can be done by planting the seed indoors or having the plants grown for you from the varieties you choose. Also, by partly preparing your soil in the fall, it will be more nearly ready for spring finishing.

### Corn

Even though corn freezes well, there is nothing in the garden to compare with corn harvested and put in the water while you and your guests are assembled. This is one vegetable where succession plantings or a choice of varieties is important. I have to travel a good bit in the summer and I find it more convenient to plant at the same time several varieties that mature at different times. The soil should be quite warm when planting corn. There are a number of excellent hybrids and a choice here really depends somewhat on personal taste. We still like Golden Bantam (not the hybrid) for eating quality, although it is not the most productive. We don't care whether we have the first corn in the neighborhood but we get good response in this connection from Golden Midget.

Of the hybrids, Barbecue is excellent and fairly early. It is one of the few varieties that seems to do a multi-purpose job—early, good fresh, and wonderful for freezing. We plant also Golden Cross Bantam for mid-season use, and Iochief, which with us is the latest of the hybrids.

If a still later harvest is wanted, try a later succession. Or the standard varieties planted late will give a late harvest, especially a white corn such as Stowell's Evergreen (not the hybrid).

We have a large garden (with the help of the five youngsters) and so allow room for popcorn. One variety is ample; we use Burpee's Peppy Pop Corn Hybrid, which matures early. We have also grown other varieties and found Hybrid South American Mushroom to be satisfactory.

For corn other than popcorn the time of harvest depends on individual preference. We like our corn slightly on the young side. For fresh use, corn may be quite enjoyable even a little older, but for freezing there is not much leeway if you want to recapture the garden flavor. And in corn it is vital to get the harvest from the garden to the freezer as promptly as possible.

## Cucumbers

Unless you make preserves or pickles you will probably have too many cucumbers. Not so for us. We use cucumbers fresh just as long as they bear—salads of various kinds, and boiled cucumbers on occasion:

### Boiled Cucumbers

Pare cucumbers and cube or dice. Simmer until tender, drain and wash, season with salt and pepper, butter or margarine. Or use a cream sauce, add the drained cucumbers and warm over hot water for five minutes before serving. Also try reheating drained cucumbers in tomato sauce or with stewed tomatoes.

We use only Burpee Hybrid cucumber, and a 50-foot row does us well for table use. Frequent removal of cucumbers is important to prolong the harvest. We like to split the planting, allowing about three weeks between sowings.

Cucumbers may be considered a luxury item in small gardens, as they do take space. We have not had this problem, but of course cucumbers can also be trained on a fence or trellis, and Burpee Hybrid does well for this purpose.

### Eggplant

Burpee Hybrid eggplant is our stand-by. Newer and earlier is Early Beauty Hybrid but we haven't grown it in our garden sufficiently to switch over. We use young eggplant, sliced and fried in egg batter, or baked with a slice of tomato and cheese. The older fruits can also be used this way. They are also excellent breaded, and corn meal can be used for this purpose. If you have an excess of eggplants you can freeze them.

### Endive

Endive is especially well known to western gardeners, as it is a rather frequent item in salads in restaurants, in California especially, where salads are apt to be served the year around. There is lots of punch to endive, and texture. Green Curled is the one we have grown, although I must confess the youngsters see little use for it. It mixes well with other greens and can be used alone if others are not available.

### Herbs

Most herbs present no problems in growing, and usually the herb is offered without choice of variety. We are particularly fond of using the seeds from certain herbs in our cooking, pickling, and baking. Notable here is anise seed, wonderful for use in almond

bread slices, among other things; caraway seeds for breads, and
dill for pickling. Here is our recipe for the first named:

### Almond Bread Slices

4 medium or 3 large eggs
1 cup sugar
1 lemon
½ teaspoon vanilla
1 teaspoon anise seeds
3 cups flour
½ cup blanched almonds
½ cup butter or oil
1 tablespoon baking powder

Beat eggs well, then add sugar (dribbled in) and continue
to beat until well blended. Add the grated rind and juice of
the lemon, the vanilla, anise seeds, and about half the flour.
Cut almonds in halves or smaller and add them, along with
the butter or oil, and the remaining flour with the baking
powder. The dough should be slightly sticky. Knead it for a
few minutes with floured hands, on a lightly floured board,
adding—only if necessary—no more than ½ cup of additional
flour. Shape into long narrow loaves about two inches in diameter. They will flatten out somewhat. We bake them on
oiled and floured cookie sheets at 325 degrees for about 20
minutes. Remove from oven and cut into ½-inch slices while
still warm. They may be used this way, though we put the
slices under the oven broiler and toast on both sides till crisp.
We like the crunchy texture this gives, but the slices are excellent either way, alone or as tea cakes.

Borage, sage, and thyme are among the other herbs we use in
cooking, and chives have a variety of uses, of course. Try coarsely
chopped chives, radishes, and cucumbers, all icy cold, in a bowl

of sour cream, for a refreshing hot-weather dish—practically a
meal in itself.

## Mustard Greens

We much prefer mustard greens to spinach, and if you live in
an area where you can pick wild mustard, you are indeed lucky.
If you must depend on cultivated varieties, Fordhook Fancy is
good. Another of the cool-weather crops, mustard greens must be
sown quite early, and must be watered frequently in times of
drought or it will bolt.

## Parsley

Extra Curled Dwarf is our choice. It requires very little care.
We use it throughout the summer, and just a little while before
frost we cut what's left, dry it, chop it, store it in tightly closed
jars, and use it throughout the winter.

Here's an idea we've used: Put your parsley in an area of your
garden which will not be plowed. The parsley will behave as a
perennial and give you fresh leaves far earlier in the season than
is otherwise possible. Such carry-over plants go to seed or peter
out sooner than do plants from newly sown seed, and it is therefore wise to make a new sowing each year. Or plant the seed in
the fall, keep it protected over the winter, and you will have early
parsley in the spring.

## Peanuts

We include these in the garden for the sake of the children. It
is educational for them to see how peanuts are produced, and
there is a sense of satisfaction when the nuts are roasted and
eaten on a wintry night.

We have gotten our best results by shelling the nuts before
planting, although either way is satisfactory. Soil must have
warmed thoroughly before planting. We like both Jumbo Virginia
and the Spanish.

*Okra*

Okra will produce over a long period if the pods are picked frequently and not allowed to get too large. We find a 50-foot row ample for our use. Clemson Spineless has slightly longer pods than Perfected Perkins' Long Pod, but we have used both and find practically no difference in flavor.

*Lettuce*

Lettuce is certainly our favorite salad component, one I enjoy plain, with just a touch of lemon juice, or with oil and vinegar, as well as with prepared dressings, and in combination with other vegetables or fruits.

Lettuce is another vegetable that likes cool weather. It cannot be successfully frozen or canned, or even stored for any length of time without seriously impairing its flavor. Uniformity of strains is so good that it is very important to have a number of succession plantings, with not too large a planting at any one time.

A few varieties have been developed that are long-standing (do not bolt to seed as quickly as others). Notable in this group are the Great Lakes crisp-head types. If you want lettuce when the more flavorful ones will not perform, Great Lakes should be part of the garden.

The loosehead type is exceptionally good for hot-summer locations. Burpee Greenhart is our choice in this group.

But for real lettuce quality and flavor, even though the season of productivity is short, there is nothing as tasty and tender as the butterhead types. Wayahead and White Boston are still among the best.

Lettuce should be grown with plenty of water. In our experience we have found that lettuce may occasionally be bitter, but this can be minimized by placing it in cool water for a few hours. This also tends to crisp the lettuce, though crisping should not be necessary if it has been well grown and not allowed to wilt after cutting.

Cos lettuce, Oak Leaf, and Ruby can be considered for table effect as well as for their eating quality.

### Peas

We grew peas quite well when we lived in cooler areas. To do them satisfactorily in areas of hot summers they should be sown early in the spring. As with beans, to avoid staking I prefer the dwarf or bush peas—Burpeeana Early for early tender quality, though it is not the best yielding pea.

Mammoth Melting Sugar is an edible-podded variety we have liked. Use these when there is just the outline of the peas showing through the pod. They can also be used as regular peas if you are not able to use all you planted while they are still at the edible-pod stage.

We use regular peas in all the usual ways, and include some in a Spanish dish, arroz con pollo, which includes in its ingredients capers (hard to find in some stores, but good in many dishes), and olives. Proportions can be varied to suit individual tastes. The tarragon vinegar in which capers are packed adds to this dish. To us, the flavor is much improved the second day, after there has been more time for blending.

*Arroz Con Pollo* (*Rice with Chicken*)
¼ cup cooking oil, olive oil preferred
4 cloves garlic, minced
1 onion, chopped
1 green or red sweet pepper, chopped
2 cups rice
Fryer chicken, 3 to 4 pounds
Salt and pepper
2 cups green olives, whole or coarsely chopped
2 bottles capers
10 or 12 whole cloves
1 cup fresh peas

Put oil in large iron skillet or frying pan. Heat almost to boiling. Add garlic, onion, pepper. Add rice, and chicken cut into serving pieces. Salt and pepper to taste. Fry until rice is golden brown. Add olives, capers, and cloves, and enough water to cover. Cook at medium heat until chicken is tender. Add peas and cook for 10 minutes longer. Serve at once or put in oven for 10 minutes more if a drier rice is desired.

Quantities of most ingredients given can be varied considerably to suit taste. For easier eating, the chicken may be cooked separately according to any favorite recipe, then boned and added after the other ingredients have been cooked as directed.

[NOTE: This recipe has true Latin-American authority. Mrs. Kantor, the former Otomie Maradiaga, brought it from her Costa Rica homeland. —K.K.]

## Onions

There is a lot of choice here, to suit uses and individual tastes. The tenderness so important with many vegetables doesn't seem to be a factor here. Other points are more important. We use both mild and strong onions, fresh and also stored for winter use.

We usually plant a row or two of Evergreen Bunching to be sure of having green onions (scallions) for some of the uses mentioned earlier, and this is supplemented by thinnings from other onions.

Southport Yellow Globe is still one of our favorites—medium size, stores well, and is strong enough for our strong-onion use. For a milder onion we like Burpee's Yellow Globe Hybrid, which is also relatively early.

We use onion sets to get the extra-early requirement of the season's first scallions and of fully grown bulbs.

A procedure we've found useful is to prepare onions for cooking ahead of time—one batch sliced, another cubed or diced, a third finely chopped—storing convenient-sized packages of each form in plastic bags in the freezer. When we use them, we thus avoid onion tears and smelly hands, and also stretch the harvest over a long period.

### Peppers

Spanish-type dishes form a rather frequent part of our menus, so we like peppers and use both sweet and hot, in just about every way conceivable—fresh, in salads, in cooking, stuffed, pickled, in sauces, etc.

We like California Wonder and grow it almost to the exclusion of all others. It is excellent for stuffing and is also good for all other sweet pepper uses. However, some pepper varieties, as is true of many other vegetables, seem to do better in some localities than do others. Burpee's Fordhook is also good, and Yolo Wonder will often do in some areas where California Wonder (to which it is similar) will not, mostly because Yolo Wonder is mosaic resistant. Peppers for cooking and flavoring can be held in the freezer in much the same way as indicated for onions.

### Pumpkins

Our only use for pumpkins is for Halloween and the youngsters. We don't grow them regularly in the garden. If we do, we of course use some for cooking, but usually depend on winter squash for so-called pumpkin cooking and baking. Big Tom is the only variety we have grown in the garden for Halloween carving.

### Summer Squash

This is one of our favorite vegetables. We now grow only two kinds—Burpee Hybrid Zucchini and Golden Crookneck. We like zucchini sliced raw in salads; we leave the skin on; the slices are attractive and have a nutty flavor.

For all cooking purposes zucchinis should be used at young stages. Very young fruits only 2 inches long and ½ to ¾ inch in diameter are very tasty when cubed and sautéed in butter, or in corn oil, if cholesterol is your problem. We take slightly larger ones—about 1 to 1½ inches in diameter, and 3 to 5 inches long —and bake them, with various toppings: bread crumbs, onions, cheese, etc. This dish is excellent with fish.

### Baked Young Zucchini Squash

8 or 10 zucchini squashes, 3 to 5 inches long
¼ cup corn oil
⅓ cup bread crumbs
1 tablespoon chopped parsley
2 tablespoons chopped scallions or chives
1 beaten egg
Pinch of salt
Pepper
½ cup grated Parmesan cheese

Simmer zucchinis in water to cover until tender—no more than 15 minutes. Scoop out the inside of each, leaving shells intact (if overcooked, this may be a little difficult). Mix the scooped-out part with rest of ingredients, reserving half of cheese. Refill shells, topping with cheese. Bake about 30 minutes at 300 to 325 degrees.

Zucchini is also fine, of course, when cooked just until tender, as is Crookneck. We tried freezing zucchini but were not as satisfied with it for this purpose as we are with Crookneck.

To keep squash plants bearing, keep the fruits picked.

### Winter Squash

We have used four varieties: Burpee's Bush Table Queen, Burpee Butternut, Buttercup, and True Hubbard.

While our catalog states that winter squashes should be harvested only after completely matured, we have found in recent years that if they are treated as a summer squash and eaten at young stages, you get an entirely different flavor than that of summer squashes.

Butternut is our bull's-eye variety and it is good, but we like the flavor of Buttercup even better. Buttercup is not very handsome to look at, but it has a very fine, sweet flavor. Both can be boiled, baked, or used for pies, and because they are smaller than Hubbard they are somewhat more versatile. We often cut Butternuts in half, remove the seeds and bake on the half shell, adding butter and salt at the table. Frequently we substitute mashed squash, plain or topped with marshmallow and browned in the oven, for potatoes or sweet potatoes.

Hubbard (True Hubbard) will probably store the best of all squashes, though its larger size may be a disadvantage to small families. It can be used the same as Butternut and Buttercup for cooking in various ways.

### Rhubarb

There are not many rhubarb varieties available from seed. From roots the choice is a little better, and choice is purely a matter of taste: some varieties are more tart. We prefer a rather tart flavor, and find MacDonald quite suitable, and also like its pinkish-red color. Victoria is even more tart, but we grow only MacDonald.

We've never had any trouble growing rhubarb. Once started, it can be divided when necessary. Seed stalks should not be allowed to form, and frequent watering and occasional light applications of fertilizer are helpful. We give our rhubarb lots of growing room—6 to 8 feet between plants, and about 6 feet to the next garden row.

All our perennial things are grouped together, and we keep rhubarb along with asparagus in with our small fruits such as berries, although a few plants—especially the red-stalked varieties—are quite decorative when grown nearer the house. In mild areas they will not die down during the winter. Where winters are severe it may be necessary to mulch the plants; we have not had to do so in the Philadelphia area in recent years.

Rhubarb is satisfactory frozen. We simply peel, dice, and pack dry, then prepare in any usual manner after thawing.

## Turnips

My earliest and favorite recollection of turnips is sowing them in cornfields about the time of the last corn cultivation, then munching on them later when we came through to harvest the corn. It was always Purple-Top White Globe, and to this day I enjoy raw turnips. Unfortunately, the rest of the family seems not to enjoy them, so turnips aren't planted in our garden as a regular procedure. Some years we do grow them, and a new variety, $F_1$ Hybrid Just Right, is good for roots and the tops can be used for cooking greens.

## Radishes

Cherry Belle has been one of the earliest with us. Burpee White is quite mild and does not get pithy, as do some varieties. It is good even when grown up to an inch and a half across, though best at smaller stages. It has larger tops than most radishes, so you cannot judge its readiness by other varieties—especially by Cherry Belle, which has exceptionally short tops. These two are the only ones we now grow, making succession plantings from early spring to early summer, and then again toward fall, for a crop before frost. In climates of cool summers, you can plant radishes right on through the season, of course.

We haven't tried to store any of the fall or winter types of radish in recent years. My recollection is that the Black Spanish is pretty hot, and the White Chinese not quite so pungent.

## Spinach

In spite of our preference for mustard, spinach is more frequently grown by most people. When we grow it, Bloomsdale Long Standing is our choice. It should be grown cool—in early spring or in the fall.

We like spinach with just lemon juice, or with sour cream. It also makes a good soup, cold or hot:

### Spinach Borsch

Chop fine:

      2 cups spinach
      1 cup carrots
      1 cup onions

Barely cover with boiling water. Simmer gently, covered, for 20 minutes. Add to this and simmer another 15 minutes:

      1 tablespoon butter
      2 cups beef or chicken stock
      1 cup tomato pulp, or stewed or strained tomatoes. (This can be omitted and an extra cup of spinach and 1 tablespoon lemon juice substituted.)
      1 cup very finely shredded cabbage

When serving, add to each bowl of soup a tablespoon of thick, sour cream (at room temperature if the soup is being served hot).

### Swiss Chard

Burpee's Fordhook Giant, green-leaved and white-stalked, is the only one we grow. It is a willing grower. Most recipes call for chard leaves as greens and the stalks cooked as is asparagus, but with younger plants we use both together, simmering until tender.

Rhubarb chard has red stalks, attractive in the garden. Since we don't try to make our vegetable garden decorative, a few plants of this variety are sufficient.

### Sunflower

We grow this to roast the seeds for nibbling. Easy to grow, it is useful as a screen or a background. It is a very heavy feeder; also, it should not be planted where it will cut off sun to other parts of the garden. North or northwest of the garden area are best locations.

## Tomatoes

In terms of food value of the harvest, this is the most remunerative crop you can grow. Start tomatoes 6 to 8 weeks ahead of outdoor planting time—and then be ready with some form of protection in case of late frost.

We do not train or prune our tomatoes every year, but let it depend on time, space, location, and so on. Pruning to a single stem spreads the harvest over a longer period. If making juice for canning, perhaps concentrated production is better. We make a good deal of juice, and freeze it, but don't grow varieties especially for that purpose. We grow for eating quality. Two hybrids make up the bulk of our selection—Big Boy and Big Early.

Jubilee, orange-colored, is mild and is attractive when used along with red tomatoes. It actually has a distinctive flavor, too, and is mild and meaty.

Hidden on one of the last pages of our catalog, without fanfare, is Table Talk tomato. It is not a hybrid, but to us is a very fine-flavored and solid tomato.

Finally, we round out our tomato planting with Red Cherry or Basket Pak. Basket Pak is slightly larger, but both are very interesting. About an inch or a little larger in diameter, Basket Pak may be eaten whole or used whole or halved in salads. It is also good for preserving and pickling. A few plants are sufficient.

## Watermelons

There is no place for these in small gardens. You have probably gathered by now that ours is a large garden, so even though we don't get well-flavored melons each year, we keep trying. Last year we were successful with Sugar Baby, a small, round, icebox size. Our results with larger watermelons have been inconsistent. Some years, on the West Coast, Klondike did well for us. The $F_1$ Hybrid Fordhook watermelon is also satisfactory.

Even if the fruit doesn't have really good flavor, the shells are handy for serving mixed fruit salads, especially if liberally sprinkled with kirsch (a cup or so to enough fruit to fit into the hollowed-out shell of a fair-sized watermelon). And, of course, you can always make watermelon-rind preserves!

Perhaps I should add this as a final note: We have used practically no power tools in our garden except for the initial soil preparation when using a new location. The rest we have done with ordinary hand tools, none being gadgets. But as our older children get ready for college, this picture may change. Probably we will cut down on the size of the garden—which I hate to do—or succumb to the power tool. I don't mind hard work, and enjoy the exercise of gardening, but if it becomes a chore, half the enjoyment will be lost. We consider the garden as partly a hobby, and probably spend more time in it as a family than is usually done.

# 27 THE WINTER GARDEN

It was a cold Virginia day in wartime 1944, and the writer and his wife were moving into a rented cottage in suburban Arlington, across the Potomac from the District of Columbia. The cottage had a little back yard—roughly 40 feet by 60—about the same as the next door property on the east. When we stepped out there, an old Dutch woman, our neighbor now, was trudging up the frozen path of this adjoining yard, and though it seemed impossible to us, she had just that minute harvested from the icy garden a head of curly endive so big she was carrying it in both hands. She had grown it in a big makeshift coldframe snuggled into the yard's northwest fence corner. The coldframe was full of green growing things, and here and there about the yard there were clumps of others, protected by little straw haycocks.

It was our introduction to wintertime gardening. Later on, when we were living on a farm in east-central Missouri—where winters were significantly colder than in Arlington, dropping well below zero—we regularly had our own winter garden.

Most of the Burpee people, both as seedsmen and as gardeners, agree that a winter garden is more practical than it may sound. Their head man, David Burpee, is one of the most enthusiastic winterers, and partly on this account he is a kind of delegate at large for the parsnip, which stores itself in the ground until you are ready for it, even if it takes all winter. Burpee once volunteered his favorite parsnip recipe during a radio talk when his seed house was opening its Midwest branch at Clinton, Iowa, and the parsnips got more fan mail than Burpee did. "The trick is to cook them well," he told his listeners. "First parboil them. Then fry or bake them like candied sweet potatoes. I've served that dish to friends at home on Fordhook Farms and said: 'Do you know what that is?' and they always replied: 'Of course. Candied sweet potatoes, the best we ever tasted.'"

Parsnips are an example of the root crops, one of the two big groups winter-garden vegetables split into. The other group is the greens—salad plants and cooking greens.

This is probably the place to separate the men from the boys, as winter gardeners might put it. Or to separate the nuts from the rest of us, as the opposition thinks. "It is my feeling that none but the most avid gardener would want to bother with a fall or winter vegetable patch," Theodore C. Torrey, director of vegetable research at Fordhook Farms, said in an interoffice memo a few years ago. "It is much more convenient and appetizing to eat quality frozen and canned vegetables put up during the summer than to try to harvest small parts of vegetable plants from the outdoors in the cold of winter."

His boss, David Burpee, takes a quite contrary view. "A favorite subject of mine is that of vegetables out of your garden all winter long in the North," he has said, adding: "You can have a lot of fun going out into your garden and gathering fresh vegetables when snow is on the ground." So there we have the two sides, as irreconcilable as usual, the conservative and the rebel, the matter-of-fact and the adventurous.

One of the best Burpee spokesmen to appear on behalf of the winter garden was a Fordhook Farms vegetable breeder, Frederic C. Streland, and what follows is his capable paper on the subject, with here and there an editorial aside.

## THE GARDEN THAT NEVER DIES
by
*Frederic C. Streland*

The ultimate challenge to the home gardener is the production of fresh vegetables throughout the year. A beginner can grow the easier warm-weather crops, and produce an overabundance of beans, tomatoes, and corn in August and September. But it takes skill and much more careful planning to extend the productive period of a garden into the winter months.

[It is also in the winter months, dietary authorities have pointed out, that vitamins—particularly A—in which *freshly picked* vegetables are so rich, are most needed by most of us to help fight the colds and other health hazards the harder weather brings. —K.K.]

Growing winter vegetables can be a rewarding experience. Many tasty and unusual dishes can be added to the winter menu. A real treat awaits you if you have never enjoyed Brussels sprouts or collards sweetened by the first freezes of early winter, or if you haven't been warmed by a potpie of salsify and potatoes on a cold winter day. [Recipe at end of chapter.] Creamed leek, celeriac diced and creamed, and kale with boiled potatoes are dishes to delight the finest palate.

Furthermore, both labor and space requirements are less than for summer crops, as winter vegetables are generally smaller than corn, tomatoes, cucumbers, etc. Often there is space available where early spring crops such as peas and radishes were grown. But don't try it if you feel you are still a beginner or if you are tired of gardening by the end of August. And don't try all of the winter vegetables at once—it's much more practical to add a few each year, depending on your taste to decide which ones.

Here are a few general hints for successful winter gardening.

Freezing is, of course, the gardener's big enemy in the late fall and the winter months. It narrows his choice of crops, but it is really surprising how many tasty and nourishing vegetables are at least partly winter-hardy. Here, now, are two basic points of winter gardening:

1. Protective covers of straw or leaves or soil are recommended after growth has stopped. It is usually just as important to protect against direct sunshine as against freezing. Repeated thawing and freezing are most injurious. And few gardeners in the United States can depend on the first snowfall's providing a protective blanket which will last until spring thaw—a convenience for gardeners in more northern areas, and one that can work wonders in preserving some root crops from injury.

2. Damage from these causes is especially severe in young plants. Therefore, *proper timing of the sowing* becomes doubly important—so as to have plants at both an edible and a more cold-resistant stage when growth is stopped by cold. Irrigation or watering is recommended in dry spells to keep plants growing, or they may be too small when cold weather comes.

Following are some of the more attractive winter vegetables, with a few hints on how to make them perform their best. *All these pointers are, of course, subject to revision for local conditions.* Suggested sowing dates are given for southeastern Pennsylvania, where tender crops such as tomatoes are killed by frost (on the average) by October 10, and where practically all vegetative growth has stopped by about November 20, even in such tough plants as Brussels sprouts and rutabagas.

*Parsnip, salsify, and the roots of Hamburg or root parsley* will withstand almost any winter we can offer, with practically no effect other than improved flavor. Cover parsnips and salsify with straw if you want to be able to dig them at all times. Hamburg parsley is not quite as hardy and had better be protected with some straw or leaves, for safety's sake, starting in early December. All three require a long growing season. Sow Hamburg parsley and salsify in late April or early May. Parsnips can be sown from April 15 to June 15, depending on size desired. Large old roots are more likely to have fibrous centers.

*Leek and chives,* among the onion family, are best for winter hardiness. Both should be sown in late April or early May. Leeks, if spaced 6 inches apart in rich soil, will produce stalks up to 2 inches in diameter, of mild, onion-like but distinctive flavor. They usually survive without protection until about the end of December, and sometimes last through the whole winter. [In a memo dated February 1, 1957, Torrey commented on leeks: "Very hardy class. Leeks now in the field at Fordhook are still in edible condition after many hard freezes." —K.K.]

Chives are usable well into November. They put out new shoots early the following April.

*Turnips and rutabagas* are old stand-by winter vegetables. Rutabagas are somewhat more cold-resistant than turnips. Sow rutabagas the first week in August, and turnips the last week in August, for best results. The soil reaction should be close to neutral for best flavor. Sow thinly, or thin to at least 4 to 6 inches between plants. Purple Top White Globe is the best turnip for fall use. American Purple Top is one of the best rutabagas.

Turnips and rutabagas may be attacked by flea beetles when young. Dust with rotenone. Turnips may become infested with aphids in later stages. Spray with malathion. Rutabagas may suffer from mildew in cool, damp weather of September and October. Spray with manzate as soon as noticed.

*Beets and carrots* will usually last well into November, even without covering. Both can be buried in a well-drained location and used until spring. The Lutz Green Leaf (or Winter Keeper) type of beet will reach huge size and still remain sweet and tender, so is strongly recommended for winter use. Burpee's Goldinhart (or Red Cored Chantenay) is probably the best all-around carrot. Sow both beets and carrots the first half of July. Neutral soil will produce the best flavor. Thin the carrots to 2 inches, and Lutz Green Leaf beet to at least 6 inches.

*Winter radishes* are a standard item of food in many parts of the world. They can be handled the same as beets and carrots, but sown later—about the middle of August. For better protection, a variety with roots mostly underground is preferable: Long Black Spanish. They should last at least until the end of November. In the early stages they will probably require dusting with rotenone for flea beetles. Thin to 6 inches or more.

*Celeriac, or turnip-rooted celery,* is easier to grow and is more cold-resistant than celery. In most winters it will last until early December without protection. Or it can be harvested, buried, and used until spring. Diced and creamed, or in salads, it has an excellent celery-like flavor. Start it in a seedbed or flat early in May. Transplant to 10 or 12 inches apart when plants are 3 or 4 inches high. Rich, light, well-drained soil is especially important for celeriac.

*Kale, collards, and Brussels sprouts* are splendid leafy vegetables for the winter garden. All can stand short periods of cold as low as 10 degrees above zero (kale can take sub-zero weather) and be improved in flavor for it. They can often be harvested until the end of the year—sometimes even later. [Of collards, Torrey commented in the memo previously mentioned: "Very hardy class. Often plants will live over the winter and start growth again in early spring. Older plants seem to winter better than younger or late planted ones." Of kale he said: "Much like collards in performance but less desirable as a vegetable in the warmer part of the summer. Frosts improve the quality and not many people would want to harvest much before October 1 or when the weather has become cooler." —K.K.]

Kale and collards can be seeded about July 20. Thin to 6 to 12 inches. Or sow in hills 6 to 12 inches apart and thin to one plant per hill. Dwarf Blue Curled Scotch is the best kale for cold resistance. Vates is the best collard; Georgia is almost as good.

Brussels sprouts had best be started in a flat or seedbed about June 1 and transplanted to stand 2 feet apart in wide rows. Jade Cross F₁ Hybrid is the best variety. In late fall or early winter the leaves can be removed from the stalk and the whole stalk with its sprouts can be hung in a cool dry cellar for late winter use.

*Cabbage* is somewhat less hardy. The red and the savoy varieties are generally better for winter use. Culture is practically the same as Brussels sprouts. Sow during the last week in June. Don't handle the heads while frozen; wait for a thaw and then harvest. [In his memo, Torrey agrees that the savoy is preferable over smooth-leaved types, and adds: "The younger, less compact heads hold longer than the fully matured. Perhaps a few edible leaves could be found after December 15, but even on that date much trimming of heads is necessary." —K.K.]

*Broccoli, cauliflower, kohlrabi, and Chinese cabbage* are less hardy members of the cabbage family. All will usually yield into late November but not much longer unless covered with straw or sash. The individual plants that last longest are, of course, those with the best natural covering of foliage. Handle cauliflower the same as Brussels sprouts and cabbage. Sow in early to late June, depending on the variety.

Broccoli, kohlrabi, and Chinese cabbage can be treated the same as kale and collards. Sow broccoli in mid-July and thin to 18 inches. Sow kohlrabi the first week in August and thin to 4 inches. Sow Chinese cabbage the first week in August and thin to 18 inches. [Regarding Chinese cabbage, Torrey has noted: "Hard freezes will ruin compact-headed types, but the loose-leaf types will survive several freezes. As in cabbage, the more immature plants survive better than the headed ones."—K.K.]

In all the cabbage family, use rotenone dust for cabbage worms and flea beetles, malathion for aphids, and manzate for mildew.

Other vegetables that will usually produce into the middle or end of November are *spinach* (sown about August 25), *dandelion* (sown in mid-July), *Swiss chard* (sown in mid-June), and *parsley* (sown in late April or early May). A single sash supported by planks or a ridge of soil or bales of straw can often keep parsley in usable condition through half of the winter. Mats or old carpets on top of the sash will prolong the harvest still further.

Unless the winter is unusually severe, many of these crops will put forth vigorous and tasty new growth early the following spring. Salsify foliage will be the earliest, often starting in February. Cut it when it is 6 inches high, for a salad. Somewhat later, depending on the weather, will come chives, parsley, dandelion, spinach, kale, and collards. Swiss chard survives some winters, the variety Perpetual or Spinach Beet being the one most likely to.

Finally, a few words about other kinds of winter damage to plants besides freezing. The main ones that may occur are water-logging, fungus and mold injury; and heaving of the earth by repeated freezes and thaws, causing erosion and excessive drying.

1. The water-logging, fungus and mold injury, and subsequent rotting, can be kept to a minimum by planting in a light and well-drained soil, preferably on a gentle slope. The site is very important. Select a corner or edge of the garden, to be out of the way of clean-up and plowing.

2. Heaving, with erosion and drying, can be controlled to a great extent by mulching, or still better by a cover crop of annual rye grass. Broadcast the rye grass about September 1, or soon enough for it to have grown about 6 inches tall when the first

really freezing weather comes. Be sure not to sow it too early or it will overrun the vegetables. A protective sod of rye grass helps stabilize the soil temperature, and minimizes erosion and heaving. It is also an excellent protection against dessication of plants by long periods of cold, dry wind, which sometimes occur when there is no protective snow on the ground.

To Frederic Streland's comments, the writer would like to add this: On the Missouri farm I mentioned, we used two or three dodges to keep ourselves in salad makings long after the winter had cracked down for good. We had a couple of simple, flat-topped cold frames, 6 feet by 3, and in one of them when we were expecting the first frost—about October 15—we crammed all the mature plants we could pack in. They were mostly lettuces, but also endive, Chinese cabbage, and celery. They were more heeled in (their roots in the moist earth) than transplanted, and jammed shoulder to shoulder, since this was not a growing arrangement but a storage one. It kept us in salads daily for the rest of the year.

The other frame was simply dropped over a bed of closely planted leaf lettuces that had been started for that purpose about a month before. With this protection they continued to grow a little, and were big enough to be used when the other frame was emptied. Both frames were given extra protection during colder spells by our piling straw and earth loosely around them, setting a bale of straw at the north end of each for a windbreak, and scattering a kind of mulch of straw over the sashes.

We supplemented the lettuce from the second frame by sprouting Witloof chicory in the basement, from roots we had grown in the garden during the summer. This is a simple thing to do and the product is a delicacy seldom found on the market for love or money. We dug the roots in the fall, trimmed away all but an inch or so of the tops, and then cut off enough of the bottoms to make all the roots about seven inches long. They are about the size of carrots. Then we planted a batch of them in nail kegs with a few drainage holes in the bottoms, putting about ten inches of garden soil in the kegs and shoving the roots down till nothing but the tops showed—about a dozen roots to a keg. We wet the earth well and then added six or eight inches of sand on top, and covered the kegs with newspaper. The tightly rolled sprouts were up and ready for salads in about a month. You get one sprout per root but if you have enough roots you can make succession plantings all winter, since they will stay dormant in a dry place until planted.

While it is growing its roots in the garden during the summer, chicory is a well-behaved plant and if you wish, you can use some of the leaves for salads or for cooking greens. The plant is also the source of the chicory in the chicory coffee of the South, the Magdeburg variety being preferred here, for its larger roots. If you want to try this yourself, here are the steps, in the words of a lady of Dixie, Mrs. Anna Wheeler Phillips, who teaches vocational homemaking in the Mississippi town of Brookhaven:

"The roots of the spring-planted crop are dried, then roasted and ground, and used with coffee to give it body. Often it is used as a substitute for coffee. The use of it in Louisiana is to add color, bitterness, and body." The chicory is used in various proportions as an additive to coffee; one part to ten of coffee by volume would be light though noticeable, and equal amounts of each would make a decidedly dark and strong brew.

Following is the potpie recipe mentioned earlier in the chapter. Winter gardener Streland has also thrown in a fritter recipe for good measure. The recipe for another winter delicacy, Butternut squash pie, is through the kindness of Miss Erna Bennink, Fordhook office manager as well as secretary, bookkeeper, and vegetable trials noter.

### Salsify and Potato Potpie

Peel and slice salsify, say about 2 or 3 cupfuls, and simmer 20 minutes in just enough water to cover. Add:

> 2 or 3 cups of peeled and sliced potatoes
> Large piece of butter or margarine
> Salt and pepper

Simmer 5 minutes more, adding a little more water if needed. Put into casserole and cover with biscuit dough or pie pastry. Bake about 20 minutes at 350 to 375 degrees.

### Salsify Fritters

Peel a few roots of salsify and simmer until tender enough to mash, about half an hour. After mashing, make them into small cakes about the size of oysters. Dip these into bread crumbs, then into beaten egg, then into bread crumbs again. French-fry in deep fat, or sauté in skillet until a light brown.

### Butternut Squash Pie

Grate:

> 2 cups of raw Butternut squash

Mix together:

> 2 tablespoons dark molasses, warmed
> ⅔ cup sugar
> 1 heaping tablespoon flour
> ⅔ cup sweet cream

Stir this into the grated squash, and add:

> 1 egg, beaten
> ½ teaspoon salt
> ½ teaspoon nutmeg
> ½ teaspoon pumpkin pie spice
> 1 teaspoon cinnamon

Pour into pastry-lined pie pan. Bake 45 minutes at 425 degrees.

# 28 WHAT YOU'LL BE PLANTING X YEARS FROM NOW

One of the small comforts of spinach-hating moppets has always been that the stuff can't stand hot weather. It goes to seed and that's that. This happiness, however, is about to end. The thing ending it is a plant from India—Malabar spinach— which Burpee's are listing for the first time this year. A vine known botanically as *Basella alba*, Malabar spinach dotes on hot weather, likes any old kind of soil, grows fast and climbs a fence like a monkey, isn't bothered by bug or blight, and makes glossy new leaves so fast half-a-dozen plants will keep the family in greens till the world looks emerald. You cook it like spinach, too.

Although Malabar spinach is already with us, it is a good pointer to many vegetables of the future if a theory of David Burpee's is on the target. His theory is that India is an almost untapped treasure chest of new plant life, so far as the United States is concerned. In years past, he reasons, when China was the source of most new plant life that we got, India was being dominated by Great Britain, whose interest was in Indian plants adapted to the cool, moist climate of the British Isles. Consequently, we know almost nothing about most Indian plants that can take hot weather, the kind of summers most Americans have. Burpee feels that many of these still undiscovered Indian flowers and vegetables will be important to us before this decade ends.

His nearly fifty years of daily experience in running the largest garden seed business of its kind makes David Burpee one of the best-qualified men in the world to tell American gardeners what good new things they can look forward to growing, in the next several years and beyond. Here is the picture as he sees it, for the home gardener.

## I PREDICT . . .
### by
### *David Burpee*

Would you like to grow a little "tree" tomato you won't ever have to stake? One you can pick fruit from as if it were a tiny peach tree?

Or how about a delicious cabbage that even a bloodhound couldn't smell cooking?

Or a crisp, vitamin-packed green celery that is actually *stringless?*

I predict that home gardeners will be able to raise all three of these superb new-model vegetables in the years to come—and many, many more improved things. Some are in the laboratory as you read these words. Others are already out in the trial rows, showing what they can do. Harder ones are waiting, some for the perfection of new techniques to give us the tools we must have to do the job.

Meanwhile, other tools—sturdy ones such as hybridizing, and polyploidy, and ray treatment plus some other ways of increasing mutation rates—are enabling plant breeders, commercial and those with the federal government, the experiment stations, and the agricultural colleges, to speed up getting you many more new plants than they could have some years ago when searching out things already growing was our main reliance. We still search things out, though, and the new Malabar spinach is one of the things found in this way. It is something else, too. It is a good example of a big reason we look for the things we do. The reason is you, the home gardener.

Because many of you have told us you would like more greens and salad plants that will thrive in hot weather, finding them is one of our pet projects, and Malabar spinach is a green that flourishes in summer heat. It is the first, we hope, of many more such new greens.

Now, before I go any farther, let me invite every reader of this book to tell me what improvements, or even what brand-new plants, he'd like to see in his garden in the next several years. We need your ideas. They are more influential than you may think, because for every person who takes the trouble to speak up, a thousand may feel the same way but say nothing. In general, we know you want in your garden vegetables good taste, tenderness, good looks, and spaced ripening—whereas someone growing fresh vegetables for sale in the supermarket must stress looks more than taste, toughness (for shipping) over tenderness, and everything in a field must ripen at the same time. But when it comes to other things about home-garden vegetables—such as a different size or shape or color or taste—we like to know what you think, and we are grateful when you tell us.

And now I'm going to predict something else—what I might term a "Minute Man" home vegetable garden of the future that you can look after in merely a few minutes a day. Some of the expected new things listed below will help make this Minute Man garden a reality. Others will be tender plants you can seed early in the open ground for a head start; bigger harvests from smaller space; plants that fight insects and diseases by themselves. And—though I suppose it sounds pretty far out—I'm expecting to get some help on this and other jobs of the future from plants we think are growing on other planets. If we find them there and can bring back their germ plasm in seeds and grow them, we may open up vast new avenues—delicious foods no one on earth has ever tasted, exotic new flowers none of us have ever seen—and the exciting chance of mating some of the space plants with earth plants, and producing something stunning: Earth-Space Hybrids, with potentials we can only dream of.

Meanwhile here are some more of the things I predict are somewhere in your earth-plant gardening future:

Good winter squashes, richer in valuable vitamins, growing on handy little bushes instead of trailing over the ground.

Tomatoes flavored to suit a wider range of tastes—from French-dressing tart to mild and mellow.

Onions you can peel without crying and cook without smelling.

High-vitamin broccoli plants that "store" their buds right in the garden—tightly closed and held at peak flavor until you need them.

A sturdy-stemmed pea that even in hot weather will produce loads of plump, easy-to-shell pods.

Sweet corn with deeper kernels and slender cobs, tailored for freezer storage. And for the little garden, a new and delicious compact-model with three-foot stalks and up to four ears on each.

A lettuce that likes hot summers.

"Zipper-podded" lima beans easy to shell, and sweeter, greener, fuller.

A seedless cucumber.

A bush cantaloupe for small gardens, and a small-fruited bush watermelon.

A smooth new extra-vitamined carrot colored deeply orange.

Beanier-tasting bush snap beans with more pods per plant. Also sweeter-flavored and deeper green.

A weatherproof tomato that will take more heat, cold, wet, and drought.

Speedy new melons—Honeydews, Crenshaws, and Persians—to beat the earliest midwest and northern frosts.

A self-climbing cucumber you can grow up a pole to save space and harvest easily.

An ever-bearing pepper with sweeter, smoother fruits more brightly colored.

A good early peanut—up to five nuts per pod—for short-summer gardeners.

And especially for the children, a little jack-o'-lantern pumpkin that grows on a neat bush.

And now what about the flowers of the future? You will remember I said of vegetables that it is you gardeners who call the tune on what we should do. Well, it is the same with flowers. Sometimes what we know of your wishes is pretty elastic and general—such as the fact most of you seem to enjoy trying out a fresh novelty each year.

A harder thing for us to do well is to detect the changes in your flower-garden needs before they grow up into full-sized trends. Because by the time they *are* trends it is much too late for us to be merely starting to commence to begin to help you, as somebody has put it. Remodeling a flower for the market usually takes three to five years, even using all sorts of short cuts. As to trends—an example of a recent one was the increasing call for dwarfer plants (lower-growing) with as big or bigger flowers. What set this trend to rolling was the ranch-type house, with its long horizontal lines. Which brings me to a prediction.

I predict that the trend to dwarfer plants has about reached its practical limit, and a new trend is building—one toward new and taller flowers with substantial but trim growth habit. My reason for this prediction is an economic one: building costs. They have kept on spiraling up, and the result is an increase in the proportion of the 1-story-plus house (1½ stories and 2 stories, and sometimes 2½ or 3) since you can get more space for less money per cubic foot that way.

I think I'll hazard a few fairly specific predictions now about the flowers you'll be planting in the future. Some of these are long-range predictions—or call them educated guesses—but in some other cases I can even give you an approximate debut date. Let's start with that famous marigold whose story Chapter 25 of this book is all about:

We believe we will have seed ready for you to grow a big, glistening, pure-white American marigold by 1968—and maybe sooner.

Undated, but somewhere following the big white, there will be a big pink marigold and a big red.

By the time you have the white marigold, you will also be able to grow still dwarfer dwarf marigolds with large flowers in all of the present colors, and in both regular and odorless foliage.

I can't give it a date yet, but a zinnia with long curving petals as big and graceful as a giant chrysanthemum will also be in the future garden.

Due by or before 1968 are heat-tolerant snapdragons in a rainbow range and with up to a hundred long-lasting flowers to a single spike.

This one is also coming in the next five years: rich new non-purpling reds, and salmon-pinks, in all the more popular types of asters.

Creeping petunias for ground cover, in many good colors. We already have a start here, with our little pink prize-winner

Cheerful. The breeding work with it is difficult—but I'm predicting eventual break-through and success.

This may surprise you, but I predict that some flowers not very popular today may be among the most popular ones of the future. This can be so for various reasons, I think, different ones in each case. For instance:

Vinca rosea or periwinkle (the annual, not the vine) has many virtues—good germination in warm ground, a simple and appealing blossom, freedom from disease and insects, tolerance to heat, and foliage that in a way is the most lustrous of any annual flower, almost like the foliage of a gardenia. It is a lovely thing in the garden and in bouquets. But it has one distressing fault—it waits too long to bloom, starting in the northern states just before the first killing frost, if it was seeded in open ground. Some day we hope to find an early-blooming periwinkle springing up among the others—a mutation, in other words—with which we can work. It is one of the things I should like home gardeners to watch for. If a *very early-blooming periwinkle* pops up in your own garden, I would appreciate your saving the seeds for me to test.

Another relatively unpopular flower today that I think is going to become much better liked if we can make one improvement in it is balsam. As you know, balsam grows its beautiful rose-like or camellia-like flowers—and in a wonderful assortment of colors —in spikes, the spikes being the stalks and branches themselves. But balsam's trouble is that the leaves grow out between the flowers, and sometimes almost hide them. Except for that, balsam has nearly everything but fragrance—easy to grow in open ground, no serious pests or diseases, grows in hot weather, and blooms from midsummer on.

So again—I am asking home gardeners if they will be on the lookout for a balsam plant *with practically no foliage showing between blossoms.* Its seeds may help lead us to a new race of beauties.

Finally, if I were asked the one flower I'd like most to be able to predict with certainty, I suppose it would be the one I've been trying for ever since my father, the first Burpee seedsman, set me on its trail when I was still a schoolboy, back in 1909. It was a yellow sweet pea. I'm more skeptical about finding it now than I was then—but still, sweet peas *are* very prone to throw mutations, and for all we know, a true yellow sweet pea has already amazed some gardener by suddenly showing up in the middle of other-colored vines. It can happen, so let me invite home gardeners everywhere to keep an eye out for *a truly yellow sweet pea*, and if they find it, to send me any seed it matures, for testing at our farms.

In asking you, my fellow gardeners wherever you are, for this sort of help, I am practicing what I have preached all my life—the immense importance of selection in plant improvement work. And so I am inviting you to participate, in a sense, in this bedrock device of all plant breeding. It is the oldest and it is also part of the newest, for without continual selection the new techniques would be no more than stunts. It is the basis of a reputable seedsman's contribution to the times he lives in and to those that follow. Luther Burbank considered it so fundamental that he once said simply: "Selection is the beginning and the end."

# INDEX